Extraordinary Justice

Extraordinary Justice

Military Tribunals in Historical and International Context

Peter Judson Richards

NEW YORK UNIVERSITY PRESS
New York and London

NEW YORK UNIVERSITY PRESS
New York and London
www.nyupress.org

Library of Congress Cataloging-in-Publication Data

Richards, Peter Judson.
Extraordinary justice : military tribunals in historical and international context / Peter Judson Richards.
p. cm.
Includes bibliographical references and index.
ISBN-13: 978-0-8147-7591-2 (cloth : alk. paper)
ISBN-10: 0-8147-7591-8 (cloth : alk. paper)
1. Military courts. 2. Courts-martial and courts of inquiry. I. Title.
K4754.R53 2007
343'.0143—dc22 2007000133

New York University Press books are printed on acid-free paper, and their binding materials are chosen for strength and durability.

10 9 8 7 6 5 4 3 2 1

To my Father and Mother

Contents

Acknowledgments

As I prepared the studies that follow, a fairly regular historiographic pattern emerged. Nothing prompts the search for missing umbrellas like a good rain shower. So, the option presented by the practice of military tribunals flares out of the darkness with the emergence of significant threats, prompting an academic, judicial flurry of claims and counter-claims. Eventually the storm of conflict passes, and the whole matter subsides again into dusty obscurity. In periods of extended peace, it is difficult to imagine a more neglected subject of scholarly consideration. In the heat of war, with the resurrection of the practice—or the mere prospect of it—the commentary proliferates in earnest. Yet as it enters a new iteration, the basic contours of the debate, modulating between the poles of liberty and order, remain relatively constant. This characteristic "punctuated equilibrium," to switch metaphors, cannot be ignored in assessing the domestic and international ramifications of a practice with the long history of the military tribunals.

The present work, alas, falls into the same pattern. Would that the circumstances that gave rise to this book had never occurred. The events of September 11, 2001, and the policy discussions that followed, first drew my attention to the subject. Professor Michael Reisman encouraged me to look into the matter further. It did not take long before I realized that the practice was far more widespread, both in American military history, and in the history of our allies, than many commentators were letting on. For some, the simple expression "military tribunal" appears to summon up a host of cliché-laden horrors: "star chambers," "juntas," "rubber truncheons" and "kangaroo courts." My own experience of nearly ten years practice as a Judge Advocate in the military courts of the United States Air Force led me to believe that such images frequently carry little or no connection to actual experience. Significant distinctions were being ignored. An important, neglected dimension of the historical record needed filling in. In particular, I saw a need for a work of synthesis, drawing together the secondary literature and readily available primary sources that would allow insight into a common practice of significance and continued value.

As such this book stands on the shoulders of earlier works such as Mark Neely's masterly and authoritative study of civil liberties in the Civil War, *The Fate of Liberty: Abraham Lincoln and Civil Liberties;* James Sefton's comprehensive record of military administration of the Reconstruction South, *The United States Army and Reconstruction: 1865–1877;* and Philip Piccigallo's invaluable account of the war crimes tribunals of the Pacific theater of the Second World War, *The Japanese on Trial: Allied War Crimes Operations in the East, 1945–1951.* I candidly acknowledge my indebtedness to the earlier labors of these scholars. As with all such acknowledgments, any errors remain my own. Yet, with the exception of Piccigallo's account, which itself addresses only the eastern theater within the wider World War, none of these works seeks to focus specifically on the practices of military tribunals as a discrete topic. Recent events arising out of the war against islamicist terror would suggest the subject merits a story all to its own. The following represents my own attempt to bring at least a larger and wider portion of that story into greater relief.

"Of the making of many books there is no end." To the extent that this book is of any value it is due in large measure to the contribution, support, and assistance of family, friends, and colleagues too numerous to mention here. I am especially grateful for the guidance, formidable erudition, and kindness of Michael Reisman of the Yale Law School, where I submitted an earlier version of this work for the degree of Doctor of the Science of Law. Without his direction and encouragement, this project would never have gotten off the ground. Others on the Yale law faculty and staff were helpful in the early stages of the work, including the additional members of my dissertation committee, Kate Stith and Lea Brilmayer; as well as Robert Ellickson, James Silk, Mirjan Damaška, Ruth Wedgwood, Harold Koh, Barbara Safriet, and Daniel Wade. Thanks also to Donald Kagan for his wise and helpful insights. The book is much the stronger for the valuable comments and insights of Gary Solis and Louis Fisher, who reviewed a draft version of the manuscript. Maj. Gen. Charles Dunlap, Michael Emerson, Earl "Marty" Martin, Michael Schmitt, Steve Lambert, and Tim Murphy, exemplary models of the scholar and officer, all provided invaluable encouragement and guidance. I have benefited greatly from the example of Harold J. Berman, Charles Shanor, and Frank Alexander at Emory University School of Law, where I had the opportunity to present some of the material from this book. The challenging and incisive classroom discussions that followed helped me to clarify and refine many of the points presented here.

I wish to extend special thanks to the members of the New York University Press for their assistance, patience, and care in preparing the work for publication, especially Senior Editor Debbie Gershenowitz, Managing Editor Despina Gimbel, and Salwa Jabado.

Thanks also to the libraries and staff of Yale Law School and the Sterling library of Yale University, Harvard University, Brown University, the Swem library of the College of William and Mary, Cambridge University, the Bibliothèque Nationale of Paris, and the Library of Congress.

Most of all, my love, gratitude, and appreciation to Johanna, Elizabeth, Suzannah, Benjamin, and Emma Grace. This book is dedicated to my parents, for whose constant support and encouragement I am truly grateful.

S.D.G.

Introduction

> The difference between a rough and a civilized society is not that force is used in the one case and persuasion in the other, but that force is (or ought to be) guided with greater care in the second case than in the first.
>
> —James Fitzjames Stephen

The al-Qaeda terror attacks of September 11, 2001, aroused a number of extraordinary counter-measures in response. Among the more controversial of these is the executive order issued November 13, 2001, authorizing the creation of special military tribunals—"commissions" for the trial of al-Qaeda terrorists.[1] The presidential order provoked a barrage of criticism that continues to surge and subside with events. Critics from left and right condemned the measure as an unnecessary and dangerous extension of government powers, as "dictatorial" usurpation, a "power grab" designed to undermine precious procedural liberties. Others upheld the President's order as a necessary policy maneuver in furtherance of vital national security interests, defending its validity in terms of international practices and local norms. Given the manifestly extraordinary nature of the practice, it is no simple matter to evaluate the effort to reestablish military commissions.

As Justice Robert Jackson famously observed in his *Terminiello* dissent, the United States Constitution is not "a suicide pact." It is probably safe to say that most constitution-makers would eschew such descriptions for their work. Extreme conditions require careful and deliberate attention to that balance between liberty and order permeating, in James Madison's view, every line of the American Constitution. It is precisely at these points of extremity that dangers to the commonwealth tend to multiply. The possibility for withdrawal of hard-won liberties rises in proportion to the perceived gravity of an external threat to a nation's security. The balance becomes more delicate, precarious.

On the one hand there is always the potential danger of overstating an external threat to national security, through excess of caution, ignorance, suspicion, or in the mere pursuit of power. In this event, civil liberties collapse under the call for extraordinary measures. The executive vests with new expansions of authority; precedents arise, difficult to undo upon clearer reflection. All this occurs for the sake of an exaggerated threat.[2]

And yet the seriousness of the threat may in fact prove genuine. Drastic action may be the only responsible option; after all, "necessity dictates the exercise of emergency powers, at times, in any republic."[3] The difficulty lies in the fact that partial information is often the best that can be obtained in assessing the magnitude of the hazard. In such times, further complications attend the need for maintaining secrecy on behalf of a nation committed in principle to transparency, democratic accountability, and open government process. Once a given danger has been overcome, hindsight's benefit and relative safety make it a difficult trick to evaluate the actual severity of a threat as it appeared to those who succeeded in putting it down. Is it possible that some lesser exertion of force, some less drastic measures, could have secured the same or even better results? What was the deterrent effect of the measures actually taken?

It is always very difficult to say what might have happened in history if events had taken a different turn. To take a salient recent example: is there a causal connection between the Bush administration's robust security measures after September 11, 2001, and the absence of subsequent attacks on American soil? Certainty evades the argument from silence. Yet policy makers can ill afford the exacting standards of proof applicable in courts of law. Nor do they enjoy the luxuries of the academic researcher who enjoys relatively limitless time and resources, ensuring that no stone remains unturned in the pursuit of an accurate distribution of historical causes and effects. Too often, the lessons of history, which ought to guide prudential leadership, become mere tools, selected and reshaped for use in partisan struggles over policy. Passionate rhetoric in time of war, as Thucydides long ago remarked, is never in short supply.

Within the panoply of potential emergency measures, the mechanism of the military juridical response—i.e., one that takes place outside of the normal Article III judicial process—has played an important part.[4] The assertion of occasional necessity raises questions that surface with every major conflict that precipitates the use of emergency measures. Why is it ever the case that ordinary courts are insufficient to the task of administering justice in crisis conditions? What are the necessary preconditions for calling extraordinary judicial forums into existence? As a matter of historical record, did these courts-in-extremity advance the ends for which they were created?

For leaders in time of national security crisis, military tribunals have offered a number of advantages over other methods. The persistence of the custom rested in part on the premise that there is no intrinsic moral or legal justification for granting all types of enemy military forces in time of war the identical range of protections given to members of one's own military. Warring enemy forces are less likely to be able to turn such tribunals to their own advantage, by manipulation of security leaks or communications media. In conditions shaped by the stern demands of military necessity, speedy means of adjudication ensure that critical resources, time, and personnel are not siphoned away in a painstaking judicial process oblivious to the larger circumstance of war. Military forums allow greater provisions for secrecy and thus may help protect sensitive information—a protection that is less available in the open discovery process of the civilian trial. In the more immediate sense, the military courts also allow for tighter courtroom security, as well as protection of witnesses, jurors, and others. Moreover, since they operate on a regular basis in the world defined by the rules of armed conflict, military professionals, rather than civilian outsiders, are found to be better equipped to adjudicate alleged violations of such standards.[5]

Given the extensive use of various types of military courts in the past, and the urgency imposed by current national and international comment, it is remarkable that the practice, especially before 9/11, received so little scholarly attention.[6] Part of the relative obscurity that still enshrouds the subject of the military tribunal arises from its hybrid nature, a quasi-judicial function operating as a military response in time of war. Military historians neglect the subject because of its limited, tangential impact on the activity of warfare itself. Rare is the work of military history that fixes on a practice that usually takes place, if at all, on the sidelines, often in the aftermath of hostilities.[7] Equally, its dislocation from the ordinary functions of the civil judicial process leaves it outside the sights of the legal analyst. Regular military courts-martial tend to fall within the exclusive domain of specialized military practitioners. For the civilian public, the scope and function of such courts remains unclear. Another ingredient for confusion may rest in the fact that the United States Congress has not actually issued a formal declaration of war in any of the nation's recent military engagements. Perhaps the fluidity of the very concept of "war" since 1945 contributes to the neglect.[8]

Moreover, though it was not always so, the subject of military law receives little if any coverage in the curricula of the nation's law schools. The neglect parallels a larger (and widening) social gap. In the words of one recent work on military law,

> Today, fewer and fewer Americans have served in the armed forces. This includes our elected representatives and senior members of the executive branch. The result is that many Americans know almost nothing about the military justice system. They are unaware of the many similarities between the military justice system and civilian criminal law and procedure, or of the considerable protections afforded a military accused, many of which exceed those enjoyed in civilian courts. At the same time, many do not know about the differences between military and civilian justice or appreciate why they exist. This lack of knowledge about military justice inhibits critical examination by those who are ultimately responsible for it and who depend on the armed forces it governs.[9]

In American law schools, one is more likely to find courses dedicated to the subject of fashionable post-modern legal theories than to the law of war.[10]

Yet, notwithstanding the earnest efforts observed a hundred years ago by Joseph Conrad, aimed at "dragging the scourge down from the skies" to transform it "into a calm and regulated institution," the ferocity of war appears to have remained a regular feature of the human condition in the fifty-odd years since the conclusion of the Nuremberg trials and the founding of the United Nations. Attempts to avoid the consequences of this reality by the enlistment of labored euphemisms tends merely to cloud decisions of policy and strategy that must be faced. Clarity and discrimination in the use of language would greatly help. In the current conflict against al-Qaeda jihadist forces, a similar obfuscation attends the use of the general, albeit religiously neutral phrase, "war on terror," the vagueness of which stirs up fears of equally vague and boundless intrusions against precious liberties.

It would be helpful to remove the veil of obscurity covering practices that have exerted significant impact on the development of the international law of war. In the studies that follow, it is my intention to examine the workings of the mechanism of what in American parlance has come to be known as the military commission, as it fits within the larger framework of extraordinary responses to national emergency.

It is helpful to begin with some working definitions. I do so with awareness of the late Karl Popper's warnings as to the value of the process of definition as a means of resolving contentious problems of policy and practice. In this case, the question becomes, how do you define "terrorism," "justice," "due process," or "the state of war"? As Popper warned, the answers to such questions often tend to produce a further series of calls for definitional clarity. The quest for a definition satisfactory to all interested parties can lead to unending, fruitless regression.[11] Academic cottage industries form in the gaps among competing formulations. The subject at hand is not immune to such problems. One scholar asks, how can an offense committed by means of box cutters, though "productive" of three thousand deaths, be categorized as an "armed attack"?[12] The question, of course, is posed with full awareness of the consequences hinging on such definitional distinctions. Still, this reasoning runs the risk of "proving" far more than its author intends, for in a technological age, many an "armed attack" ostensibly reduces to the manipulation of switches, buttons, data, and levers—none of which in isolation is tied intrinsically or necessarily to the use of military force. This is to fix on one link at the expense of an entire chain of purposeful acts by knowing human agents. Lawyers tend to revel in this kind of argument and thereby, perhaps, overestimate its value.[13]

Another "interpretive" approach treats the events surrounding 9/11 as a kind of "unreal" symbolism, in which distinctions between action and response become reversible components to the same meaningless "spectacle": "The repression of terrorism spirals around as unpredictably as the terrorist act itself. No one knows where it will stop, or what turnabouts there may yet be. There is no possible distinction, at the level of images and information, between the spectacular and the symbolic, no possible distinction between the 'crime' and the crackdown. And it is this uncontrollable unleashing of reversibility that is terrorism's true victory."[14] Such "post-modern" essays in moral equivalence may or may not tell more about their author than about the events they purport to understand. Nevertheless, as efforts at accurate, meaningful verbal description, they give the lie to the professed incommensurability between words and events.

Still, some ambiguity clings to the notion of a "military tribunal," making necessary a few points of clarification. The term has been used to describe the unprecedented international trials of Nazi and Japanese war criminals at the end of the Second World War, as well as the international ad hoc forums convened in the 1990s to try war crimes in the former Yugoslavia and Rwanda. The term has also been applied to the courts convened on the part of national military authorities for the trial of wartime offenses on the part of enemy forces. In American practice, at least since the Mexican War, these national military courts have gone by the name of "military commissions."[15] The term "commission" was first adopted in order to distinguish these types of courts from the "court-martial." The American military commissions have proved to be a flexible tool adaptable in a wide variety of situations. As we shall see, in the Mexican War, the commissions originated as a means for administering discipline to U.S. Army troops in an unprecedented situation—occupation of a foreign nation by American armed forces. Now, the term "court-martial" is reserved for the internal discipline of United States armed forces around the world.

French military courts for the trial of war crimes are known as *conseils de guerre,* literally, "councils of war." However, the same term applies to the ordinary trials of members of the French military. Similarly, British practice applies the simple label, "military courts." As we shall see, this use of one generic name should not be understood to mean that there have not been significant differences in application in historical practice. Potential for confusion exists with any of the available terms. Use of a common universal term carries the danger of blurring important distinctions. I chose not to use "military commissions" in the title to this study, since the term is unique to the American context, even as the type of court it describes extends far beyond the practices of the American military. Given these circumstances, "military tribunal," while it runs some risk of confusion with the extraordinary international trials of major war criminals, seemed to me the best choice of the lot. In his recent work on the subject, Professor Louis Fisher opts for the same term, for somewhat different reasons, acknowledging that "commission" and "tribunal" are virtually "interchangeable."[16]

Identification of a point of departure for such a study is somewhat arbitrary—the practice of military adjudication of offenses against wartime codes of conduct is almost as old as the practice of war itself. The long reach of custom bears out Maitland's famous remark about the historian's plight, forced to tear the "seamless web" of the past by the simple task of *beginning.*[17] The Australian international lawyer Timothy L. H. McCormack notes the markings of an early military tribunal in Xenophon's account of the Spartan commander Lysander's treatment of Athenian prisoners after the naval battle at Lampascus near the close of the Peloponnesian War in 405 B.C.: "by calling together the Allies, Lysander effectively constituted a tribunal for the express purpose of deciding the fate of Athenian prisoners against whom war crimes allegations had been made."[18] The account hints of striking parallels to much later developments: "the calling together of victorious Allies to determine the subject-matter jurisdiction of the tribunal and to set up the processes for the trial of alleged offenders, and the punishment of convicted criminals."[19] The Allied tribunal applied what amounted to an emerging consensus on the law of the Greeks to decide the fate of the Athenian prisoners.[20]

The historian Maurice Keen found in the medieval chroniclers' accounts of the Hundred Years War clear evidence to support a "striking claim": namely, "that military tribunals at least claimed cognisance of the offences not only of soldiers of their own side, but of soldiers generally, even those of the enemy."[21] The principle was sourced in a universal chivalric standard, to which all sides were accountable. "War was fought by knights, and in war the rules of honour applied universally, binding princes and men at arms equally. Offenses against these rules could therefore be tried by anyone who had a right to try the offences of soldiers, whatever the offender's allegiance."[22]

In the American context, military commissions featured in the War of Independence and in many subsequent military engagements. The theoretical underpinnings of the line of analysis I propose to follow extend back at least to John Locke, the theorist "in whose name the American Revolution was made."[23] Locke, of course, left open the possibility of prerogative executive powers in the course of his outline of government in the *Second Treatise*.[24] The following work concentrates on the manner in which this notion of prerogative power worked itself out in the modern era as the Western powers responded to external (and/or internal) threats of varying magnitude. I make no attempt to provide an exhaustive historical catalogue. Rather, a series of discrete, modern examples—from the American Civil War, the Second Boer War, the First World War, and the Second World War—will provide, it is hoped, contextual relief, a background against which current and future responses may be more helpfully evaluated.

Nor do I mean to underestimate lasting and important differences in the conception of political rule as it has arisen among the Western democratic powers. To be sure, the distinctly American separation of powers sets limits on the value of a comparison with British practices. Yet the British model merits consideration, for—as is the case with so many other features of American political and military institutions—American military justice practices have British roots. Moreover, this feature of the problem, regarding institutional checks on executive authority, has generated a vast amount of political debate and scholarly scrutiny, going back, at least, to the contest between *Helvidius* (Alexander Hamilton) and *Pacificus* (James Madison) over President Washington's proclamation of neutrality.[25] I do not presume to resolve a contest that is perhaps at the end of the day insoluble—at least in the abstract. In the words of Justice Jackson, again, "The actual art of governing under our Constitution does not and cannot conform to judicial definitions of the power of any of its branches based on isolated clauses or even single Articles torn from context."[26]

Still, it is something of a truism that "it is of the nature of war to increase the executive at the expence of the legislative authority."[27] The breadth and durability of a widespread practice, giving evidence of a "common law" custom of wartime adjudication, lends support to an elastic view of the Constitution's separation of powers provisions.[28] That commanders repeatedly had recourse to the practice of military commissions in the major armed conflicts of American history, and that similar practices characterize the experiences of other Western powers, sets the argument over the extent of executive versus congressional authority—an argument lately renewed in the Supreme Court's 2006 *Hamdan v. Rumsfeld* decision—in perspective.

History and custom support the notion that Congress's resolution of September 18, 2001, recognizing the President's authority "to use all necessary and appropriate force" against enemies responsible for the attacks of 9/11, includes the ancillary authority traditionally ordered among the duties of military commanders to convene military courts for addressing enemy offenses.[29] Yet, in *Hamdan,* the Supreme Court's most recent pronouncement on the subject of military tribunals, a five-member majority rejected this claim. Despite some rather straightforward recent guidance from Congress, the *Hamdan* Court nevertheless held that insufficient legislative warrant exists for the tribunals initiated by President Bush after the 9/11 attacks. The opinion, widely viewed as a stern rebuke to presidential policy, could potentially signal the practical conclusion to a longstanding military practice. But that is not likely. Indeed, with the passage of the Military Commissions Act of 2006, the judicial assertions of *Hamdan* were countered, less than six months later, by an equally forceful response from Congress, seconded by the President.

The last time public discussion of such matters occurred, George Orwell wrote on the subject of war crimes tribunals on several occasions. In one essay, Orwell recommended "some hurried, unspectacular way" of dealing with the war criminals of the Second World War. The phrase captures one of the principal virtues of the forum, its "unspectacular" quality. At the same time it carries the right note of ambivalence: the "hurried" character of the trials means that wrong judgments do occur, that the choice of military tribunals is hardly an unalloyed good, but a prudential measure for damage control in times of extremity—not necessarily, in the words of Michael Ignatieff, "a lesser evil," but rather, a device calibrated to the extraordinary circumstances of war for the securing of first-order public goods, the basic necessities of safety and order. "Above all," Orwell opposed the "solemn hypocritical 'trial of war criminals,' with all the slow cruel pageantry of the law, which after a lapse of time has so strange a way of focusing a romantic light on the accused and turning a scoundrel into a hero."[30] In a day when the "slow, cruel" spectacle of Slobodan Milošević in the Hague, a melodrama cut short only by the defendant's untimely death, vied for the spotlight with the courtroom "histrionics" of a resuscitated Saddam Hussein, such observations deserve another look. Orwell recognized what many of our experts in the law fail to see: that "international justice" is not a kind of zero-sum dream, in which the world surrounding the proceedings remains static, in which there are no important trade-offs or costs involved in maximizing procedural rigor in a given case, and in which the measure of procedural correctness applied becomes the sole test of the wisdom and justice of the event.

I cannot pretend that the problems to which I have referred remain confined to this subject. Neither can this work presume to provide the universal solvent for their correction. Though there is widespread acknowledgment of the fact that law is not generated *ex nihilo,* American understanding of the practices to which international law applies often lingers under the fog of a more general historical and cultural amnesia. My goal is to remove the analysis from the realm of arid legalistic abstraction in order better to evaluate practical consequences. The following study, it is hoped, will offer the vantage point of historical understanding for a widening of perspective, a release from what T. S. Eliot described as our "parochial" fixation with the ephemeral present. This cross-section from among the major military conflicts of the past two centuries offers a mass of recent evidence for the existence of what is identified here as a customary "common-law" practice of war crimes adjudication. It also assists, it is hoped, in bringing clarity amidst the disorientation and dismay that still characterize the West, so rudely awakened that clear September morning from its decade of dogmatic slumber. At a time when calls for global American intervention alternate with cries against American imperialist overreaching, examples from the historical experience of once-similarly situated Western forbearers and allies, allowing for differences occasioned by the passage of time, deliver an illuminating prospect. Moreover, the project points the way for further contextual examination of events situated in the shadowy borderlands between academic disciplines. While the activities of military tribunals may not adhere to the tidy lines of discrete scholarly specialties, whether in law, military history, strategy and tactics, or international relations, the history of this custom merits an examination that necessarily transcends such boundaries. Recent political, military, and legal events lend a new note of urgency to the task, underscoring the need for conscientious, dispassionate analysis. Whether the following study fulfills such requirements remains for its readers to decide.

1

American Practices from the Founding through the Civil War

The New Nation

It was a common perception from the very beginnings of the republic that the nation's geographical circumstances set it apart for its ability to maintain the peace and security of its inhabitants. In an early number of *The Federalist,* the anglophile Alexander Hamilton noted the "felicity" of the "insular situation" of the British kingdom as providing the basis for its enjoyment of relative freedom from "substantial military establishments" and identified it as a model for the new United States to follow. In the event the people were "wise enough to preserve the Union," Hamilton asserted, the nation might "for ages enjoy an advantage similar to that of an insulated situation" and reap the benefits of peace and prosperity of "a country seldom exposed by its situation to internal invasions."[1]

Hamilton's prognosis proved accurate enough. In his 1948 study on the extraordinary recourse to "constitutional dictatorship" in times of national crisis, Clinton Rossiter noted that the nation's relative isolation, the wealth and variety of its natural resources, the existence of a "safety valve" in the westward-moving frontier, and the resilience of the American economy in the nineteenth century together attended a situation characterized by a "lack of serious crisis and the concomitant lack of crisis government."[2] By comparison to the other Western democracies it most closely resembles, the United States has enjoyed precious little disruption to its constitutional political order in the form of exogenous shocks, having had to face "exactly one invasion and one revolution" over the course of more than two centuries.[3] Yet America's "insulated situation" ended on September 11, 2001.

The precariousness of the new country's position among the nations made it necessary to give due attention to matters of peace and security. In his assessment of "the authorities essential to the care of the common defence," Hamilton emphasized that "[t]hese powers ought to exist without limitation, *because it is impossible to foresee or define the extent and variety of national exigencies, or the correspondent extent & variety of the means which may be necessary to satisfy them.* The circumstances that endanger the safety of nations are infinite; and for this reason no constitutional shackles can wisely be imposed on the power to which the care of it is committed. This power ought to be co-extensive with all the possible combinations of such circumstances."[4] Implicit in Hamilton's remarks was a conviction as to the implausibility of a prefabricated comprehensive plan for national security. The means of confrontation would be dictated to great extent by the future, unknown content of the "national exigencies" to which they would be tailored. The unforeseeability of the nature, "extent and variety" of the array of threats to be addressed meant that the mechanisms of response would necessarily be reactive, in large measure, and that they would place a high value on the executive qualities of speed, efficiency, secrecy, and decisiveness.

Even before the adoption of the Constitution, the War of Independence witnessed the use of military tribunals as an extraordinary response to the exigencies of war. The trial of enemy violators of the laws of war in these forums was recognized as an established practice under the law of nations. Washington's determination to prevent the nation's downward slide into military dictatorship[5] set the character and tone of the tribunals organized under the auspices of the armies of the new republic. The tribunals provided an institutional means of securing restraint and order in the midst of circumstances that could swiftly spin out of control.[6] In urging his men to refrain from violent retaliation, Washington evinced a desire to uphold a code of virtue and honor in war. Responding to British destruction of a New Jersey captain's home and farm, he asserted, "Tho' my indignation at such ungenerous conduct of the enemy might at first prompt me to retaliation, yet humanity and policy forbid the measure. Experience proves, that their wanton cruelty injures rather than benefits their cause; that, with our forbearance, justly secured to us the attachment of all good men."[7] As difficult as it would be to refrain from retaliation, the cruelty of the enemy and forbearance of friendly forces could together win credibility for the new nation and its cause.

Numerous incidents of enemy espionage occasioned the convening of military tribunals, perhaps most notably in the case of Major John André, a collaborator with General Benedict Arnold.[8] André, deputy adjutant general in the British army, conducted a secret correspondence with

Arnold in 1779 to arrange the surrender of West Point. The two met in September 1780, and New York militiamen captured André at Tarrytown as he sought to recover to British lines in disguise. General Washington ordered the hapless British officer to be hastened before a military tribunal composed of fourteen general officers, in Colonel Alexander Hamilton's words, "to prevent all possibility of misrepresentation or cavil on the part of the enemy."[9] Basing its findings largely upon the voluntary confession of the accused, the board determined that André "ought to be considered as a spy and that agreeably to the laws and usages of nations he ought to suffer death."[10] Despite zealous efforts to avert the sentence on the part of the British command, André was executed two days later.[11] The contemporary chronicler of the war David Ramsay noted that "the necessity of discouraging further plots, fixed his fate, and stamped it with the seal of political necessity."[12] Alexander Hamilton's account of the *ad hoc* court provides a poignant glimpse into the gentlemanly nature of the proceedings that characterized the short trial. Even when allowance is made for the hyperbole introduced by eighteenth-century decorum and sentiment, the display of elevated regard for the enemy is virtually unthinkable by current standards:

> Never perhaps did any man suffer death with more justice, or deserve it less. . . . [In] the whole progress of the affair, he was treated with the most scrupulous delicacy. When brought before the Board of Officers, he met with every mark of indulgence and was required to answer no interrogatory, which could even embarrass his feelings. On his part, while he carefully concealed everything that might involve others, he frankly confessed all the facts relating to himself; and upon his confession without the trouble of examining a witness, the Board made their report. The members of it were not more impressed with the candor and firmness mixed with a becoming sensibility, which he displayed than he was penetrated with their liberality and politeness. He acknowledged the generosity of their behaviour towards him, in every respect, but particularly in this, in the strongest terms of manly gratitude. In a conversation with a Gentleman who visited him after his trial, he said he flattered himself he had never been illiberal; but if there were any remains of prejudice, in his mind, his present experience must obliterate them.[13]

The military courts of Washington's continental army preceded the establishment of a system of federal civil courts. In implementing tribunals such as the group of officers who tried Major André, General Washington was acting under the auspices of the Articles of War passed by the Continental Congress. The Articles of War, adopted from the British model, governed the administration of American military justice into the second half of the twentieth century, with only slight amendments over time. Throughout the Revolutionary War, no jurisdictional distinction was made between the forum used for American military offenders and the trial of enemy spies and other offenders for violations of the laws of war. Following the British practice, all types of cases were heard in courts-martial. An important amendment to the Articles of War eventually carved out a specified jurisdiction for "military commissions" for the adjudication of offenses against the law of war not normally subject to courts-martial.

Interestingly, there was very little direction given in the Revolutionary War Articles regarding the long-standing military practice of trying enemy combatants for violations of the laws of armed conflict. The custom was simply assumed without comment. The Continental Congress paid greater attention to what may be called the moral government of officers and enlisted men fighting on behalf of the United Colonies. The first substantive provisions dealt with rules of decorum and the conditioning of moral character. In Section I, article 2, it was "earnestly recommended to all officers and soldiers diligently to attend divine service." Penalties were assigned for those who behaved "indecently, or irreverently, at any place of divine worship." The following article provided penalties for "prophane cursing or swearing." Next, chaplains who abandoned their assigned postings without leave were to be court-martialed. The prominence bestowed upon moral propriety and self-discipline in the Articles of War reflects the urgency with which these matters were viewed. In the section addressing rules for the administering of military courts, the members of courts-martial were enjoined to "behave with calmness and decency." The Articles of War as a whole were "to be read and published once in every two months, at the head of every regiment, troop or company, mustered, or to be mustered in the service of the United States."[14]

It is important not to overlook the military context within which the courts-martial took place. Patterns and practices here became established that would shape the entire future course of American juridical mechanisms of response to infractions of laws of war. Undeniably, prisoners of war on both sides suffered deprivation and cruelty. The British treatment of captured Americans met with steadily increasing crescendos of protest and outrage. Retaliation and reprisals occurred as the war dragged on.[15] Maintaining good order and discipline among the troops was a constant struggle, one exacerbated by the unseemly practices of irregulars on the fringes. Such practices provide a reminder "that the War for American Independence was in many ways and in many places a civil war, that the imperial contest overlay preexisting levels of local social, religious, and political tensions of varying intensity and complexity. The reality that a civil war was intertwined with British efforts to suppress a rebellion had a powerful, corrosive effect on the ability and willingness of men on both sides to moderate their actions and avoid involving civilians in military operations."[16] Thus, the new army's own tribulations took the form not only of hostility and brutality, but also assailed it from the society out of which it had come, especially as the initial euphoria of 1775 faded with time. For all these reasons, Washington's army became the crucible in which the new republic's foundational elements of "citizen virtue and moral commitment" received their greatest testing by fire. The temptation to lash out in vindictive violence against enemy prisoners and violators of law of war must have been severe. In the concatenation of circumstances that increased frictions between the army and the wider society, the army and in particular, its officers, proved

> capable of subordinating self-interest to the public welfare, the essential ingredient of a virtuous citizenry when put to the test. Because of that restraint, a military coup, with some American Caesar rising out of the ashes, did not eventuate . . . The army remained on the side of liberty and republicanism while tempted, even dared by civilians who withheld support and encouragement from 1777 on, to go the other way. When most sorely tried it reaffirmed subordination of military to civil authority. Paradoxically, this same hard-core group of regulars, so damned by so many patriots (and feared by ideologues as the antithesis of the republican ideal of the militia) set the highest example of selfless behavior in Revolutionary America.[17]

Any signs of incipient military dictatorship should have made their first appearance in the army's treatment of enemy spies and violators of law of war. The exigencies of war prompted the creation of these military tribunals and necessarily imbued them with urgency, severity, and finality. Yet in these early manifestations of military justice, the virtues of restraint and order, inculcated in the Articles of War and on display in the treatment of Major André, set the conditions for the most part in which enemy combatants and spies were treated. The character of the tribunals, the tenor of their operations, is best seen as a reflection of the complex culture and conditions, both military and civilian, in which they arose.

The Early Nineteenth Century

In the aftermath of the War of 1812, General Andrew Jackson convened a court-martial for the trial of the naturalized Frenchman and member of the Louisiana Legislature, the civilian Louis Louaillier on charges of spying and other offenses. The Battle of New Orleans, fought on January 8, 1815, and resulting in a lopsided victory for Jackson and the Americans, had been followed by tension and disorder in the city. Jackson imposed martial law and suspended the writ of *habeas corpus.*[18] The general was holding out for the official news of the peace, which failed to arrive until mid-March. On March 3, Louaillier had published a newspaper article criticizing Jackson's refusal to lift martial law. The article, like "a match to powder," was followed by a mutiny of Louisiana troops and the defiant refusal of a company ordered to replace them.[19] Jackson ordered the court-martial of Louaillier on seven charges, ranging from mutiny to espionage.[20] When Louaillier petitioned the local Federal district judge, Dominick A. Hall, for a writ of habeas corpus and received it, Jackson responded by arresting Hall and sending him to jail. Louaillier's court-martial, presided over by the conscientious Brigadier-General Edmund P. Gaines, Regular Army, deliberated two days and declared itself to be without jurisdiction on all but the spying charge, on which the court entered an acquittal.[21] An enraged Jackson rejected the court's findings and ordered Louaillier to be returned to confinement. Finally, two days later, on March 13, 1815, official word of ratification of the Treaty of Ghent arrived in New Orleans, upon which Jackson revoked the order of martial law and released his military prisoners, including Louaillier. After the turmoil had subsided, Judge Hall ordered the hero of New Orleans to appear before him "to show cause why he should not be held in contempt for his refusal to recognize the writ of habeas corpus in the case of Louis Louaillier,"[22] asserting that "the only question was whether the Law should bend to the General or the General to the Law."[23] Judge Hall found Jackson in contempt and assessed a thousand-dollar fine (later to be remitted, with interest, by Congress in 1844).[24] In Lincoln's responses to critics during the Civil War, the case would reemerge as a precedent to lend support for the proposition that "the Constitution is not, in its application, in all respects the same, in cases of rebellion or invasion involving the public safety, as it is in time of profound peace and public security."[25]

Similar controversy attended the 1818 Florida court-martial of two Englishmen, Alexander Arbuthnot, who in trading with the Indians had over time become their advocate and spokesman, and Lieutenant Robert C. Ambrister, an adventurer with the Royal Colonial Marines. The trial took place as just one aspect of Jackson's controversial campaign in Florida, in which he exceeded his presidential mandate to push the hostile Seminole tribes back to the limits represented by the Spanish forts in Florida. Moreover, Jackson instituted military control over the region, the purchase of which the Secretary of State was in the process of negotiating. Arbuthnot, an elderly white-haired gentleman, whose "only friends were Indians,"[26] faced charges of aiding and abetting the Indian tribes in their war against the United States, as well as of spying. The evidence against him included "appeals [in his writing] from [various hostile chiefs] to the British Governor at Nassau for troops, arms and ammunition with which to fight the Americans; communications in the Indians' behalf to the British Minister at Washington and to the Governor of Havana; statistics on the strength of the hostile Indians and the munitions they needed to wage war."[27] Ambrister was arraigned upon the charge of making war against the United States at the head of the Indian tribes. The presiding officer in the court-martial was the same General Gaines who had adjudicated in the Louaillier trial in New Orleans three years earlier. Arbuthnot was found guilty and sentenced to be hanged. Upon convicting Ambrister for levying war against the United States, the court initially recommended execution. But before the sentence was finalized, one of the court members asked for a reconsideration, and in the end the court "substituted therefor the milder punishment—which thereupon became the legal and only sentence—'to receive fifty stripes on the bare back and be confined with a ball and chain to hard labor for twelve calendar months.'"[28] In his review of the case, Jackson disapproved the court's revision of the sentence and ordered the accused to be shot in accordance with the initial rendering. The execution speedily ensued. Commenting in 1886, William Winthrop correctly judged that "for such an order and its execution a military commander would *now* be indictable for murder."[29]

In Washington, the House of Representatives met to consider the record of Jackson's purported abuses of authority in Florida, to include the executions of Arbuthnot and Ambrister. After the House Committee on Military Affairs had concluded its report condemning Jackson's behavior, the matter went before the full House, which cleared its docket in order to devote itself to the case. Lighting up the House "in a blaze of eloquence,"[30] the Whig Speaker, Henry Clay, at the head of Jackson's political enemies, strove mightily to make the case against the general. The speech, with Clay taking the role of Jackson's accuser in the advance billing, attracted foreign ministers and ladies of fashion; the galleries and aisles were crowded to overflowing; the Senate adjourned its business in order to attend.[31] Clay "denounced Jackson for conducting unauthorized war on Spain and for the brutal murder of two British subjects; closing, he warned the nation against the dangers of a new Caesar."[32] Yet when the House came to a vote on the matter: "Resolved, That the House of Representatives . . . disapproves the execution of Alexander Arbuthnot and Robert C. Ambrister," the noes outnumbered the ayes by ninety to fifty. The other related votes came to a similar vindication of the general and of his practices in the Pensacola campaign. In England, despite passionate outbursts of denunciation in both the Whig and Tory press, the British Government, "after a careful investigation of the facts, if not acquiescing in the rightfulness of the action of the court-martial, at least made no complaint of it as involving a violation of international law."[33] For policy reasons, the result, though illegally obtained, was not called into question.[34]

The Mexican War

Historians generally acknowledge James K. Polk's Mexican War of 1846–1848 as the event that brought about the formal recognition of the military commission in America as a practice separate and distinct from the court-martial.[35] If Jackson demonstrated a somewhat high-handed disregard for legal niceties in his use of military tribunals, the inventor of the forum known as the military commission, General Winfield Scott, exercised considerable prudential judgment in his own use of the extraordinary military courts. For the most part, the General Order that provided for trial by military commission identified criminal offenses normally cognizable by civil courts in time of peace.[36] The jurisdiction of the commissions extended to such crimes "whether committed by Mexicans or other civilians in Mexico against individuals of the U.S. military forces, or by such individuals against other such individuals or against Mexicans or civilians."[37] Plainly, the chief reason for the distinction had to do with the need for a legal body equipped to address criminal activity by civilians and/or military members peculiar to the time and circumstances of war.[38] Specific violations of the laws of war were tried and punished in separate tribunals, designated by General Scott as "councils of war." These councils were responsible for adjudicating charges of "Guerilla Warfare or Violation of the Laws of War by Guerilleros, and Enticing or Attempting to entice soldiers to desert the U.S. service."[39] Resort to the councils was rare in the Mexican War.

The war itself had begun under rather dubious circumstances.[40] After the acquisition of Texas in December 1845, President Polk ordered General Zachary Taylor from Louisiana to Texas, to protect the army's southern flank along the Rio Grande. In reality, the boundary stretched approximately 150 miles north, in an area between the Rio Grande and the Nueces. With Taylor's army blockading the Rio Grande near the Mexican position at Matamoras on the opposite side, an American reconnaissance patrol met with attack from a larger Mexican force. Several Americans were killed in the skirmish; the rest, taken prisoner. Upon receiving the news of the confrontation, Polk promptly sought funds from Congress, arguing that a state of war was already in existence as a result of the aggressions of the Mexican army—on American soil. The appropriations bill, complete with a preamble asserting that "a state of war exists," sailed through the Democrat-controlled Congress, with a declaration of war, a $10-million appropriation, and a call for volunteers. Senator John C. Calhoun objected as to the existence of a "state of war," arguing that "the president's action, forcing a declaration of war on Congress without deliberation or reflection, effectively divested that body of the war-making power."[41] The main source of opposition to the war was concentrated in the Northeast.[42] New England Whigs denounced Polk's manipulation of the boundary dispute with Mexico.[43] Radical Whigs feared that the war was really part of an effort to enlarge slave territories. Nevertheless, widespread enthusiasm for the war, at least in its first year, conflated to aggressive expansionism in the "All Mexico" movement, seemingly fed in part by bigotry against the Mexican people.[44] Opposition to the war focused mainly on Polk's apparently blatant violation of the *ius ad bellum*, rather than on particular aspects of the conduct of the war itself. The greatest number of trials by military commission occurred in 1847, and probably proliferated, at least in part, in response to the guerrilla tactics of the Mexican military, which managed to prolong the war despite an unbroken string of decisive American victories on the battlefield.[45]

Yet, as the historian Mark Neely observes, many of the offenses catalogued in General Scott's order "could have been perpetrated *only on the enemy in occupied territory by Scott's own troops*" (italics in original).[46] This puzzling peculiarity is resolved with recognition of the narrow focus of the jurisdiction of the military courts under the Articles of War. The general rule, inherited from British military practice—if not from Parliament's legislative record—limited the powers of courts-martial to those cases in which some impact on good order and discipline in the military could be discerned.[47] "Ordinary" civilian offenses normally remained the province of the civilian courts. The question presented itself: "How are crimes to be punished which are committed in territory occupied by force of arms, but which are not of a military character nor provided for in the military code of the conquering state?"[48] In what for Americans were the unique circumstances of the Mexican War, the need for a new type of forum for criminal justice arose out of the lack of discipline prevailing among the volunteer components of the U.S. army, a contingent Scott described as "the wild volunteers," as "miscreants" and "barbarians."[49] A greater means of self-restraint was needed in the foreign territory of Mexico, "for by the strange omission of Congress, American troops take with them beyond the limits of their own country, no law but the Constitution of the United States, and the rules and articles of war. These do not provide any court for the trial or punishment of murder, rape, theft, &c., &c.,—no matter by whom, or on whom committed."[50]

In his *Memoirs,* Scott noted that his order imposing martial rule met with embarrassment and hostility among "all the authorities," who "touched the subject as daintily as a 'terrier mumbles a hedgehog.'"[51] Scott himself counted the order a great achievement toward the maintenance of "the discipline and honor of the army," and said that he could never have reached Mexico City without it.[52] Scott listed a number of reasons for the success of the order:

> It was successively republished at Vera Cruz, Puebla, and the capital, so that it might be familiarly known to every man in the army, and in a translation, it was also extensively circulated among the people of the country. Under it, all offenders, Americans and Mexicans, were alike

> punished—with death for murder or rape, and for other crimes proportionally. It will be seen that the order did not in the least interfere with the administration of justice between Mexican and Mexican, by the ordinary courts of the country. It only provided a special American tribunal for any case to which an American might be a party. And further, it should be observed, that military commissions in applying penalties to convicted felons, were limited to "known punishments, in like cases, in some of the States of the United States"—the latter, as such, being without a common law, or a common criminal code.[53]

With some measure of characteristic hyperbole, "Old Fuss and Feathers" celebrated his own vindication as against "the cowardice of certain high functionaries on the subject"; for "it has been admitted by all that the order worked like a charm; that it conciliated Mexicans; intimidated the vicious of the several races; and being executed with impartial rigor, gave the highest moral deportment and discipline ever known in an invading army."[54]

After the imposition of martial law, Scott sought to ensure that justice was meted out with swiftness, impartiality, certainty, and, especially in the case of American army offenders, due severity. Scott, a student of the art of warfare, had learned important lessons from the excesses committed by Napoleon's army during the Peninsular campaign and sought strenuously to avoid the same mistakes. The imposition of martial law developed as a critical element in Scott's overall *military* strategy. Keeping in mind the larger political objectives for the war, Scott determined to avoid a long, frustrating "cat-and-mouse" struggle with Mexican guerrilla forces. The problem of the military commander in occupation of foreign territory was a rather new one in American military history. The gauge for determining success or failure necessarily required a new breadth and range of perspective: "An army operating in a hostile country is vulnerable because it must deal not just with an enemy army but with an entire population that has the power constantly to harass and to withhold needed resources." It would be senseless—militarily and politically counter-productive—to follow a "scorched-earth" policy, either by design or by simple lack of discipline, since, as Napoleon had learned, such measures would leave in the resulting wreckage a populace in the occupied territory embittered and keen to exact revenge—the source of new recruits for indigenous guerrilla forces. The key to avoiding such a potentially disastrous result was in "maintaining strict discipline within his own army, paying for all provisions acquired in Mexico, guaranteeing Mexican property rights, and recognizing the sanctity of religious structures. He designed his martial law order to accomplish these objectives."[55]

Scott was largely successful: "Instead of leaving anger and hostility in the army's wake as it passed through the country, it left law and order. Realizing that successful guerrilla activities depend on an environment hostile to the invading army, Scott used martial law in a way that both protected American soldiers and created a more conducive atmosphere for peace talks."[56] Thus, the imposition of martial law by no means represented a degradation of the rule of law in the regions where it was applied. The success of the military commissions as a tool of discipline and of military strategy resulted from the prudential military and political statesmanship that attended their application: "In practice the combination of a reliance on local officials to deal with purely Mexican matters and the military commissions to handle those involving Americans or American interests worked well. It gave a degree of stability and competence of administration which had not been seen in some areas within the memory of living man. It is not surprising, therefore, that there grew up in Mexico a movement for the incorporation of the nation within the United States or, if that failed, to offer the control of the nation to Scott."[57]

The tale has an ironic postscript. Polk's ongoing quarrel with Scott makes for an interesting case study in civil-military relations. From the heights of his triumph, Scott's fall from grace followed with rude alacrity. By April of 1848, he had been removed from command and returned home. The ostensible proximate cause was the squabbling among glory-seeking generals under his command, for which Scott was held responsible. The larger explanation was the "greed" of Polk in desiring to extend the conquest of Mexico beyond what Scott deemed to be militarily, economically, politically, and morally sensible.[58]

The Civil War

Notwithstanding the impact of earlier manifestations, Clinton Rossiter is surely correct in maintaining that it was in the Civil War "that the peculiar pattern of crisis government in the United States was first set."[59] The establishment of military commissions as a means of adjudicating wartime offenses emerged in the flow of a series of controversial measures undertaken by Lincoln in the critical early months of the conflict, between the opening volleys at Fort Sumter in April 1861 and the President's special address to Congress upon its reconvening on July 4. In this crucial eleven-week period, Lincoln virtually "was the government of the United States," acting "on no precedent and under no restraint."[60] His actions during these weeks have been the source of much controversy among historians and scholars. The actual institution of military commissions came later; the first such courts convened in the autumn of 1861, in the volatile border state of Missouri. But Lincoln's orders of the first eleven weeks of the war set the stage for the later establishment of the special military courts. On April 15, 1861, Lincoln summoned the militia "of the several States of the Union to the aggregate number of seventy-five thousand" as his initial step toward the suppression of the rebellion set in motion by the secession of seven southern states. In the same eleven-week period, Lincoln ordered a blockade of the seaports of the southern states—a measure of questionable legality under both the Constitution and international law. He followed up the initial call for militia with an entreaty for volunteers, seeking to enlarge the army and navy by over 42,000 troops—a blatant intrusion upon the congressional war powers in Article I, section 8 of the Constitution. In the same period, the President ordered the Post Office to be closed to "treasonable correspondence"; in addition, he "caused persons who were represented to him as being or about to engage in disloyal and treasonable practices to be arrested by special civil as well as military agencies and detained in military custody when necessary to prevent them or deter others from such practices." Drastic action had been necessary to respond to circumstances in which, Secretary of War Stanton stated, "every department of the Government was paralyzed by treason."[61]

Most important for the later establishment of military tribunals, Lincoln issued an order for the suspension of the privilege of the writ of habeas corpus—this despite the widespread conviction that the power for such drastic action constitutionally belonged to Congress alone, since the clause limiting suspension of the privilege except "when in Cases of Rebellion or invasion the public safety may require it" rests in a list of restrictions on the powers of Congress in Article I, section 9. Pressing problems created by mass support for the Confederate cause, not to mention outright insurrection, had arisen, especially in the border states of Missouri, Maryland, Delaware, and Kentucky. The same conditions would surface in the southern sections of Ohio, Illinois and Indiana. Yet the initial order limited itself to a narrow geographical area, the military line between Washington and Philadelphia, and later, Washington and New York. Lincoln's "mental struggling" seems evident in the communications he made to explain the rationale for resorting to what he deemed a truly drastic measure.[62] Despite a prolonged and puzzling reticence on the part of Congress,[63] the order was later ratified by the legislature, but only after thousands of arrests had already been made under its authority. The judiciary was not so circumspect. Litigation over the constitutionality of Lincoln's decree followed in quick succession upon the order itself. As part of his duties on circuit, Chief Justice Roger Taney heard a case involving a secessionist drill lieutenant, Merryman, who had been arrested in Maryland and confined at Fort McHenry. In *Ex parte Merryman* Taney returned the opinion that Lincoln's order exceeded the bounds of executive authority under the Constitution and issued the writ ordering Merryman's production. In the course of his decision, Taney raised the specter of military dictatorship, voicing the fear that the arbitrariness introduced by the order could remove the protections available "under a government of laws"; every citizen would be reduced to holding his "life, liberty and property at the will and pleasure of the army officer in whose military district he may happen to be found." Notwithstanding the admonition of the Chief Justice, the commander in charge of the military department, General George Cadwallader, refused to obey the court order. When Taney issued a writ of attachment for contempt in response, the marshal serving the writ was denied access to the fort, and the matter came to a standstill. To be sure, the pronouncement of a lone justice riding on circuit would have failed to carry the force of an *en banc* opinion of the full court in any event. Nevertheless, the status of the judiciary as "the weakest branch" was exposed. Neither Lincoln nor his generals gave heed to the Chief Justice's constitutional criticisms of the President's order, and the privilege of *habeas corpus* remained suspended throughout the course of Lincoln's administration. After March 3, 1863, however, all further presidential suspensions of the privilege of *habeas corpus* occurred at the behest of Congress, for the "Habeas Corpus Act" granted such authority to the President "whenever, in his judgment, the public safety may require it."[64]

It seems that the extraordinary character of the activity of civil war stirred up fog and confusion with regard to the distinctive legal mechanisms set in motion in response. Lincoln, his cabinet, and his generals appear to have assumed that the suspension of *habeas corpus* legally sanctioned the application of the Articles of War to civilians, and thus, the trial of civilians by *courts-martial*, although it was actually the declaration of martial law that the Articles contemplated as the threshold event for the institution of the special tribunals known as *military commissions*. Denial of the privilege of *habeas corpus*, the post-war *Milligan* court would make clear, was not tantamount to a declaration of martial law. Yet the distinction remained ambiguous throughout the course of the war itself. Indeed, generals in the field apparently introduced the practice of trials by military commission without the awareness of the Lincoln administration; and "Washington officials often used the terms 'suspension of the writ of habeas corpus' and 'declaration of martial law' interchangeably."[65]

"The Government's Hour of Trial"

From these beginnings in legal uncertainty and confusion, military commissions came to be used with great frequency in the course of the Civil War—an undeclared war and one in which President Lincoln's unilateral assertions of authority in his role as Commander-in-Chief led to charges of high-handed, "dictatorial" disregard of civil liberties.[66] On September 24, 1862, Lincoln issued "his most sweeping cancellation of the writ."[67] The scope of the campaign for the maintenance of civil order was broadened to apply suspension of the privilege of *habeas corpus* to draft resisters, persons who "discouraged voluntary enlistments," and those who participated in "any disloyal practice affording aid and comfort to rebels against the authority of the United States."[68] All such persons became subject to martial law and trial by military commission, or court-martial. From this point, trials by military commission were linked with arrests under martial law on a regular basis.[69] After this order, myriad citizens were arrested and sent to confinement in military prisons, including state legislators, newspaper editors and owners, businessmen, war protestors, and pastors.[70] Yet many such prisoners, housed in military detention facilities such as Fort Lafayette in New York Harbor, received little if any due process. As James Randall observed, "Subordinates sometimes acted under a misapprehension of the extent of their authority, erroneously supposing that because the 'writ was suspended,' all forms of law were gone. In disregard of restraining instructions from Washington, prisoners were sometimes taken on trivial charges, such as 'being a noisy secessionist,' giving sympathy to the 'rebels,' selling Confederate 'mottoes and devices,' of 'hurrahing for Jeff Davis.' An Episcopal minister of Alexandria, Virginia, was arrested for habitually omitting the prayer for the President of the United States as required by the church service."[71]

In his July 4, 1861, Special Message to Congress, Lincoln had demonstrated an early awareness of the tragic dimensions of the nation's dilemma. The test posed by the seceders had thrown down the gauntlet to the very existence of constitutional republican principles everywhere: "'Is there, in all republics, this inherent, and fatal weakness?'" asked Lincoln referring to the seceders' rhetoric; "'Must a government, of necessity, be too *strong* for the liberties of its own people, or too *weak* to maintain its own existence?'" Set in these starkly existential terms, the urgency of national self-preservation loomed proportionally greater in the calculus of necessity than the risk of abuse of civil liberties.

> The whole of the laws which were required to be faithfully executed, were being resisted, and failing of execution, in nearly one-third of the States. Must they be allowed to finally fail of execution, even had it been perfectly clear, that by the use of the means necessary to their execution, some single law, made in such extreme tenderness of the citizen's liberty, that practically, it relieves more of the guilty, than of the innocent, should, to a very limited extent be violated? To state the question more directly, are all the laws, but one, to go unexecuted, and the government itself go to pieces, lest that one be violated? Even in such a case, would not the official oath be broken, if the government should be overthrown, when it was believed that disregarding the single law, would tend to preserve it?[72]

Acknowledging that the extremity of the response should be commensurate with the scope of the danger did not obviate the agony of the choice. If the Constitution was not to be given the last rite of extreme unction as a kind of mutual death pact, the fateful, lawless step must be taken for the sake of preserving the law. Ultimately, no paradox lingered here.[73] As Harry Jaffa has observed, Lincoln understood his assertions as to "the strength of his government" to be harmonious with the rule of law. Far from serving as "a pretext to undermine the liberties of the Constitution," the necessary measures had been taken as first-order exercise of the natural proclivity to self-preservation. Lincoln's argument presupposed that "just as there is no assignable limit to what is permitted to individuals by the law of self-preservation in the state of nature, there can be no assignable limit to what a government may do on behalf of those to whose care that preservation has been entrusted."[74]

Moreover, the measure calling for suspension of the *habeas corpus* privilege could not properly be deemed extra-constitutional—the Framers of the Constitution themselves had anticipated the self-evident requirement for means adapted to the unforeseeable and indefinable variety of future national exigencies. Extraordinary conditions demanded an extraordinary response. Even the instrumental fact of the provision for suspension of *habeas corpus* in Article I, among the legislative powers, could not override the "dominating purpose" of the text, "to enable the government to provide for the public safety in the case of a rebellion."[75] Lincoln later explained that his purpose with the restraining measures was "for *prevention,* and not for *punishment*—as injunctions to stay injury, as proceedings to keep the peace."[76] Still, it could not be gainsaid that the broad ranging authority placed in the hands of military officials as a consequence of the suspension of the privilege opened the door to abuses.

Under these circumstances, the military tribunals served as something of an (albeit imperfect) check on the caprices of army officials charged with carrying out martial law in decidedly precarious conditions:

> Trials by military commission restrained United States forces in the Civil War mainly by imposing systematic record-keeping and an atmosphere of legality on the army's dealings with a hostile populace. Military commissions played a role in preventing martial law from degenerating into what the cynical Duke of Wellington had called it, "the will of the general." No Union general in Missouri could, according to Winfield Scott or Henry W. Halleck or Ulysses S. Grant, order summary justice for a civilian offender and march on without so much as recording the event . . . Military commissions dictated not only record-keeping but also system, regularity, review, and some safeguards for defendants' rights.[77]

Given the divided jurisdiction wrought by the institution of martial law, inevitable clashes occurred between civil and military authorities. The *Merryman* case provides an early example of the attempts made by the civilian court system to maintain control over the administration of justice. Yet "Military authorities sincerely believed that they could not leave matters to the ineffectual efforts of the judiciary." Such efforts were "ineffectual," because of the "basic physical inability of the judicial arm to cope with a situation involving turbulence and widespread violence." In the view of military officials charged with maintaining peace and order in the midst of chaotic conditions, "the complexity, delay, and clumsiness of judicial procedure were felt to be unsuited to the effective handling of a threatening situation."[78]

The jurisdiction of the tribunals addressed an expanded array of circumstances. For obvious reasons, the conditions that in the Mexican War had made necessary the creation of the new type of tribunal no longer obtained. American troops were not fighting this war on foreign soil. Moreover, the bulk of the cases involved the adjudication of civilians for whom the jurisdiction of the civilian court system was at least theoretically available and applicable. In the border state of Missouri, where it first came into use, the measure served as a means of enforcing the state of martial law declared by General John C. Frémont in August of 1861. Here, civil war unfolded in "microcosmic" version.[79] By the summer of 1861, outbursts of street fighting had escalated into full scale violence. After a bloody battle at Wilson's Creek in August of 1861, "neighborhood war, bushwhacking, sniping, and guerilla fighting . . . of a most sanguinary sort . . . [had become] rampant" in the state.[80] To some degree, the presence of Federal troops and the imposition of a state of martial law served to escalate the level of disorder, for it succeeded in "driving thousands into the Confederate ranks," while it "also occasioned many kinds of obstructive tactics and acts of violence on the part of those enemies who remained out of uniform."[81] Still, the commission of wartime offenses such as sniping, espionage, and bushwhacking by civilians, not regular, uniformed combatants, made necessary the implementation of special forums for the adjudication of these uniquely wartime offenses. Military commissions came into usage as a means of providing a modicum of stability in the midst of appalling brutality and civil disorder. Similar conditions operated in the other border states. The bulk of the cases heard there had to do with guerrilla activities, horse stealing, "bridge burning, tearing up railway and telegraph lines, and like offenses."[82] In these strife-worn regions, "the widespread guerrilla warfare . . . forced awful choices on Union authorities as well as on the individual citizens of a state."[83] In one exemplary case,

> Robert T. Johns of Greene County was tried by a military commission in the county seat, Springfield, in the fall of 1862 for violating the laws of war by letting rebels lurk in his neighborhood without reporting them to

> the U.S. military authorities. He pleaded guilty but explained that one of the men lurking in the high brush was his brother-in-law, on whom he did not want to inform. He had discovered the men hiding in the brush only by accident and did not wish either to harbor them or to inform the authorities about them. But neutrality in areas involved in guerrilla warfare often proved impossible. The commission sentenced Johns to six months at hard labor.[84]

To be sure, further hard choices attended the task of discerning between "legitimate popular resistance forces and illegitimate guerrilla bands," which remained a vexing problem throughout the war.[85]

Although the majority of cases had to do with civilians in violation of the laws of war, combatant soldiers also appeared before the commissions, which in this particular operated in a manner similar to the commissions in the Mexican War—as a check on the activities of "wild" volunteers. Such a case was that of Private William T. Cox of the 8th Cavalry Regiment, Missouri Volunteers, whom a military commission found guilty of various offenses, charged together as a violation of the laws of war. On the night of October 18, 1862, Cox had left the encampment and, along with an armed band of unknown ruffians, forced his way into the home of a private citizen, Richard Rose, in Green County, Missouri, stolen a horse, and plundered the house while "cursing, maltreating and abusing" the inhabitants. Before the spree was over, Cox had also raped Rose's wife, Nancy, and robbed and plundered the houses of other neighboring citizens. The commission found Cox guilty and sentenced him to be shot to death. [86]

Neely's numerical summaries for the trials by military commission is revealing: out of a total number of at least 4,271 cases, 1,940 cases were heard in Missouri, as compared to 1,339 in the eleven Confederate states combined. More than nine times as many cases occurred in Missouri as in either of the other border states of Maryland or Kentucky, which together with Missouri accounted for the greatest amount of activity by military commissions. The conclusion is inescapable: "The incidence of military commissions was a function of civil disorder." Largely due to the record compiled in two particularly well-known Supreme Court cases, Lincoln's reputation would suffer from his use of military commissions in the Civil War. Yet, despite allegations of lawless authoritarianism, "trials by military commission in the Civil War were marked by procedural regularity. The best proof of this is the records themselves"—records which contain a better, more exhaustive account of the trials in question than that which existed in the contemporaneous civilian criminal justice systems. Since all such trials were recorded, in contrast to contemporary civilian criminal and civil trials, the evidence concerning the conduct of the trials is "manageable, comprehensive and exhaustive."[87]

Trials by military commission were reviewable by the departmental commander and by the Judge Advocate General, who from 1862 was the loyal Kentuckian, Joseph Holt, "a punctilious lawyer and military administrator who repeatedly overturned the decisions of trials by military commission (as well as courts-martial) for what can only be called legal technicalities."[88] The General-in-Chief also exercised reviewing authority. Sentences awarding the death penalty were subject to automatic presidential review; the President had the discretion to review other cases—"and Lincoln's clemency saved many a life."[89] On such occasions, the point in issue often had to do with fundamental concerns as to the proper jurisdiction of the commissions. In early 1863, three Maryland citizens had been "taken prisoner while in arms in the ranks and uniform of the rebel army," charged before a military commission and convicted of treason. The death sentences of the three Marylanders, James R. Oliver, Samuel C. Betts, and James Rider, were overturned by order of the Secretary of War. The proceedings in their cases had been disapproved by the President, for the record demonstrated that they were to be designated as prisoners of war "and should be treated as such and exchanged."[90]

The Dakota Trials

During the dark days of 1862, with the Union cause at low ebb, the Lincoln administration learned of another crisis exploding on the western frontier in Minnesota. A month before the bloody stalemate at Antietam gave Lincoln the needed breathing space for delivering the Emancipation Proclamation, there came news of massacres in the western part of the Minnesota territory. Sioux warriors were killing men, women, and children. Invidious corruption in the governmental administration of Indian affairs, severe crop shortages and starvation, and general friction between white settlers and native tribes had flared into murderous war, at the worst possible time. As is so often the case for governments in times of crisis, the quantity and varying quality of reports from Minnesota made it difficult to get an accurate grasp of the magnitude of the danger. In settlements up and down the western frontier, in the army, in newspaper reports of massacres, panic set in, raising the specter of a massive conflict with the Indians.

The fact that war on this scale never finally materialized did not work retroactively to eliminate the need for prudent responsive action at the time: "responsible officials in Washington had no way to evaluate the information and were forced to consider the possibility of a frontierwide conflict."[91] Lincoln's problems were compounded by a severe manpower shortage, which prompted a plan for arming and sending Union prisoners paroled by the Confederates. There was also the rumor of conspiracy in the air: it was said the Dakota massacres were part of a Confederate plot to distract men, resources, and attention away from the war with the South.

By the ninth of October, General Pope could report that the Sioux war was over. In late September, Colonel Sibley convened military commissions for the trial of Indian captives. Many of the 1,500 Indian prisoners were women and children. In the army, among the Minnesota settlements, the urge for vengeance was fierce. Pope would have dispensed with trials, preferring summary executions. The trials proceeded with speed and few evidentiary or procedural safeguards. By the end of proceedings a month later, the commission had issued 303 death sentences. Upon his review of the case transcripts, Lincoln discovered that "the trials had become shorter and shorter as they progressed."[92] Lincoln and others in the administration absorbed intense pressure from correspondents, politicians, and concerned observers, who demanded executions for the condemned and warned of reprisal actions against Indian women, children, and other noncombatants in the event of an overly lenient response. Despite his own need for political support at a critical time in the war with the South, Lincoln commuted or pardoned a large majority of these sentences, authorizing a total of forty executions in the end.

Like the initial threat of all-out frontier war, the political damage to Lincoln, as well as the massive mob retaliations, never actually materialized. Critics point out the real shortcomings and racial prejudice displayed by Lincoln, Pope, Colonel Sibley, and others.[93] That such wrongs occurred is undeniable—but they were by no means unique to Union military leaders. Projection of abstract modern standards about race and justice into the decisional landscape of 1862 is unhelpful for assessing the options realistically available to Lincoln at the time.[94] The progressive impulse is commendable, but fails to factor in the likelihood that eschewing the methods of military tribunals does not necessarily produce a general uplift in conditions of justice and fairness. Rather, exercise of this option assisted at the time to prevent the downward torque into anarchy and further violence. In this, "the largest mass execution in American history," the judgments of the Dakota military commission were precipitous and unfair in many cases, but as Carol Chomsky's account shows, in all likelihood, the mob would have been far worse.[95] That abuses occurred, that the military tribunal could and should have been conducted with greater procedural fairness, is beyond dispute. That some better forum for dealing with the problem was ready to hand is much less certain. The passion for vengeance had heated to such a pitch among both settlers and soldiers that it is difficult to see how even full-scale civil trials could have significantly improved the final result. It is because the trials were held and records were kept that later generations could learn from and critique the military process. The process and records also made possible the clemency review that ended in the release of a far greater number than were executed. The Dakota trials demonstrate the inescapability of political judgment and the great need for corrective prudential statesmanship—arguably on display in Lincoln's clement treatment of many of these cases.

Vallandigham and the Corning Letter

The brunt of the criticism against the use of military commissions surfaced in response to their less common use in situations further removed from the fog and friction of war. Under the aegis of Lincoln's Order of September 24, 1862, General Ambrose Burnside had declared a state of martial law in the Department under his charge, an area that included the state of Ohio. In light of the emergency conditions attendant upon invasion in one state, and its imminent threat in the other three under his authority,[96] Burnside's Order No. 38 declared that those "who commit acts for the benefit of the enemies of our country will be tried as spies or traitors" and would face the penalty of death.[97] Clement Vallandigham, a retired Democratic congressman from Dayton and a vociferous anti-war agitator, subsequently delivered a speech at Mount Vernon, Ohio, responding to the President's State of the Union address, in which he condemned Lincoln's conduct of the war, "a wicked, cruel and unnecessary war," he said, that was being waged "for the purpose of crushing out liberty and erecting a despotism, . . . a war for the freedom of the blacks and the enslavement of the whites," etc.[98] The firebrand politician was arrested at his home, and swiftly brought to trial by military commission under the order. The commission afforded him the benefit of legal counsel, the opportunity to cross-examine witnesses, and compel production of his own witnesses.[99]

After Vallandigham had delivered a personal statement contesting the authority of the commission to try him, the tribunal found him guilty and directed his confinement "during the continuance of the war." He was sent to military prison at Cincinnati. Vallandigham's plea for a writ of *habeas corpus* disputed the constitutionality of the military commission to try him. As a civilian non-combatant, he was immune from prosecution in the military court system. After the federal circuit court in Cincinnati declined to act on his appeal, Vallandigham applied to the Supreme Court for a writ of *certiorari.* For its part, the Court "beat a prudent retreat to the fortress of technicality"[100] and refused to countenance the appeal, citing its lack of authority as an Article III court to oversee the doings of military commissions.[101] Lincoln, who had regretted Burnside's move in arresting the martyrdom-seeking "Mr. V," commuted the sentence of the tribunal to removal behind Confederate lines. Months later, the "wily agitator," nominated by Ohio Democrats as their candidate for governor, was allowed to return to the North, "and from this time forward continued unmolested in his violent public tirades against Lincoln and the Union cause."[102]

As Randall and others have observed, the timing of the Supreme Court's disposition of the *Vallandigham* appeal is critical to making sense of it in light of the later *Milligan* decision. In early 1862, the editor of the *New York Tribune,* Horace Greeley, had identified "the greatest danger now facing the country" as treason: "treason in Washington, treason in the army itself, especially the treason which wears the garb of Unionism."[103] A year and a half later, with Gettysburg still two months away, such fears had resonated with Burnside, who in his response to Vallandigham's *habeas corpus* petition warned against the demoralizing and subversive effect of speech such as Vallandigham had indulged in—especially for the soldiers of the field who faced real privations and a hostile enemy, and who were generally in the habit of "hearing their public men speak" and "of approving what they say."[104] Vallandigham had indulged in the exercise of mere license, not true liberty. The responsibility of public men and the public press was to use caution and to remember the context of basic security in which alone liberty in any meaningful sense could flourish.[105]

By the summer of 1863, it had become apparent that the administration's incursions against civil liberties sorely wanted a clearly articulated defense. With the rising tide of arrests, public opinion had begun to mount against the President; even members of Lincoln's own cabinet began to voice their doubts about the wisdom of policies that had led to the arrest and imprisonment of the likes of Clarence Vallandigham. The resolutions of a meeting of Democrats at Albany, New York, provided Lincoln with an opportunity to articulate his reasons for the arrest of Vallandigham, for his policy regarding the suspension of the privilege of *habeas corpus,* and for the government's resort to the use of military tribunals. Exercising "exceptional care in preparing his response," Lincoln seized upon the chance to take his own arguments directly to the public. The so-called Corning letter received an initial airing in the *New York Tribune,* saw a reissue in pamphlet form, and further reprints by the Loyal Publication Society, so that a total on the order of ten million people came to read some half-million available copies of the letter.[106]

In his argument, Lincoln shifted the emphasis that had been used by the Albany protestors in their own criticism.[107] Yes, it was true that constitutional protections, such as the right to a speedy and public trial before an impartial jury of peers, had been "secured substantially to the English people *after* years of protracted civil war" and adopted in the U.S. Constitution "at the *close* of the Revolution." The distinction must be candidly acknowledged; such guarantees had been established after, and not during, the course of long and violent armed conflicts, the resolution of which had been clear only with the passage of extended periods of uncertainty and deprivation. Once the dangers of bloody internecine war had been safely negotiated, the blessings of civil liberties could be duly chartered, but to absolutize the nature of the protections was to ignore the very real preconditions of military and political security that alone could give such liberties a chance of survival.[108]

Further confusion came as a result of the Albany critics' refusal to distinguish the flexible conditions articulated in the Constitution itself. The arrests made in these cases failed to trigger the protections applicable to trials for treason, capital, or other crimes, or to criminal prosecutions more generally. The very nature of civil war changed the terms of analysis in such a way as to dislocate the normal operations of the criminal justice system. The fomenters of rebellion could not expect to find refuge under the security of the Bill of Rights, when it was "liberty of speech," "liberty of press," and "habeas corpus" that they sought to use as weapons for undermining the constitutional order itself. In the altered state of things precipitated by civil war or invasion, the very notion of an offense against that order must necessarily undergo redefinition, if the society itself was to be preserved: "Nothing is better known to history than that courts of justice are utterly incompetent to such cases. Civil courts are organized chiefly for trials of individuals, or, at most, a few individuals acting in concert; and this in quiet times, and on charges of crimes well defined in the law. Even in times of peace, bands of horse-thieves and robbers frequently grow too numerous and powerful for the ordinary courts of justice." The efficacy of criminal justice as a means of preserving a flourishing civil order depended upon its maintenance within clear boundaries, and upon clear, identifiable definitions for both offenses and the processes for their adjudication. It presupposed a manageable number of cases and offenders, a prevailing sense of orderliness imposed by the rule of law. The challenge imposed by what was in the current situation "a clear, flagrant, and gigantic case of rebellion" upset all calibrations of the finely tuned and erstwhile smooth-functioning systems of criminal justice. "But what comparison, in numbers have such bands ever borne to the insurgent sympathizers, even in many of the loyal States?" A system to absorb the shocks and jolts occasioned by the periodic outburst of lawlessness or injustice now stood in danger from an inundation of such disturbance on a massive scale. With the increasing threat to security rose the corresponding necessity for vigilance, a necessity that upset the balances provided in the normal ordering of criminal justice. "Again: a jury too frequently has at least one member more ready to hang the panel than to hang the traitor. And yet, again, he who dissuades one man from volunteering, or induces one soldier to desert, weakens the Union cause as much as he who kills a Union soldier in battle. Yet this dissuasion or inducement may be so conducted as to be no defined crime of which any civil court would take cognizance." The very fact that the framers of the Constitution had contemplated situations ("cases of rebellion or invasion") in which the privilege of the writ of *habeas corpus* could be suspended offered a demonstration that the ancient liberty could not be considered in absolute terms, but rather as inevitably conditioned by time and circumstance.[109]

Lincoln stressed the deep cleavages wrought by the conditions of civil war. Arrests undertaken "by process of courts" were "directed at the small percentage of ordinary and continuous perpetration of crime." Those conducted "in cases of rebellion" proceed upon a different basis—

"directed at sudden and extensive uprisings against the Government, which at most, will succeed or fail in no great length of time"; such arrests occur, "not so much for what has been done, as for what probably would be done." The purpose is proactive and "preventive," rather than retrospective and "vindictive." The drastic nature of the change in criteria became apparent with the recognition that a significant number of Confederate worthies, including Generals Breckinridge, Lee, Johnston, Magruder, and Preston had all been within the authority and jurisdiction of the Federal government at the time of the commencement of the rebellion "and were nearly as well known to be traitors then as now." None had committed any cognizable crime under state or federal civil codes—indeed, all, if arrested, would have been released under the normal workings of *habeas corpus*. And, of course, none had been arrested. Yet it was also apparent that the Confederate cause would have been immeasurably weakened by their apprehension. When applied to such conditions, the civil liberties guarantees of the Bill of Rights simply failed the test of relevance. Lincoln asserted, "I think the time not unlikely to come when I shall be blamed for having made too few arrests rather than too many."[110]

In the course of his arguments, Lincoln was not attempting to map out a utilitarian calculus for maximizing the happiness, or minimizing the pain, of the greatest possible number of Americans. Rather, the extremity of the peril to basic minimum conditions of public safety produced a *chiaroscuro* effect that clarified the purposes and motives of men. At least human motivation was easier to discern "than in cases of ordinary crime." Ignoring perhaps the perplexing ambiguity of the border-state conflicts of loyalty we have noted earlier, Lincoln reckoned silence itself could not be interpreted as neutrality in the present situation: "The man who stands by and says nothing when the peril of his Government is discussed, cannot be misunderstood. If not hindered, he is sure to help the enemy; much more, if he talks ambiguously—talks for his country with 'buts' and 'ifs' and 'ands.'"[111]

This much was clear: the links of causation between inflammatory speech and violent action showed a greater propensity to form a solid chain in conditions of rebellion or invasion. By "laboring, with some effect, to prevent the raising of troops; to encourage desertions from the army; and to leave the Rebellion without an adequate military force to suppress it," Vallandigham in his speechifying had actually caused damage to the Army, "upon the existence and vigor of which the life of the

Nation depends." In these circumstances, his "warring upon the Military" meant that the military had the "constitutional jurisdiction to lay hands upon him." Military law prohibited the offense of desertion upon pain of death. It would surely be a perverse rendering of justice to spare the one fomenting disruption and insubordination at the expense of the simple offender who acts on such cues: "Must I shoot a simple-minded soldier boy who deserts, while I must not touch a hair of the wily agitator who induces him to desert?" If justice was the goal, then justice required a rather different outcome. "I think that in such a case to silence the agitator, and save the boy is not only constitutional, but withal a great mercy." Where, in the heightened conditions of civil war, speech readily translated into action, it must be treated as such in order to avoid a destructive subversion of the very principles for which the protections of the law had been established in the first place.[112]

Lincoln rejected the contentions of detractors who raised the fear of the slippery slope, that this merging of speech and action, once entertained by government, would be difficult, if not impossible to abandon once the justifying emergency had passed.[113] The argument was no more valid than to suggest "that a man could contract so strong an appetite for emetics during temporary illness as to persist in feeding upon them during the remainder of his healthful life." Implicit in Lincoln's argument was the conviction that the health of the body politic was the norm, and disease the exception; and that the responsibility for avoiding addiction to the harsh "emetics" of martial rule lay not only with the governors but with the people themselves.[114] It presupposed also the belief that the government retained its essential representational character, despite the fact that its own representatives, *in extremis*, had been forced to administer a drastic purgative cure. The skill required went beyond the mere punctilious adherence to legal rules. A good ruler, like a good doctor, would know when to ease off from application of the powerful medicine, before it debilitated or killed the patient. But the treatment must be allowed to have its effect. A government of, by, and for the people would not perish from the earth through the prudentially responsible actions of representatives committed to its preservation.

Lincoln finished the letter with a politic appeal to the example of Andrew Jackson in the waning days of the War of 1812. Jackson—like Vallandigham and his allies, a Democrat—had administered the strong physic of martial law at New Orleans and had taken much-criticized actions in its furtherance with the arrest and imprisonment of Louiaillier and Judge Hall. Yet Jackson, too, had respected the extraordinary and temporary character of the measures, had quickly moved to reestablish Constitutional protections as soon as he deemed it prudent to do so, and had paid his fine in respect for the rule of law. To be sure, the application of emergency measures such as the suspension of *habeas corpus* and the establishment of martial rule and military tribunals lay open to the possibility of abuse. But the possibility that a governmental action could be abused provided no real argument against it, when the alternative options only further increased the danger to public security. Abuse of power was always a potential concern. In times of extreme threat, prudential statesmanlike control of the necessary levers of power had charted the safest course.

Similarly, in a response to further protestations on the part of Ohio Democrats, Lincoln explained the context underlying Vallandigham's trial: incidents of armed resistance against the arrest of deserters, assassinations of draft enforcement officials—countered by military force, bloodshed, and death. Lincoln placed the blame for these escalations of violence squarely in the corner of the rabble-rousing "Mr. V."[115] Though the tide in the war had turned in the North's favor by February of 1864 when the case reached the Supreme Court, much danger still lay ahead. The court took its position of deference to the Executive at a time when the outcome of hostilities was still far from clear.

Milligan and Reconstruction

Military commissions continued to operate in the South during the Reconstruction era. It was of course in this same period that the well-known *ex parte Milligan* decision reached the Supreme Court. In October of 1864, Milligan, a lawyer from Indiana, a Democratic politician and a prominent member of the "Copperhead"[116] "Sons of Liberty" organization, had been arrested by order of the commander of the military district of Indiana for "[conspiring] against the government, [affording] aid and comfort to rebels, and [inciting] the people to insurrection." Milligan was implicated in a plot to stage an armed uprising and free eight thousand Confederate prisoners of war in Illinois as part of a larger plan to separate the "Northwest" from the Union, join forces with the South, and squeeze the Union in a pincer movement.[117] Under the authority of Lincoln's Order of September 24, 1862, and the Habeas Corpus Act of 1863, a military commission convened in Indianapolis to try the case, found Milligan guilty, and sentenced him to be hanged on the date of May 19, 1865. In the interim, a civilian grand jury declined to indict him on the same facts. Milligan's appeal was granted certiorari at the Supreme Court on *habeas corpus* grounds. The Court heard arguments in March of 1866 and made its ruling in July, but did not issue a written opinion in the case until December. In its opinion, a five-member majority of the Court declared that the subjection of civilian citizens to military trials and martial law was illegal wherever normal civilian courts were "open, and in the proper and unobstructed exercise of their jurisdiction."[118] The Court in *Vallandigham* had declined jurisdictional authority to address very similar issues in 1864, but "*then,* considerations of safety were mingled with the exercise of power"; by contrast, "*now* . . . the public safety [was] assured." With hostilities safely concluded, and confident in the security of the Union, Justice Davis, writing for the majority in *Milligan*, could boldly rebuke the policy of the Lincoln administration:

> The Constitution of the United States is a law for rulers and people, equally in war and peace, and covers with the shield of its protection all classes of men, at all times, and under all circumstances. No doctrine, involving more pernicious consequences, was ever invented by the wit of man than that any of its provisions can be suspended during any of the great exigencies of government. Such a doctrine leads directly to anarchy or despotism, but the theory of necessity on which it is based is false; for the government, within the Constitution has all the powers granted to it, which are necessary to preserve its existence.[119]

Since a court not ordained and established by Congress had tried Milligan, a civilian and a citizen, and since it had denied him the "inestimable privilege of trial by jury," his trial had gone forward in violation of the Constitution. The regular civilian courts had been available; and "Martial rule can never exist where the courts are open, and in the proper and unobstructed exercise of their jurisdiction. It is . . . confined to the locality of actual war." Not only did the majority ascribe to the position that the commission in this case lacked jurisdiction over the defendant; they also went on to assert in dictum that Congress lacked constitutional competence to authorize such a court outside the sphere of military operations at all. It was on this limited point that the dissent took issue with the majority. Agreeing as to the unconstitutionality of this particular commission—because Congress had not granted the authority to such courts in Indiana—the dissent was unwilling to concede that such a grant was beyond the constitutional scope of Congress in the exercise of its war powers.[120]

Given the "thunderously quotable language" of the *Milligan* decision, it does appear ironic that the practice of trials by military commission continued as late as 1870. With the passage of time, the holding of Milligan has been read narrowly to say that the Constitution forbids the trial of civilians who are citizens by military commission in areas where the civil courts are open—"but it is little else."[121] The decision, lauded as a bulwark of constitutional liberty, nevertheless subsided into practical "irrelevance."[122] Perhaps the harshest verdict on the case belongs to Edward Corwin, who averred that the opinion shows little else but that "two or three years after a grave emergency has been safely weathered and the country has reaped the full benefit of the extraordinary measures which it evoked, a judicial remedy may be forthcoming for some of the individual grievances which these produced, and a few scoundrels like Milligan himself escape a deserved hangman's noose."[123]

While the practice of using military commissions did decline over the course of the postwar period, the *Milligan* decision did nothing to put a halt to the more than 1,435 trials by military commission that took place from the end of April 1865 to January 1, 1869.[124] By 1870, the Supreme Court of Tennessee could pronounce the military commission "a tribunal now as well known and recognized in the laws of the United States as a court-martial."[125] It was probably the widespread usage of military commissions during the course of hostilities, along with their effectiveness in maintaining some degree of balance between the demands of justice and those of military expediency in the midst of the chaotic conditions of mass warfare, that led to their continued use after the war's conclusion. Race riots in parts of the South, accompanied by the victory of radical elements in the Republican party in the 1866 congressional elections, led to the passage of a particularly onerous version of the Reconstruction Act in March, 1867. The Act denied legal status to those state governments in the former Confederacy which had refused to ratify the Fourteenth Amendment.[126] The statute divided the ten "unreconstructed" Southern states into five military districts and placed them under martial law. The military commanders of the districts enjoyed the power to convene trials by military commission. In some areas, the rule of the U.S. Army Generals in the conquered territory of the South served to perpetuate the prevailing disorder, resentment, and confusion, and thus probably contributed to the workload of the military commissions.[127]

On the whole, military commissions mainly functioned "as substitutes for the local courts, in cases where, in the opinion of the commander,—for the statute invested him with the sole discretion in the matter,—a resort to the military jurisdiction was essential to the due administration of justice."[128] The need for military commissions occurred wherever the civil court system was not yet in functioning order, or in cases where such courts, though operating, could not provide for the impartial administration of justice.[129] In addition, the commissions continued to "mop up" the effects of the war, addressing still unresolved incidents that had occurred before the "stillness at Appomattox."[130] As in the war itself, this sometimes meant the disciplining of Northern volunteer forces assigned to police the territory under reconstruction.[131]

In this period, the trial and execution of Captain Henry Wirz, Swiss commandant of the Southern prison at Andersonville, ranked among the most controversial of the cases decided by military commission. The case symbolically functioned as a quasi-judicial referendum on the South's treatment of Union prisoners. Wirz had never exercised supreme command at Andersonville; he had arrived there only in March 1864. Yet, as the notorious prison's standing commander at war's end, the unfortunate Wirz served as lightning rod for the collective wrath of a morally and psychologically exhausted North. The problem worsens with the retrospective recognition that it is extremely difficult to controvert the *tu quoque* response. Civil War prisoners in both the North and the South suffered horrendously—the official records of prison deaths, through maltreatment, exposure, starvation, and disease number upwards of 30,000, on both sides, though actual numbers were likely much higher. Almost one-third of the 48,000 prisoners confined at Andersonville had died in the abysmal conditions.

The military commission convened to hear Wirz's case in August 1865. Wirz was charged with numerous counts of injuring, torture, and murder of Union prisoners in his custody. The trial lasted two months and generated over 5,000 pages of recorded testimony. Wirz had argued in his defense that the terms of General Johnston's surrender had rendered him immune from future prosecution. The fact that the trial went forward at all was considered a confirmation of "the vindictive nature of the whole proceeding," for "postwar psychology . . . demanded the head of Wirz; and his destruction was promoted by Secretary of War Stanton, Judge

Advocate Holt, and even President Johnson, who approved the sentence of the military commission."[132] The conviction and execution of Wirz raised a hue and cry among radical Republicans, who saw the case as a political perversion of justice. Wirz is often counted as one of the few Confederate defendants convicted for war crimes in the Civil War. It is certainly true that there was no general blood-letting in the wake of Wirz's death. However unfair as to the individual defendant, the trial appeared to have its desired effect. There is no question that, even if Wirz can be deemed guilty of culpable negligence in some sense, many other offenders, on both sides, and many of greater guilt, managed to escape his fate.[133] The case fully exhibits the tragic dimension of war and explains the recurring public fascination with extraordinary justice. It displays the deep, abiding human drive to achieve a modicum of justice in circumstances of such enormity as to overwhelm the capacity of the usual juridical mechanisms. The wretchedness of the Civil War prisons defied the categories and capacities of criminal jurisprudence allocated for measuring and dispensing justice.

Surely the most sensational case involved a military commission convened to try John Wilkes Booth's eight alleged co-conspirators in the assassination of President Lincoln. President Andrew Johnson issued an order for the convening of the commission; seven generals and two field grade officers were assembled to hear the case, from May 12 to June 13, 1865. All eight of the defendants were found guilty of at least a portion of the charges against them.[134] Questions as to the validity of some of the convictions have fed into a seemingly endless stream of literary investigations, as well as litigation.

These were the exceptional circumstances to which an extraordinary remedy came to be put to use. In assuming governmental functions throughout the South, the army entered a legal and political situation that was without precedent. The lessons to be drawn from the army's experience in military government in the Mexican War were of limited value in the post-bellum South. The meaning attached to the condition of "martial law" varied widely among commanders and military districts. The wide latitude allowed to the generals extended to the use and quality of adjudication supplied by the Reconstruction military commissions. Nevertheless, while "frequent conflicts of jurisdiction with the reopening civil courts occurred" and legal difficulties abounded, "the wonder is not that some irregularities and unfortunate situations arose, but that there were not more of them."[135]

Since the commissions were being used in order to ensure that crimes would be punished and injustices prevented, the wiser generals saw the commissions as an important instrument, though no panacea, for regulating volatile racial tensions in the areas under the army's jurisdiction.[136] In a General Order, President Grant "instructed the Army to protect Negroes from being punished more severely than a white man would be for the same offense."[137] Thus, while the army generally sought to maintain positive relations with civil officials, it was not always possible to defer to them, especially when the adjudication of interracial crimes came into question. In one noteworthy case related by James Sefton, General Slocum, Commander for the Department of Mississippi, refused to comply with a writ of *habeas corpus* issued in the local court on behalf of a white man, Joseph Jackson, who was accused of the murder of a Negro. Slocum had arranged for Jackson's trial by military commission at Vicksburg and, in an action reminiscent of General Andrew Jackson's performance at New Orleans, had ordered the arrest of the judge, Daniel Merwin, who issued the writ. Merwin appealed to the Mississippi governor, condemning Slocum's move as "a blow by the mailed hand of military power against the civil authority in the exercise of its most valued and hitherto most respected function," and the governor accordingly appealed to President Grant via Secretary of State Seward. After receiving the advice of his Attorney General, Grant forwarded his conclusion that "it was still inexpedient to restore the privilege of habeas corpus," and the matter came to an abrupt end.[138]

To be sure, the Jackson case impugned the integrity of the Mississippi civil apparatus. While it may be impossible to know for sure what would have happened to Jackson in a state criminal proceeding, it is hardly difficult to imagine the likely result, given the overall cultural climate of the post-bellum South. Nevertheless, motives on the part of Federal and army authorities were hardly unalloyed. Assistance rendered to blacks in the South was thought to smooth the way to ensuring Republican votes from the beneficiaries. The anti-political General Sherman was not conjuring a mere shibboleth when, in explaining his lack of support for Negro suffrage, he described it as a ploy "whereby politicians may manufacture just so much more pliable electioneering material."[139] Yet the fact that pure motives were hard to come by hardly diminishes the importance of the military courts as a significant interim measure for obtaining decently fair, impartial conditions for administering justice at a time when such commodities were often in short supply. Limited time, manpower, and resources meant that military trials were mainly confined to felonies and serious crimes.[140] Moreover, the military commissions were viewed as only one component of the system for the administration of justice in the South, which also included the use of courts-martial; the military provost courts, convened for minor offenses; and, as they returned to operation with greater frequency over time, local civilian courts.

2

British Military Tribunals and Martial Law in the Boer War

Long-settled tradition as to the limits of martial rule in English law had to be reconsidered with the onset of new, unprecedented conditions of warfare in the modern era. Parallel experiences had come for the Americans in the Mexican War and to a much greater extent in the Civil War, where methods of emergency rule had to be adapted to the unprecedented nature of these conflicts. Means configured to the unique circumstances of the Mexican campaign were found to suit the exigencies faced by Lincoln and his generals in a conflict that came to assume massive proportions, presenting unprecedented seepage of the theater of operations into civilian areas and threatening the very existence of the nation.

Rather than massive invasion, the critical conflict that prompted Britain to adapt its emergency juridical response came in the form of a war conducted entirely on a remote colonial territory. Despite the remoteness of the conflict, the war generated intense debate throughout British society over the nature and limits of war aims, the effectiveness of military strategy and tactics, and eventually the very legitimacy of the war endeavor itself.[1] The war placed a severe stress on the ongoing viability of British colonial interests in South Africa. As it continued, the conflict sustained a profound transformation. Nineteenth-century methods and practices, characterized by the set battle piece, gave way to an equally bloody yet indeterminate style of guerrilla warfare. Technological changes in communication, logistics, and weaponry precipitated parallel changes in the "face of battle." The unprecedented conditions and amorphous boundaries of the new, modern style of warfare brought about a corresponding reconfiguration of long-established principles of emergency rule.

The dilemmas posed by the use of military tribunals in the South African war represented an especially virulent strain of the general problem of imperial administration in the context of an emergency and, as such, proved to be especially intractable in wartime conditions. Surely it was no coincidence of history that the flowering and proliferation of liberal political and economic principles throughout the West after 1815 witnessed the subjection of those principles to a series of cruel and demanding tests, in fairly short order. For one thing, liberal ideals necessarily absorbed a shock where interests of state policy carried their extension into new territories—with the backing of force. The acquisition and maintenance of imperial power often led to the spawning of hitherto unrecognized and unacknowledged interests within colonial territories, dedicated to the establishment and flourishing of political liberty. In its better moments, imperial rule was a form of benign dominion dedicated at least in part to the transplantation of liberal ideals. For Britain, it was at this point of friction, between the assertion of imperial rule, the successful flowering of such transplants, and the eventual germination of independent-minded interests at odds with imperial policy, that the question of martial rule repeatedly flared up to test the limits of those ideals. When it did, the controversy seldom remained in the exclusive domain of legal specialists.

Indeed, the outstanding intellectual forces of the nation joined the argument. Among others, John Stuart Mill, Thomas Carlyle, John Ruskin, and Thomas Huxley weighed in on an especially fierce controversy involving the governor of Jamaica, Edward John Eyre, in 1865.[2] Under the auspices of an imperial Council of War, Eyre had imposed martial law after an outbreak of native violence at the Morant Bay courthouse issued in the death of a magistrate and ten other white colonials. Eyre limited the area under martial law to Surrey County, where the incident had occurred. After the initial state of emergency had died down, but before lifting the decree, Eyre had singled out one of his most vociferous critics, George W. Gordon, as fomenter of the anti-British outburst and procured his removal to Surrey County. A court-martial thereupon tried Gordon, convicted, and executed him.

The case provoked a fury of criticism, from both sides. The supporters of Eyre's martial law policy argued on the basis of the perceived dangers endemic to the situation—the vastly outnumbered British force would have had no chance in a full-scale native revolt such as had only recently occurred in Haiti.[3] Exigent circumstances on the ground had rendered necessary his swift and stern response—indeed, the incident had unraveled largely as the result of an initial softness on the part of the governor in refusing to place the entire island under martial law to begin with. Critics countered that Eyre's actions—far from being a legitimate response to a real threat—represented an unjustified and arbitrary exercise of power; the declaration of martial law was a cynical smoke screen for the rapid disposition of inconvenient political opponents.[4] The Eyre controversy prompted a massive official inquiry, and the Royal Commission generated evidence that became fodder for a prolonged exchange of volleys between "liberal" and "conservative" elements. In the end, a London grand jury refused to forward the indictment against Eyre. Nevertheless, he was rebuked for having ordered the arrest of Gordon outside the bounds of the district circumscribed by martial law, as well as for having tried him *ex post facto,* the incident leading to his arrest having preceded the martial law declaration. Yet the questions stubbornly persisted: Had Governor Eyre overstepped his legal and moral authority? How much force was enough? Was it possible to fix *a priori* boundaries and adhere to them in all circumstances? Or was a certain measure of discretionary prerogative a necessary feature of executive administration? If so, could the legislature grant such a prerogative?

The dilemma appearing in the Eyre controversy represented a specific application of the problem of imperial rule, which had spawned what, in a perceptive and influential work, the British Artillery Officer Charles Callwell identified as "small wars." Callwell asked:

> Why are the European nations involved in small wars? Small wars are a heritage of extended empire, a certain epilogue to encroachments into lands beyond the confines of existing civilization, and this has been so from early ages to the present time. Conquerors of old, penetrating into the unknown, encountered races with strange and unconventional military methods and trod them down, seizing their territory; revolts and insurrections followed, disputes and quarrels with tribes on the borders of the districts overcome supervened, out of the original campaign of conquest sprang further wars, and all were vexatious, desultory, and harassing. And the history of these operations repeats itself in the small wars of today.[5]

The vexatious questions would be repeated with greater urgency in the South African conflict. Indeed, the difficulty of resolution mounted with the introduction of new methods of warfare: "The problem of defining a state of war, of recognizing the point at which public safety was endangered, was still more difficult, and was to become increasingly so as open insurrection became rarer and lower-intensity, guerrilla-type resistance became more common. Likewise the extent of a warlike or insurrectionary threat grew more difficult to define, as new military and civil technology—especially in the sphere of communications—transformed old patterns of warfare."[6]

A Small War of Great Consequence

In its initial phase, the Boer War remained for the most part confined within the perimeters of the British colonial territories in South Africa. These opening movements of the war followed a familiar nineteenth-century pattern involving the parry and thrust of opposing armies seeking decisive advantage in a succession of discrete large-scale battles. The sheer geographic scale of the country proved to be a great challenge for the British commander, Sir Redvers Buller. The distances were vast—Cape Town lay some 800 miles from the Transvaal capital, Pretoria—and the lack of roads meant the infantry could not stray from the lifeline of the single-track railways. Buller, awaiting reinforcements, sought to move his relatively small and scattered forces (approximately 30,000 British members of the army and colonials) in a series of columns: one went up the railway leading to the Orange Free State capital of Bloemfontein and further on to the Transvaal cities of Johannesburg and Pretoria; another followed the parallel western line leading to Kimberley and Mafeking. Buller himself commanded a force in Natal seeking to bring relief to Sir George White's besieged garrison at Ladysmith. After a series of embarrassing setbacks for the British—the disastrous "Black week" in December 1899—Field Marshal Lord Roberts was appointed commander-in-chief; Lord Kitchener his chief-of-staff. With the new year, the war shifted to new territory, literally and figuratively, spilling into the Boer republics, accompanied by new techniques and tactics meant to address unprecedented circumstances.

Hardly a mere insignificant, localized warm-up to the total war unleashed in 1914, the South African conflict, which was Britain's largest military engagement since the close of the Napoleonic wars, wrought far-reaching constitutional changes with regard to the traditional conception of martial law.[7] The dramatic break is noted by other commentators. In the words of Charles Fairman:

> War is no longer confined to the area between two hostile camps; it exists not merely at the place where the King has raised his standard in the

> field. And while the instrumentalities of war increase, the courts must find commensurate powers for the military authorities. The courts will take notice of unusual dangers growing out of new methods of war. The situation which obtained in South Africa, whereby civil courts followed the army as it drove out the invaders, and exercised under military aegis jurisdiction over nonmilitary offences and minor breaches of martial law regulations was an eminently suitable arrangement. If the existence of these courts on sufferance was to be invoked to hamper the military authority in necessary operations, then the commander-in-chief need only withdraw his support and the processes of the court would cease to run.[8]

As a matter of strict legal doctrine, there had traditionally been considerable question as to whether it was possible even to speak of "martial law" as a legitimate juridical category. The Duke of Wellington had famously pronounced that martial law was in fact "no law at all."[9] To the extent martial law was acknowledged as a legal position, the long-standing view on its defined limits had been articulated by Sir James Mackintosh before Parliament:

> The only principle on which the law of England tolerates what is called martial [law] is necessity: its introduction can be justified only by necessity; its continuance requires precisely the same justification of necessity: and if it survives the necessity on which alone it rests for a single minute, it becomes instantly a mere exercise of lawless violence. When foreign invasion or civil war renders it impossible for courts of law to sit, or to enforce the execution of their judgments, it becomes necessary to find some rude substitute for them, and to employ, for that purpose, the military, which is the only remaining force in the community. While the laws are silenced by the noise of arms, the rules of the armed force must punish, as equitably as they can, those crimes which threaten their own safety and that of society: but no longer; every moment beyond, is usurpation: as soon as the law can act, every other mode of punishing supposed crimes is itself an enormous crime.[10]

The vigorous protection of civil liberty simply required rigid limits upon the existence and operation of military rule, the operation of which came into effect only upon the manifest inoperability of the civil courts. The position paralleled that of Justice Davis in the *Milligan* case. No doubt this high and impregnable position as to the personal liberties of Englishmen owed something, as Alexander Hamilton had observed, to the felicitous geographical position of the island nation, which had not faced the ignominy of a foreign military invasion since the Norman Conquest. With the national interest now tied to belligerent conditions in the far-flung reaches of the empire, the traditional standard came into question.

Martial law was imposed nearly simultaneously with the outbreak of hostilities in some regions. In Natal, on October 15, 1899, martial rule descended upon Newcastle, Dundee, Klip River, and Upper Tugela; the next day, it spread to Mafeking, Vryburg, Taungs, Barkly West, Kimberley, and Herbert in the Cape.[11] In the following month, it was extended to encompass the entirety of Natal and Zululand, as well as spreading to additional districts in the Cape. As Leo Amery's *Times History* observed, the political complexities of the region tended to erode the clarity of battle lines, and consequently to increase the danger to security: "When the Boer forces invaded British territory they did not enter an entirely hostile theatre of operations. Both in Natal and the Cape Colony, the Transvaal and Free State forces met with many active and secret sympathizers. On the Cape side, in the districts occupied by the Boer commandos, the majority of the able-bodied British subjects of Dutch extraction either openly joined the invaders or aided the enemy by indirect means." The calculus of necessity made it plain that "[o]rdinary measures were inadequate to deal with invasion combined with rebellion. The situation demanded exceptional powers."[12]

Kitchener's order of January 30, 1900, stated "the object of proclaiming Martial Law" in terms of necessity: "to enable persons resisting the authority of the Government, or aiding and abetting the enemy, to be arrested summarily and punished promptly."[13] In British territories, this did not mean that the ordinary civil courts were superceded by the judicial authority of the commander: "When practical it [*viz.*, martial law] should only supplement, but where the Civil Government is paralysed, it must of necessity replace the ordinary civil procedure."[14] Rather, the civil courts were to work in conjunction with the military tribunals—their jurisdiction included the typically military offenses of spying and giving assistance to the enemy.[15]

Yet it was deemed appropriate to provide supplemental instruction in the Circular on Martial Law on the treatment of "colonists of Dutch extraction," who were in danger of being charged with disloyalty on the basis of "information which is very often biassed by political and personal influences."[16] Thus, the mere sale of supplies to enemy invaders "who would otherwise probably take them by force" could not be considered an offense.[17] Nor could the mere "feeling of sympathy with an enemy of their own race."[18] Such qualifications palpably demonstrate the difficulty under which Kitchener and the other British commanders labored in seeking to impose institutional self-restraint and a sense of prudential balance in the ferocious heat of conflict—especially at this early stage in the war. Illuminating is the comparison with a further supplemental order issued by Kitchener over a year later, in April 1901, which registers a rigid terseness not found in the earlier proclamations. It is a short, one sentence notice, alerting the residents of the Cape Colony that those who take up arms against the King or in some other way provide assistance to the enemy "shall immediately on arrest be tried by Court-Martial, . . . and shall on conviction be liable to the severest penalties of the law."[19] Noticeably absent are the earlier references to the need to take time to establish sufficiency of proof.[20] It shall become apparent that the change is best explained from within the context of the larger British war effort. The April 1901 order came in the midst of what appeared at the time to be a severe threat to the safety of British interests in the Cape Colony—a Boer commando invasion of the colony, which was actually a second invasion that had succeeded upon the granting of liberal and generous terms to an earlier group of enemy raiders and insurgents.

The Boer War demonstrated in a deadly way a new reality of armed conflict: its expanding, shifting spatial and temporal boundaries. The first year of the war had largely followed conventional lines, with the armies of Buller and Louis Botha squaring off in bloody encounters at Colenso and Spion Kop in the northwest corner of Natal along the Tugela River; the armies of the western frontier surged up and down the northbound railway lines, with Roberts's massive force eventually securing the British advance into the Free State at Paardeberg. Operating from a fatal miscalculation of the enemy's true "centers of gravity,"[21] Lord Roberts had made his celebrated return home to England after the quick and successful capture of the capital cities of Bloemfontein and Pretoria, believing the war to be "practically over" by the autumn of 1900. Yet in many ways, as the war slogged on into its second year, the worst—at least for tens of thousands of unfortunate civilians—remained ahead.

The marauding guerrilla bands of the great Boer generals, De Wet, Smuts, and De la Rey, would continue to plague Kitchener's "mop-up" contingent for nearly two more years. The cat-and-mouse game, it seemed, could continue almost indefinitely over the wide and barren surface of the veld: "The struggle . . . took shape and dissolved like a fog. There were no lines or fronts, no battles—mere skirmishes with an invisible enemy, whose only aim, apparently, was to run faster than their pursuers."[22] Consequently the magnitude of the continuing threat became exceedingly difficult to define. The nebulous and invisible enemy could still inflict death and mayhem with startling efficiency, and bid fair to continue on indefinitely. Kipling encapsulated the elusiveness and dangerous tactics of the Boer enemy:

> Ubique means "They've caught De Wet, an' now we shan't be long."
> Ubique means "I much regret, the beggar's goin' strong!" . . .
>
> Ubique means the dancing plain that changes rocks to Boers.
> Ubique means the mirage again an' shellin' all outdoors.[23]

Upon the capture of Bloemfontein and Pretoria, Roberts received authority to annex the Boer republics. The decision in favor of annexation created some legal controversy; as the unfolding of events would affirm, the mere capture of the capital cities hardly equated to a de facto military conquest of the entire territories under their aegis. Nevertheless, Roberts favored annexation, believing it to be the most effective means of facilitating the return of the Boers to their former ways as "peaceful farmers."[24] With the annexation, Roberts formed a military administration over the territories of the Orange Free State and the Transvaal in short order.

At the end of May 1900, the Free State, now designated the Orange River Colony, was placed under martial rule. On September 1 of the same year, martial law was imposed in the Transvaal. The former Boer republics were geographically divided into military districts. Although the apparatus of the Boer civil government was not dismantled wholesale—existing law remained in place unless preempted by the strictures of military necessity—many of the personnel charged with its administration were replaced by British military officials, who were company and field grade officers for the most part. Within the administration of the district governors, military courts were established for the trial of serious offenses. The form and process of the courts mirrored the earlier order given by General Buller for martial rule in the Natal region.[25] The military courts were composed of not less than three officers and followed basic courts-martial procedure. Accused were afforded representation of counsel, cross-examination of government witnesses, and the opportunity to call defense witnesses. Trials were public. As to sentencing, application of the death penalty required a unanimous panel and ratification by the commander-in-chief, Kitchener. These military tribunals addressed a wide range of military and civilian offenses, committed by civilians and Boer combatants, including rape, murder, violation of the oath of neutrality, spying, treason, and treachery.[26] The arrangement made for a vast expanse of territory subject to martial rule. Throughout much of this later phase of the war, it included most of the Cape Colony, the former Boer republics, Natal, and Zululand. The quality of administration of the military governors in the republics varied greatly according to the capabilities of the officers themselves. Criticism of the uneven administration of justice surfaced, as personal caprice and individual temperament flowed frequently into the gaps and fissures left by the absence of a rigorous system.[27] Administrative efforts at improvement were made during the course of the war, with varying degrees of success. But the French notion of *l'état de siège,* the legal emergency provision of the republican tradition—one that would receive a severe testing in the Great War some fourteen years hence—had no counterpart in the British constitution.[28] Precisely because the whole machinery of British martial rule was, legally speaking, an anomaly, a makeshift provision for extraordinary occasions, there was no systematic structure in place to ensure equity and uniformity in its administration. The very liberalizing features of the constitution that had made a "French" exigent response mechanism unsavory and even, in the view of some, dangerous, suffered all the more intensely with the shocks of emergency introduced by modern war.

With no end of the war in sight, the personal factor became increasingly important; the administrative failings of Roberts and of Kitchener would permanently mar their accomplishments in South Africa. "Kitchener of Chaos" became the epithet "applicable to Kitchener's treatment of civilians in the Boer republics."[29] Roberts, though often distinguished from his successor in command as an epitome of military virtue and magnanimity, actually initiated all of the questionable methods which eventually won Kitchener himself such a dubious place in history.[30] The two generals' management of the conditions peculiar to the guerrilla warfare of the conflict's denouement left perhaps the blackest mark upon the

British record in South Africa, a mark that carried ominous portents for the century to come.

For as the guerrilla war slogged forward, both sides found it increasingly difficult to sustain the illusion that this was a civilized "gentleman's war" subject to traditional legal constraints. Cruelty from one side begat brutal reprisals from the other.[31] A British policy of widespread farm-burning, which included driving away animals and livestock, was adopted to eliminate the lingering pockets of "banditti" resistance; imposed to cut off Boer sources of sustenance, the policy imposed a harsh penalty upon their civilian support structure. Yet the law of unintended consequences set in with a vengeance. The need to contain and control the ensuing flow of refugees and to protect relatives of surrendered Boers from the brutal reprisals of their own commanders in the field prompted the establishment of a system of relief "laagers." Kitchener's "concentration camps" would serve as his dubious, lasting legacy in South Africa, setting a curse upon British imperial policy for the remainder of the life of the empire.

Despite Afrikaner protests to the contrary, the camps were never intended to implement a policy of genocide.[32] Resort to the use of the camps began shortly after the taking of Pretoria in June of 1900, as a part of "Roberts's general policy . . . to put pressure on civilians in the expectation that their hardships would induce the men in the field to lay down their arms."[33] After assuming command in late November, Kitchener opened more camps. Surrendered burghers, along with non-combatant Boer families, displaced to the camps in increasingly unmanageable numbers. Separate camps began to be established for Africans in March of 1901. Around this same time, control over the camps was transferred from military to civilian control. The change was celebrated at the time as the inauguration of a profound improvement, but such announcements proved overly optimistic. As the tide of refugees swelled, sanitary conditions rapidly deteriorated. The humanitarian observer Emily Hobhouse, who visited the camps in the spring of 1901, found most of them to be ill-equipped, poorly situated, unhygienic, and overcrowded.[34]

Still, the tightening of the vice seemed to be exerting the desired effect. In June, Jan Smuts wrote to President Kruger: "Our cause has reached a state of great anxiety . . . Most farms and most foodstuffs have been destroyed; almost all families are held in the camps where the treatment is not good and the misery very great. The two Republics are a desert where food for the troops is more and more scarce. The families who are not captured, are refugees in the bushes and mountains; several families have in the end been murdered by the Swazis and the Zulus; almost all the Native tribes in the North are excited and commit atrocities. A certain number of our burghers are fighting against us with our enemies. Our whole people has suffered extremely and there is no hope for a speedy end to all these miseries."[35]

As the year wore on, Kitchener's administrative deficiencies mushroomed to produce a disaster of epidemic proportions. Typhoid, influenza, and measles rampaged through the camps; the death toll mounted, peaking in October. It was Emily Hobhouse's protest movement that ultimately brought notice of the horrendous sanitary conditions to the attention of the British public. By the time the camps were finally shut down the following year, the death toll in the camps would be measured in the tens of thousands. It remains impossible to fix a precise figure to the number of deaths; one of the reasons is that no data is available for assessing the vast number of native Africans, who probably suffered worse in the camps than the Boers did.[36]

Given the fact that non-combatant women and children received such putatively non-punitive treatment during the course of hostilities, it is little to be wondered that Boer military regulars, combatants, criminals, and others who found themselves before the British military tribunals experienced occasional injustice, administrative deficiencies, and arbitrariness in the process.[37] Such problems were accompanied by rigorous self-scrutiny on the part of the British army. Perhaps the most well-known, if not notorious, of the military courts conducted by the British in the Boer War was the trial of "Breaker Morant." This was only one of many courts of inquiry that were conducted by the British in the interest of self-examination. Most of these courts of inquiry had to do with determining the legitimacy of troop surrenders to the enemy.[38] Thus, to take one early example, Captain S. Duncan, of the Gloucestershire regiment, was charged with having unjustifiably raised the white flag in the humiliation at Nicholson's Nek in the opening days of the war, on October 30, 1899.[39] A court of inquiry convened to investigate the matter in April of the following year. Upon the court's finding of misconduct, Duncan was removed from the service—despite the subsequent intervention of Lord Roberts himself. Appeals and further inquiry into the circumstances of the matter—Roberts appointed a special committee to examine the case—persisted for another two years, well beyond the conclusion of the war itself.[40] Moreover, a Royal Commission assigned "to inquire into the military preparations and other matters" produced four massive volumes of evidence and testimony over the course of some fifty-five days of hearings, subjecting the British army's conduct of the war to a meticulous investigation and self-assessment.[41] Given the anxieties and uncertainties of the situation on the ground, what remained most striking about the British administration of military law in regard to enemy combatants was its relative mildness. Criticism at the time focused not on the harshness of the punishments meted out, but upon the soft treatment of captured Boer sympathizers, supporters, and combatants. The view was prevalent that it was the very leniency of the British that encouraged the continuation of the commandos' guerrilla campaigns. This was especially apparent with the treatment of rebels in the Cape Colony.

After the disastrous setbacks of the early weeks of the war, Sir Alfred Milner, High Commissioner for South Africa, suffered constantly under the threat of an invasion of the Cape from the Boer republics. Moreover, the potential for an uprising in a population composed of approximately two-thirds Afrikaners, it seemed, only wanted the spark of ignition. Even the British third was "not true-blue British,"[42] and as such, promised to cause trouble as well. Initial incursions into the border territory of the Cape, in November of 1899, held out the promise of a significant strategic advantage to the Boers—though they finally failed to capitalize on it. Steyn's invading forces met with little opposition after crossing the Orange River. In defiance of their British overlords, thousands of Dutch sympathizers from the Cape joined the Boer insurgency; even prominent Afrikaners from the colonial legislative council openly sided with the commandos.[43] In such circumstances, even a partial and measured application of martial law in limited areas "did nothing in many ways to dampen the spirit of rebellion, but merely inflamed it because many Afrikaners thought it meant they would be conscripted to fight their Boer brethren."[44]

In the early months of the war, the British were still awaiting significant reinforcements from the homeland and colonies. The danger was acute. A convergence of inauspicious circumstances in the Cape appeared to join against Milner, such that even measures taken, ostensibly, with the goal of enhancing security, appeared to exacerbate the threat. "Because of the shortage of regular troops, the British authorities had to rely on colonial volunteers to administer martial law, and some . . . had pre-war scores to settle. The arming of Africans and coloureds and their use in law courts to denounce their former Afrikaner masters, all added to the sense of grievance and inspired many to rebel."[45] It was at least in part due to this delicate political tension in the region that British authorities responded with leniency after turning back the invasion in early 1900.[46] A general amnesty was given to those rebels who agreed to take an oath of neutrality.[47] Most of the Cape rebels accepted the offer. The Cape parliament suspended the martial law decree in early October of 1900. Roberts had taken Bloemfontein and Pretoria with ease, and the war appeared to be nearing conclusion.

The Boer failure to seize the early initiative in the Cape proved to be fatal to the prospects for a general insurrection. Yet this retrospective vantage point was unavailable to the participants. For both sides, at least for a time, the perceived strategic significance of the promised invasion and rebellion increased almost in direct proportion to the decrease in likelihood of its actual occurrence. Ironically, although it carried less potency in terms of actual numbers it was the second Boer invasion of the Cape Colony, late in 1900, that led to the uniform application of martial law throughout the colony.[48] Movements of the general populace were placed under heavy restriction. The greater measure of harshness eventually worked the desired effect, though it would be many months before the bitter potion could prove its cure. In combination with the nearly universal imposition of martial law, a 10,000-strong loyalist militia was formed. Then, "as if by magic, Kritzinger's invasion began to fizzle out."[49]

Yet in January of 1901, Botha's assistant Jan Smuts still anticipated the longed-for victory, with great confidence in the strategic catalyst of a Cape invasion—which had now become a significant strategic priority for the Boers: "The enemy has diminished very much in the Republics; it seems to me that almost all his strength—except the town garrisons—is now in the direction of the goldfields; and my expectation and hope is that if we throw ourselves into the breach in the Cape Colony, so many troops would have to go there to quell a rising that the remaining commandos would be strong enough to hustle the enemy altogether out of the Republics: In any case I wish very much, even if it were personally, to go to the Cape Colony to help the Afrikaners in the execution of a general revolution and declaration of independence. If once we achieve that, I regard our cause as won."[50]

As it turned out, Smuts's dream, Milner's nightmare, never materialized. The momentum of the war shifted enough to cause Cape Afrikaners to hedge their bets; many resigned themselves to the ultimate defeat of the Boer cause. The supply of weapons dwindled. Under the British crackdown, many of the most capable leaders were captured and held as prisoners. Yet the psychological calculus available to the administration at the time could not be sufficiently calibrated to measure this shift of opinion with the accuracy that hindsight now supplies. For Milner especially, the possibility of rebellion in the Cape long remained an acute sore spot. It had been his opposition to a proposal for amnesty for the Cape rebels that, in large part, aborted the peace talks initiated by Botha in February of 1901. As both sides observed throughout the period, the threat of insurrection in the Cape made a bidding to upset the military balance in the whole of South Africa, and still had the potential to produce a debilitating reversal upon the British.

In his own account of the treatment of the Cape rebels, Milner sought to put criticisms of the administration of military law into perspective by emphasizing the remarkable leniency of its execution. Thus, in the summer of 1900, he could write:

> By far the most formidable of the powers which may be arrogated to themselves by the military under martial law is that of trying and punishing persons guilty of rebellion. In the present case, except while the rebellion was actually in full swing, nobody has been tried for acts of rebellion or treason by military courts. Even while the rebels were under arms by thousands, the number of persons so tried was exceedingly small, and as soon as rebellion was stamped out in any quarter trial by military courts (except for breaches of mere disciplinary regulations, involving trifling punishment) was entirely suspended. Scores of rebels have been captured in fight, thousands have surrendered their arms, but there are not six persons present in prison in this Colony who have been confined and sentences passed on them by military courts for acts of rebellion. No single rebel has been put to death, and the heaviest punishment inflicted on any of them at the hands of the military is two years' imprisonment with a fine of £1,000. The persons arrested by the military for high treason—with very few exceptions—have either been brought to trial before the ordinary tribunals of the land, or they are detained pending the decision of Parliament to establish a special court to deal with their cases.[51]

The second, doomed Boer invasion force in the Cape Colony, though never amounting to more than a couple of thousand strong, nevertheless succeeded in rattling the British command throughout the better part of the war's second full year.[52] Kritzinger's "Lilliputian" Boer commando stayed on the loose for over seven months, through the end of the summer of 1901,[53] prompting increasingly harsh counter-measures designed to finally stamp out the threats it represented. The first of a number of executions of citizens of the Cape Colony occurred in March of 1901. Three additional Cape rebels were tried and executed the same month at De Aar, on the Cape Town–Kimberley rail line, with more executions following in June. Some rebels from the Cape were captured, convicted before military tribunals, and condemned to undergo public executions at Dordrecht (in the Stormberg mountains where Smuts was soon to lead his own commando in a daring escape from under the noses of General John French's much larger contingent). Local inhabitants were compelled to observe the executions as spectators.

On August 7, Kitchener issued a decree—a drastic, long-resisted measure to which the Cabinet had finally and reluctantly acquiesced—promising banishment for all armed Boer leaders and members of the republican governments captured after the deadline of September 15. Kitchener began placing civilian hostages on the supply trains to Kimberley and Pretoria as a means of preventing ambushes or sabotage by Boer guerrillas. During the period of Kitchener's command, an initial number of some seven hundred Boers, civilian and military, received the death sentence from military tribunals. Of this number, approximately thirty-five were executed after Kitchener had affirmed their sentences. The remainder were commuted to various terms of imprisonment. Some forty-four burghers were executed in the Cape Colony over the course of the entire war. Executions in the Transvaal and the Free State amounted to approximately forty-six.[54] Most of the executed "rebels" were British subjects, captured while assisting or fighting on the side of the enemy. Some were Boer combatants, tried and convicted for violations of the law of war.

Among the most prominent defendants in this second group tried in the British military courts was the Boer Commandant Gideon Scheepers.[55] Scheepers had entered the Cape on November 15 with Kritzinger's commando. The two commanders had divided forces after penetrating into British territory. The goal was to stir up an insurrection among Boer partisans that would precede the large-scale invasion that never finally came. After nearly a year of harassing maneuvers, and hair-breadth escapes, Scheepers became severely ill and finally surrendered on October 10, 1901. The trial commenced on December 18, 1901, and lasted until the 28th, with numerous delays caused by the poor health of the defendant. The court heard fifty-three prosecution witnesses and three witnesses for the defense, along with the testimony of the defendant himself. He was convicted on twenty-nine different counts, including murder, attempted murder, ill treatment of prisoners, flogging British subjects and natives, destroying railways and trains, and arson. The court, consisting of Lieutenant Colonel A. Sprot of the Carabineers and Captain Wilson and Lieutenant Dawson of other regiments found him guilty on all counts but one of the murder charges and sentenced him to death by hanging. Kitchener confirmed the sentence on January 14, and Scheepers was executed on the 18th.[56]

In July, Kritzinger had issued an order that would be the subject of momentous controversy in later assessments of the conduct of the military tribunals. The order called for the summary execution of natives captured in British military service—armed or unarmed. The Boers, whose particular customs and ways fixed upon the racial inferiority of the "Kaffirs," had always contended that the conflict should remain a "white man's war"[57] and were outraged by the massive influx of Blacks into regular British ranks as the war continued. It was Scheepers's execution of the dubious order that probably largely determined the disposition of his case in a trial for war crimes. Seven of the charges against him had to do with his own orders for the execution of African spies. In his defense, Scheepers had admitted to most though not all of the executions, contesting that he had simply engaged in carrying out a lawful superior order. Of the rebel cases tried in the British military courts, six or seven other notable Boer defendants, including Commandant J. C. Lötter, also faced conviction and execution for the murder of native spies or combatants.[58] In the matter of these trials British motives were far from pure—the enlistment of some 20,000 Africans into the ranks of Kitchener's columns could not be said, after all, to have been a response of newly discovered enlightened understanding as to their racial equality. But neither can it be said that these subsequent military trials and executions amounted to an indiscriminate and Draconian imposition of British "methods of barbarism." It is surely likely that British resentment over the amnesties and leniency granted to fomenters of the first Boer invasion of the colony spilled over to color the treatment of Scheepers and other similar cases. With the depressing experience of another year of guerrilla conflict, and no end of it in immediate sight, the flow of leniency had now largely dried up.[59] A Boer policy that required the summary execution of any and all prisoners—combatants, spies, or mere support troops—simply on the basis of their race, was itself a practice that threatened to torque the cycle of bloody retaliation further, and uncontrollably downward, and demanded a stern and unequivocal response. From the absolute perspective granted by hindsight, such a response probably produced comparative injustices in individual cases. Scheepers and others may well have been less deserving of their punishment than others who received amnesty. Yet more significant, surely, was the success of the British command in containing the use of the tools of martial rule and military trials within strictly defined limits.

Toward the end of 1901, the laborious, painstaking incrementalism of Kitchener's blockhouse and barbed-wire strategem began to yield significant results. From now on, the war proceeded according to "grouse-moor principles"[60]—British columns "flushing" the guerrillas into the massive enclosed areas between the blockhouses, then trapping, or "bagging," the catch. The great Boer general De Wet, one of the more successful in eluding capture within Kitchener's nets, described the "thousands of miles of blockhouse lines" as forming "a sort of spider's web of the South African Republics."[61] With the corresponding attrition caused by deteriorating Boer morale, the war finally ground down to its inevitable conclusion. Parallel to this gradual forward press of the armies proceeded a corresponding extension of martial rule: "civil courts followed the army as it drove out the invaders, and exercised under military aegis jurisdiction over nonmilitary offences and minor breaches of martial law regulations."[62]

In August 1902, at the conclusion of the war, Joseph Chamberlain commissioned an official inquiry into the adjudication of martial law in South Africa. In particular, the Royal Commission conducted a clemency review of martial law sentences in which either penal servitude, imprisonment, or fines had been adjudicated, investigating whether "it might be expedient, having regard to all the circumstances relating thereto, that such sentences or fines should be remitted or reduced."[63] Thus, the focus of the inquiry was limited to examining the appropriateness of the adjudged punishments in light of the changed post-conflict circumstances of the territories—the Cape, the Orange River colony, Transvaal, and Natal. The Commission reported on 794 cases, the vast majority of which (721) had been tried in the Cape Colony in the wake of the second abortive Boer invasion. The most common offense among this number had been high treason, followed by murder and assistance to the enemy. Out of the total number, the commission recommended that over one hundred (111) should be released outright. For a slightly larger number (145), the recommendation was "no alteration." Nearly all of these cases involved lighter initial sentences, usually confinement of less than five years. The majority of recommendations for clemency were reductions from life imprisonment to shorter terms of two to three years.[64]

Of the remainder of the cases, fifty-nine arose in the Transvaal and Orange River colonies, and fourteen in Natal.[65] The commission's clemency recommendations for these regions reflected similar proportions in the adjustment of sentences. The vast number and severity of sentences in the Cape Colony in comparison to the other territories reflects Milner's judgment as to the militarily and politically strategic significance of the colony, for both sides. Only one death sentence had been originally delivered in Natal, in the high treason case of Ignatius Marthinus Kok; this sentence was commuted to six years' penal servitude at the time of sentence confirmation, and was further reduced by recommendation of the commission to three years.[66] By comparison, in the Cape 326 initial death sentences were issued most of which were commuted to various terms of imprisonment. The area at greatest remove from the theater of combat—to the degree, at least, that such a term still had meaning given the fluidity of the guerrilla-style engagements of the war's final years—had by war's end become the region of the most intense and widespread application of martial law. The exposure of British interests in the Cape, the complex political volatility of the region, and its very remoteness from the mass of the imperial armies sent for its protection rendered the territory vulnerable to marauding enemy commandos; the gradual introduction of correspondingly severe measures sought to address these threats.

In Natal, by contrast, where the set battles of the early months of the war had raged with greatest intensity and "the magnitude and progress of the Boer invasion [were] recognized [immediately],"[67] the uniform application of martial law had occurred almost simultaneously with the outbreak of war. On the other hand, the demographics of the region meant that fewer Boer sympathizers had to be reckoned with, and the danger of backlash in the form of rebellion was correspondingly reduced. A more nuanced policy had been applied to the political powder keg in the Cape, where authorities seesawed back and forth, reluctant to alienate an Afrikaner faction seemingly ripe for insurrection. The governments at the Cape and in London repeatedly clashed with military authorities over appropriate limits and boundaries for the application of martial law. Universal imposition of martial rule had only come with the late discovery of the leakage through the Cape ports. The gradualism and indecisiveness of the responses of the Cape authorities, a mixture of uncertainty followed ultimately by severity, produced bitterness and rancor on all sides.

The Boers also exercised stern justice with prisoners. As the war continued and the British made increasing use of native African troops, the Boers—who found this practice to be a violation of the terms of "white man's warfare"—exerted brutal summary punishment upon the "Kaffirs" when captured. Kritzinger, the leader of the Boer commando in the Cape, "sanctioned the killing of armed or unarmed Africans who were helping the British or were suspected of giving aid in any form."[68] In November 1901, Kitchener wrote to Brodrick, "Cold-blooded murder of natives by Boers are frequent. On 10 November, 2 dead bodies of natives, with hands tied behind them, were found in mine shaft near Graylingstadt. They had not been shot. Sworn evidence is being collected."[69]

Ex Parte Marais: Martial Rule in Modern Warfare

The war severely tested the integrity of Britain's imperial identity and its commitment to liberal principles. British interests in South Africa tended to tug in conflicting directions. The Boer republics which sought through war to assert their right to ongoing existence—against an Imperial Unionist desire to accomplish their eventual absorption into a federal South Africa and, consequently, into the larger empire—were actually populated by many citizens of British blood, who were quick to assert their rights as British subjects when captured or detained. The seat of British rule in South Africa, the Cape Colony, contained many law-abiding Afrikaners who were both loyal to the Crown and yet sympathetic to the cause of their fellow Afrikaners.[70] The tension of conflicting loyalties echoes the American colonial experience at the time of the War of Independence, for many Boers identified themselves both with the Boer republics and as British subjects. The test of competing loyalties came with the capture or detention of these British-oriented Boers. What rights did such individuals enjoy vis-à-vis the British courts?

The altered standard, announced most decisively in the case of *ex parte Marais*,[71] stipulated that the normal civil courts could not sit in judgment on acts of the military—as long as "actual war is raging."

Moreover, the fact that *some* civil courts were still sitting and performing *some* normal functions did not dispose of the critical question of the existence of "actual war" nor, by extension, of the appropriateness of emergency measures such as the use of military tribunals. The actual existence of a state of war was to be determined by factual inquiry, not inferred as a certain legal consequence upon ascertaining the open status of the courts.

The case was decided in November and December of 1901 by the High Court for the Imperial Dominions, the Judicial Committee of the Privy Council. In August of the same year, the petitioner François Marais had been arrested in the town of Paarl, about thirty-five miles from the Cape Colony capital. Thus, the arrest occurred at some remove from the theater of hostilities—to the extent that one could still be identified in the cat-and-mouse chase that the war had by that time become. Suspected of a violation of the martial law regulations forbidding active assistance to the enemy and endangerment of "the safety of His Majesty's forces or subjects," Marais was transported to a military detention facility at Beaufort West, some three hundred miles further up the Kimberley line. The petitioner sought special leave to appeal an order of the Cape Town Supreme Court denying his application for release from military custody. Petitioner's counsel, Lord Richard Haldane contended, "the special feature of the case was that the district where the arrest was made was undisturbed, and that civil courts were still exercising uninterrupted jurisdiction. That being so, and it appearing that the ordinary course of law could be and was being maintained, a state of war did not exist, and martial law in that case could not be applied to civilians."[72] The claim seemed strong enough—Haldane was merely arguing in terms of the traditional test, grounded in the ancient Petition of Right, that looked to the availability of the civil courts for resolution of the question of the appropriateness of martial law.

Both sides in such cases sought to establish a bright line test.[73] Appellants attempting to deflect the application of martial law rulings frequently sought to establish a footing on the basis that the regular courts were still open—thus, by definition, obviating the need for martial law. State prosecutors on the other hand perpetually sought for judicial approval of the proposition that a state of martial law exists wherever the government proclaims it to be so. The Privy Council, through Lord Halsbury (who had served as defense counsel for Governor Eyre in the earlier Jamaica controversy), retorted that neither was correct. The question was not to be resolved by a determination of the status of the civil courts, nor by simple resort to the positive pronouncement of a government decree. Rather, the key to the inquiry lay in the factual determination as to whether "actual war is raging."[74] The Judicial Committee's response was unequivocal: "the truth is that no doubt has ever existed that where war actually prevails the ordinary Courts have no jurisdiction over the action of the military authorities."[75] To be sure, the Lord Justices acknowledged, "cases of difficulty" might arise in the context of insurrection, riot, or rebellion where the existence of a state of war would prove problematic. But this was not such a case: "once let the fact of actual war be established, and there is an universal consensus of opinion that the civil Courts have no jurisdiction to call in question the propriety of the action of military authorities."[76] As Edward Corwin later observed—in the spectral lull between global wars, it might be added—the committee's mid-conflict opinion "was substantially the reverse of that reached by the [American] Supreme Court in the earlier [*Milligan*] case."[77] Yet the decision was on a par with the discoveries of Lincoln and his generals amidst the carnage of the Civil War, and even, to an extent, in its chaotic aftermath. French executive authorities would make a similar finding in the course of the First World War: the mere fact of the ongoing existence of normal functioning civil courts, in some areas, and for some purposes, simply could not be equated with an assertion of the non-existence of emergency conditions. The benefit of clear hindsight in peaceful conditions afforded to the *Milligan* court was unavailable at the time the Privy Council's Judicial Committee decided *Marais*. The fog of war had not yet dissipated. Moreover, it wasn't as if the traditional requirement defined as "necessity" had been abandoned. Rather, the fluid dynamics of modern warfare required that the meaning of "necessity" be sensibly accommodated to actual conditions on the ground.

As we have seen, in the British-held Cape Colony where, on August 15, 1901, Marais had been arrested and confined under martial law, the threat of a Boer uprising had persisted as a constant thorn in the side of the British administration. Indeed, the perceived danger to the colony persisted—it was not until October 9 of the same year that martial law was finally imposed upon the Cape ports, which, military authorities learned, had been serving as conduits of men, arms, and supplies to the lingering enemy commandos in the veld. Marais had fallen into the noose of British authorities in the midst of a concentrated tightening of the vice of martial law, an increase in the level of judicial severity, which, though it assisted in squelching the movements of Boer commandos, produced "innumerable complaints from those who, hitherto, had been accustomed to sympathize with, or indirectly assist, the invader with little risk to themselves."[78] In the midst of the general war weariness, members of Parliament were "inundated" with grievances and petitions. A Board of Review was established for the purpose of addressing such complaints. The Board was not authorized to inquire into the proceedings of the military tribunals, but did provide correction and oversight to the administration of martial law in the colony.[79]

The *Marais* case prompted an important symposium in the *Law Quarterly Review,* dedicated to an examination of the law of martial rule in the light of current military conditions.[80] In perhaps the most forceful defense of the *Marais* court's adaptation of emergency rule, H. Erle Richards argued the rightness of the Privy Council opinion, asserting that "the necessity for taking action which infringes on rights of property or liberty can not depend on the fact that the courts continue or do not continue to sit: it depends on the necessity created by the presence of an enemy in the country." To categorically insist upon a definition of the existence of war made contingent upon the status of the civil courts was legalistic folly. The mere creation of an academic, legal, and contingent relationship between the two things did not mean the artificial template corresponded meaningfully to the reality of actual events. The fact of the ongoing functioning of the courts might provide some evidence, assisting in providing a context for the determination of the appropriateness of martial rule, in any given set of circumstances. But it would be tantamount to a suicidal absurdity to make this factor alone the pivotal hinge upon which the determination of a lawful state of war or peace should turn: "there is no authority which lays down the general proposition that in the view of the law, war does not exist when in fact it does exist. War is self-evident, and the fact that courts may continue to sit cannot prevent the existence of war." The theme was the necessity of a standard of review that fitted the application of martial law to the actual exigencies of war.[81]

Cyril Dodd considered the character of strained unanimity lying just under the surface of the Privy Council opinion. Since, in such a case, "no dissentient minority of the Privy Council is permitted to express in public its reasons for differing from the majority, nor is any report of a dissentient minority submitted to the King,"[82] to allow both views "would appear to leave upon the Crown the ultimate responsibility of deciding between the opposing views presented, with the assistance only of the general principle" ordinarily preferring the majority.[83] An important distinction must be maintained, and a common misunderstanding dispelled: that proclamations of martial law occur during "times of war or warlike disturbance" was plain; "but [contrary to the erroneous opinion of some,] it is not the proclamation which creates the martial law or justifies it. The proclamation is rather the statement or notice of the existence of a state of facts than the creation of those facts."[84] The condition giving rise to martial law was necessity—the state of emergency—into the circumstances of which the courts enjoyed a power to inquire, "so far at any rate as they reasonably can without injury to the State arising from the disclosure of matters contrary to the public interest and endangering the public safety."[85]

To be sure, there was the ancient and well-recognized rule, dating back to the Petition of Right in the time of Charles I, "that when the Courts are open it is 'time of peace' for all legal purposes and in all courts of law."[86] Yet the rule had been promulgated at a time when "justice was to a great extent administered by the aid of legal fictions, and there was to the then legal mind nothing revolting in the assumption of facts which were opposed to actual knowledge."[87] The *Marais* court, then, had merely moved in the direction of dispelling the long-persisting abstraction, fitting the law to the reality to which it ought to correspond. The adjustment was especially critical at such a time, given the new circumstances created by innovations of modern technology in communication, transport, and the conduct of warfare:

> [T]he area now affected by a war, the area over which martial law is a necessity, and, because of that necessity, lawful or excusable, is much larger, much more extended, than was the case prior to the increased facilities afforded for locomotion by railways and other improved modes of travel, and prior to the improved modes of transmitting information and orders by telegraph and the like. So that whilst in primitive times the area of disturbance was little more than the locality occupied by the rival encampments of the two bodies in conflict, in which area no Court could or would be found to sit for any purpose, in modern times it extends to long distances and comprises a large, it may [be] a vast, area.[88]

The fiction that a legal "state of peace" exists wherever the courts are open and functioning should finally be laid to rest. Public safety and security—the very reason for which governments exist—ought not to be sacrificed to prop up an abstract legal principle. To say this was not to allow, of course, that the existence of a state of war exempts "the soldier from all liability to answer after the war for all acts done during war." Nor did it mean that the executive authority was unaccountable before the courts throughout the continuance of hostilities. Rather, a delicate balance must be maintained between the judicial interest in pursuing justice in concrete cases and the countervailing state burdens to curtail "danger to public safety" and secure "the proper prosecution of the war."[89] No one interest could be viewed as absolute, pursued in the abstract.

The eminent historian Frederick Pollock saw the case as occasioning an inquiry into the most basic moral, juridical, and practical problems associated with the state's application of coercive force:

> First, what is a state of war? Must there be, then and there, actual fighting or disorder? Must life and property be in imminent danger? Must the enemy be visible in force, or the sound of his guns audible? Then, are the kinds of acts which may be necessary for public defence limited to the use of physical force against persons, by way of restraint or summary punishment? If not, what other kinds of acts may be required and justified?[90]

Regrettably, "the old books" provided precious little guidance. This was not, primarily, because of their displacement by "new books," new legal developments that had permanently altered the terrain of juridical responses to emergency. Rather, the legal response to emergency must be adapted to changes in modern conditions of warfare.[91]

> An enemy's army has landed in force in the north and is marching on York. The peace is kept in London and Bristol, and the courts are not closed. It is known that evil-disposed persons have agreed to land at several ports for the purpose of joining the enemy and giving him valuable aid and information. Bristol is one of the suspected ports. What shall the Lord Mayor of Bristol do? I submit that it is his plain moral duty as a good citizen (putting aside for a moment the question of strict law) to prevent suspected persons from landing, or to arrest and detain them if found on shore, to assume control of the railway traffic and forbid undesirable passengers to proceed northward, and to exercise a strict censor-

> ship and inquisitorial power over letters and telegrams. All these things are in themselves trespasses (except, probably, forbidding an alien to land); some of them may perhaps be justifiable under the statutory powers of the Postmaster-General, but summary restraint by way of prevention must be justified by a common law power arising from necessity, if at all. Observe that I say nothing for the present about trial or punishment. The popular (and sometimes official) notion that martial law necessarily means trial by court-martial has caused much confusion. Summary punishment may or may not be necessary. In that respect the Mayor's authority would be like that of the master of a ship.[92]

Not absolute, in other words, but amplified, enhanced to address the extraordinary conditions and exigencies of the situation. It was not necessary to speculate as to the consequences resulting from a failure on the part of the mayor to responsibly exercise such powers—the actual mayor of Bristol had seen his city set on fire in the Reform Bill riots of 1827. In such a situation, it was surely futile to claim that effectual response would have been unlawful and thus unavailable due to the legal existence of a "state of peace." The absence of positive justification in the form of superior orders, prescribing a plan of responsive action, could not excuse the magistrate from his own prior, independent duty to preserve public order. Nor was it the case that the emergency response should be regarded as a necessary and temporary detour from normal legality, "a kind of splendid offence,"[93] but, quoting Justice Kingsmill, "'justifiable and lawful for the maintenance of the Commonwealth.'"[94]

Moreover, there had to be an element of positive, preemptive power attached to the magistrate's repertory of emergency response. This required greater elasticity in assessing the geographical limits of the area circumscribed by necessity: "It also seems that the range of those acts must extend to the prevention of aid and comfort to the enemy beyond the bounds of places where warlike operations are in sight." For the state to perform its most basic function, the preservation of public order, such flexibility was critical, if providing advantage, opportunity, and surprise to the enemy was not to be made a keystone of state policy. "In many places there may outwardly be peace, and yet modern means of communication may admit of important aid being conveyed to the enemy in the shape of information, supplies and personal adherents. In this manner, the effective radius of a state of war has been multiplied tenfold or more." In the process of acknowledging and accounting for technological, logistical, and military changes, law does not manufacture new conditions of reality; rather, it adjusts and accommodates itself to the reality of such change. "By recognizing this fact we do not alter the law, but apply it to the facts as they exist; nor do we disparage the wisdom of our predecessors who declared their opinion of the law in a form appropriate to the facts as known."[95]

Interestingly, the Judicial Committee took occasion to revisit the question of martial rule in the context of the native uprising in Natal, in 1906.[96] Writing for the Judicial Committee, the Earl of Halsbury saw fit to reinforce the principle of *Marais,* elaborating on the differences between courts under martial law conditions and other courts of justice. Halsbury distinguished "between the proceedings of a military court sitting under . . . the Mutiny Act, and proceedings which are not constituted according to any system of law at all"—revisiting the much-repeated observation as to the oxymoronic character of the term "martial law."[97] The analogy between the two types of proceedings was "totally inaccurate." Since "the right to administer force against force in actual war does not depend upon the proclamation of martial law at all,"[98] the question of the appropriateness of martial law depended on the existence of a state of war. This established the legitimacy of the proceedings of military tribunals on the basis of a showing of necessity. The committee's statement of the position, via Justice Halsbury, is worth noting in detail for the uncompromising sharpness with which it outlines these distinctions:

> If there is war, there is the right to repel force by force, but it is found convenient and decorous, from time to time, to authorize what are called "courts" to administer punishments, and to restrain by acts of repression the violence that is committed in time of war, instead of leaving such punishment and repression to the casual action of persons acting without sufficient consultation, or without sufficient order or regularity in the procedure in which things alleged to have been done are proved. But to attempt to make these proceedings of so-called "courts-martial," administering summary justice under the supervision of a military commander, analogous to the regular proceedings of Courts of justice is quite illusory. Such acts of justice are justified by necessity, by the fact of actual war; and that they are so justified under the circumstances is a fact that it is no longer necessary to insist upon, because it has been over and over again so decided by Courts as to whose authority there can be no doubt.[99]

The function of martial law, and of the military tribunals organized under its authority, was to provide a modicum of order and procedure in the midst of the most violent and disorderly of human activities. The features of consultation, order, and regularity erected security fences against a precipitous decline into indiscriminate vengeful bloodletting. Yet at the same time these features did not obviate the summary nature of the proceedings, which operate as an appendage of the commander in the field, and not as a temporary auxiliary of the civil judicial system. The Judicial Committee saw the function of military tribunals as one aspect, albeit limited and tangential, of the commander's authority "to repel force by force." This meant that the primary limitation of martial law came about by means of the tightly circumscribed boundaries of its application, and not through the active supervision of appellate courts. Martial law was "unknown" in this sense only, that "it did not comprise a set of rules and regulations to be invoked when circumstances demanded; its content varied in each crisis depending upon what measures the situation warranted. The restoration of order, the administration of tribunals, and infliction of punishment were empowered by the reality of violence."[100] Operating within the orbit of legitimacy determined by the conditions of actual war, it was "convenient and decorous"—even "necessary"—to allow commanders the flexibility to impose some modicum of order upon the field of combat in this way. As Richard Cosgrove rightly observes, "the *Tilonko* case set the seal on the transformation in martial law produced by the Boer War."[101]

The great American naval historian Alfred T. Mahan opened his own account of the Boer War—the publication of which anticipated the conclusion of hostilities by nearly a year—with a remark upon "the general rule that the origin of current events is to be sought in the history of the past."[102] The observation was no less true with regard to the smaller sphere describing the administration of martial law. For an island nation that had enjoyed centuries of freedom from outside invasion, the measures imposed by Bullers, Roberts, Kitchener, and their subordinate commanders as the South Africa campaign dragged on had an appearance of harshness and brutality. Such criticisms still resonate with the passage of time. Administrative inequities arising with the absence of any systematic, pre-existing emergency juridical response exacerbated the problem. The rigorous critical commentary upon military juridical policies throughout the war arose from a fertile soil flourishing with the strenuous exercise of an expanding body of legal and political liberties—a history inseparable from the skein of the nation's unique geographical and political advantages. It was a history too that proudly made little place for the stern necessities of martial rule. In this regard, the *Times History's* admonition as to the relative mildness of British punitive measures in the war bears keeping in mind:

> The defects of our system of military government reflect in great measure the defects of the British race. As a nation we have small regard for system, and little capacity for prevision. Moreover, on this particular issue our national ignorance of the meaning of war inclines us towards mistaken leniency in dealing with our enemies, whom we try to conciliate during hostilities, often at the expense of our friends. Martial law and military government, as these terms are understood by the great military powers of Europe, were never enforced throughout the war, and possibly never will be under our present system of party government. The French, Germans, and Russians in South Africa considered our martial law regulations mild to the verge of weakness, while the majority of the British and Colonials, who did not understand what war is, considered the same regulations far too drastic. How drastic martial law can be, may be realized from the study of Davoust's military administration of Hamburg in 1807, or of the system enforced by the German army in France in 1870–71. Should British territory ever be invaded—and many thinking soldiers consider this by no means impossible—the sternness with which martial law will be enforced will strike terror to the heart of a population accustomed to regard human life as the most sacred thing in the universe.[103]

For all its brutality and violence, fighting in the conflict had been conducted at a comparatively high level of respect, decency, and decorum. In his final dispatches to London—almost as if he were commenting on a hard-fought cricket test—Kitchener could commend the Boer leaders Botha, De la Rey, and De Wet for having "played their part [in the conclusion of hostilities] with loyalty and in a thoroughly straightforward manner."[104] Yet, as Amery's fellow imperialist Kipling had prophesied, severer tests were soon to come.

3

France and the *Conseils de Guerre* of the First World War

In France, the context for the operation of the military tribunals (*les conseils de guerre*; literally, "councils of war") convened during the course of the First World War resides in a peculiar legal concept dating back to the formation of the republican form of government: namely, the state of siege (*l'état de siège*), "the fundamental crisis institution of the French Republic."[1] Both "a product of history and eminently an institution in law," the French state of siege has operated as a unique juridical response to conditions of national emergency, as a regime "foreseen and methodized in detail by laws of Parliament."[2] As we shall see, the fact of this statutory institutionalization of the crisis mode of government makes for critical differences with the Anglo-American ad hoc method of emergency response.[3]

As the name suggests, the political notion of the state of siege grew out of military practice. When a fortified city or town came under attack, the common response was to give the military commander in charge of the defending forces full powers of government over the fortified area and its occupants. After the French Revolution, *l'état de siège* came to be identified as the legal response to conditions of national emergency, providing for the military assumption of many of the processes of government, for a limited time and purpose. The law regarding the state of siege took its present form in two basic legislative enactments, both transparently developed in the aftermath of crisis conditions. Thus, the original law of 1849,[4] adopted subsequent to the turmoil of the year of democratic revolutions, received significant modification in 1878, after the lessons of the Franco-Prussian War.[5] A few additional adjustments have been made, but both of these nineteenth-century enactments remain in force today.[6]

Only declared in time of imminent danger arising from a foreign war, an invasion of French soil, or armed insurrection—and only in those territories under threat—the state of siege had been invoked in one other analogous situation, during the 1870 Franco-Prussian war. Even then siege conditions did not apply throughout the country. The 1878 statute required that the declaration of a state of siege could only be made by the Parliament or by the president and cabinet, if Parliament happened to be adjourned. In this case, the president would be required to call the Chambers which then would have the responsibility either to ratify or to lift the state of siege. The law required the designation of a fixed date upon which siege conditions would be terminated, at which time civil authorities would resume normal functions. The current constitutional provision respecting the state of siege seeks to balance the needs of energetic response with democratic accountability by assigning responsibility at different stages to both the executive and the legislature.[7] Article 36 of the 1958 Constitution stipulates that the power to decree the state of siege lies with the Council of Ministers. Parliament must intervene to authorize any extension beyond twelve days.

Under a state of siege, the military assumes police powers normally exercised by civil authorities. Law enforcement and the maintenance of order at the local level largely transfer from civil to military authorities. This shift of authority carries with it a considerable extension of the scope and rigor of available police powers.[8] Thus, the statute explicitly grants auxiliary powers in four separate areas: to conduct searches by day or night in the homes of citizens; to deport non-residents; to search for and confiscate arms; and to forbid publications and assemblies deemed likely to incite disorder.[9] In addition, and most important for our purposes, the military courts are given jurisdiction over all crimes and serious offenses against order, security, and public safety.[10]

Crisis, the "Doomsday Machine," and Response

In actual practice, the French government declared a state of siege before the outbreak of hostilities in the First World War. Compared to the application of the state of siege in the conflict most closely analogous to the situation facing the French nation in 1914, the 1870 war with Prussia, the government now took more drastic measures.[11] Lessons learned from the experience of the earlier war, when internal breakdown of order had attended the conflict's waning days, the current general favor of public sentiment, and the relative sense of extraordinary crisis, together contributed to the vigor of the response—a response without precedent in French experience.[12] Indeed, "[e]vents transpired so quickly and constituted such a grave danger that French statesmen had little room for maneuver and could not even afford the time to reflect on the motivations that drove their actions. French policy was reactive and instinctive. It was, if anything, over-determined, and can easily be explained by a simple appeal to the requirements of self-defense."[13] The declaration of August 2, 1914, issued on the day of Germany's general troop mobilization, summarily imposed the state of siege throughout the entire national territory, including the three departments of Algeria. The proximate cause for the sweeping decree was the unprecedented order for general mobilization in France, itself issued in the panic of reaction and response that triggered the "doomsday machine" [14] of total war. A subsequent decree, issued three days later, temporally extended the state of siege to coincide with the duration of the war.[15]

By this time, of course, the war had begun with the German army's invasion and occupation of neutral Belgium, on its way into the French heartland. After serious Allied setbacks on the frontiers, the five German armies pushed numerically inferior French and British forces to within thirty miles of Paris. Before the solid Allied resistance at the Marne led to a partial German retreat and the subsequent stalemate of the trenches, the Germans—in accordance with the timetable of the Schlieffen Plan[16]—had very nearly succeeded in achieving all their objectives on the Western front within the first forty days of the conflict.

The assault on Belgium, which violated treaty guarantees and international law regarding neutrals,[17] precipitated some of the worst atrocities against civilians to occur throughout the war. Beset by memories of 1870,[18] the Germans were apparently overcome by the delusion of a putative organized resistance movement, a *Franktireurkrieg* carried out by guerrilla fighters (the so-called *franc-tireurs*, or free-shooters, snipers) among the civilian population of Belgium. In fact, no such *franc-tireur* resistance movement existed. [19] In a psychologically bizarre and lethal paroxysm of fear, haunted by the specter of a "People's war" that threatened to undermine standing German ideals for the proper conduct of war[20] and bring the momentum of the Schlieffen plan to a grinding halt, German troops scattered violence upon Belgian and French civilians throughout the path of invasion.[21] Incidents of rape, massacre, and massive destruction of property occurred between the months of August and October—the period of mobilized war, before the stalemate of the trenches on the Western front—leaving some 6,427 civilians dead, the majority of whom were Belgian; approximately one-fourth were French.[22]

Of course, the full details surrounding the German assault in the opening months of the war would remain enshrouded in fog and confusion for many years after the event. Yet the outrage and horror inspired by the incidents prompted the speedy movements of juridical response. By September 2 the French government had shifted to the relative safety of Bordeaux, and the supreme commander, Joffre, "had incorporated the capital into the Zone of the Armies, where he ruled with total power, on 31 August."[23] At least for the city of Paris and its environs—now in the status of an "Entrenched Camp" under its Military Governor—the state of siege condition extended beyond the political and legal fiction to approximate the original military meaning of the term. Moreover, appalled by the apparent scope of German atrocities and concerned that similar methods of terror were spreading to French soil with the German advance, French authorities began to use military tribunals, the conseils de guerre, in October, for the purpose of trying war crimes.

The declaration of the state of siege itself had served to amplify the responsibilities of a pre-existing network of military tribunals throughout the country, which operated in each of the military districts into which the country was sub-divided:

> Submerged . . . below the surface of Europe's civil geography was a secondary, military geography of corps and divisional districts. France, a country of ninety administrative departments, created by the First Republic to supplant the old royal provinces with territorial units of approximately equal sizes, named for the most part after the local river . . . was also divided into twenty military districts, comprising four or five departments. Each military district was the peacetime location of a corps of the "active" army, and the source in war of an equivalent group of divisions of the reserve. . . . From the I Corps District (departments of the Nord and Pas-de-Calais) to the XVIII (Landes and Pyrenees) the military replicated the civil geography of France at every layer.[24]

In a manner analogous to the ad hoc system established during Reconstruction in the post-bellum South, each section of this grid of the "military geography" contained its own corresponding juridical component—in this case, a permanent functioning military court system. Thus, with the issuance of the state of siege decree of August 2, 1914, the entire nation ostensibly underwent an instantaneous shift to the jurisdictional authority of the military courts. In effect, this was mitigated by the fact that the establishment of military jurisdiction did not supplant the civil court system, which continued to operate in tandem with the military courts.[25] In practice, the decree simply subordinated the civil courts under the authority of the military system and gave military officials discretion and responsibility for deciding on the disposition of individual cases—in itself still an extraordinary transformation.[26] The point received, perhaps, its most emphatic official expression in an opinion of the Cour de Cassation rendered in November of 1915:

> Whereas, under the regime of the state of siege, according to the terms of articles 7 and 8 of the Law of 9 August, 1849; it appertains to the military authority, endowed by the fullness of the law with all of the powers vested in the civil authority for the maintenance of order and security, to remove ordinary judicial oversight of crimes and misdemeanors against the security of the Republic, against the Constitution, against public order and peace, whatever the status of the principal actors and their accomplices; that this power of removal rests within the discretion of the military authority; that it may neither be contested, nor refused, nor even delayed; that therefore, there are in this regard, no grounds for either litigation, or, consequently, for further debate.[27]

Again, while the context was rather different, the work of the conseils de guerre, in its scope, paralleled that of the military commissions working in the southern United States during Reconstruction. Those cases with a public dimension, impinging on public safety and order, were to be handled by the military courts.[28] In the context of the wartime jurisdiction of the First World War conseils de guerre, the French statute cut out a wide-ranging field subject to military control, extending well beyond the traditional unique categories of offenses associated with warfare and military discipline: "Assaults upon or resistance to citizens charged with some public duty, frauds in connection with the quality of provisions furnished the armed forces or in their sale, attempted robbery in a railroad station, insults to public officials engaged in their duties, the misdemeanor of vagabondage, the embezzlement of letters by a post-office agent," as well as violations of the prohibition of the sale of spirits and prostitution—the partial list of examples of offenses provides some indication of the vast extent of the jurisdiction of the conseils de guerre.[29] Notwithstanding the ongoing jurisdiction of the normal civil courts, the conseils de guerre enjoyed a broad range of discretion that was unprecedented in scope.[30]

Thus, the psychological complexities of reaction and response that contributed to the onset of war shaped and colored the juridical responses to its continuation. The paranoia and undisciplined violence of the German occupation forces in Belgium helped to provoke a response on the part of French authorities which included drastic curtailments of the civil liberties of Frenchmen. The brutal reality of "total" war amplified the urgency of calls for counter-measures against enemy espionage activities. Those engaging in commerce with subjects of the enemy powers faced stern punishments. Yet the severity of the response was attributable in part to the nature of the state of siege regime itself, an emergency measure of last resort, provided in advance, by statute, for the imposition of martial law conditions. No amount of legislative foresight could have been expected to articulate a perfectly modulated, harmonious balance of order and liberty for application in conditions of war on an unprecedented scale. [31] In the current context, the relevant nineteenth-century French legislation established a martial judicial system that reached far beyond a simple application of the laws of war.

Given the wide latitude of discretion they enjoyed, the conseils de guerre could act with seemingly arbitrary harshness. In one case, a Paris merchant had received an order from a Swiss cloth dealer, Grunberg & Cie of Zürich, for the provision of a quantity of first communion items, for delivery to a German firm located in Strasbourg. The merchant, M. Just, expressed reluctance in his response, citing the French prohibition against commercial activities with subjects of belligerent nations, but leaving an opening, hinting that he could still deal with neutrals. Grunberg renewed the request, arguing this was a legitimate transaction, to be carried out at the behest of a subject of a neutral nation. It appears that both parties knew the deal was deliberately designed to circumvent the French prohibition. The Strasbourg firm had been an old and important customer, with which Just desired to maintain close ties. Just finally acquiesced, though the deal eventually fell through before it could be completed, due to intervening circumstances. The Conseil de Guerre of the 2nd region (Paris) found Just guilty of attempting to violate the prohibition—his criminal intent was evidenced by the fact that he had begun to execute the transaction. The Conseil de Guerre condemned Just to two years imprisonment and a fine of 2,000 francs in accordance with the relevant statutes.

On appeal, the *Conseil de Revision* (courts of limited appeal, discussed *infra*) found that the matter was within the proper sphere of jurisdiction of the military tribunals, since the law placed criminal sanctions upon all commerce with subjects of the German and Austro-Hungarian empires, "by reason of the existence of a state of war, and in the interest of national defense." Thus, as a matter of definition, Just's crime constituted an offense against "the security of the Republic, against the Constitution, against order and public peace," and thereby came under the cognizance of the conseils de guerre. The *Conseil de Revision* affirmed the sentence of the military tribunal.[32]

Perhaps more than any other single source, it was the critical threat and fear of espionage, both actual and potential, which provided justification for the wide array of security measures. Thus, activities designed or having the tendency to undermine the war effort most frequently fell under the purview of the conseils de guerre. The offense of espionage was a common charge, and even if not charged, the reality of the phenomenon lurked beneath the surface, and perhaps assists in elucidating the apparent harshness of judgments like the Just decision. A prominent French treatise analyzing the war from the perspective of international law averred that all the prominent Allied nations had been "infested, before 1914, with an extraordinary army of spies, both male and female, who . . . sought to lay the groundwork for war and smooth the way for invasion."[33] Nineteen months into the war, Malvy, the Minister of the Interior, announced before the Senate, "German espionage activity in France, both before and during the war, is a reality."[34] Malvy became the object of severe criticisms in the press and in the government for the perceived inadequacy of government measures for providing security against infiltration of the interior by enemy spies.[35]

In March 1916, with the bloody German offensive at Verdun already a month old, fractious debate in the upper Chamber of the French Parliament focused on the sufficiency of governmental counter-espionage provisions. Senator Gaudin de Villaine rebuked the government for its feeble and inadequate response to the threat, reciting a long list of Germans either naturalized or granted extended visas, as well as prominent German businessmen and other foreign nationals who enjoyed unrestricted freedom of movement, uninterrupted communications, and commercial relations with organizations and individuals in enemy lands. The disparity of conditions suffered by French nationals in the territories of the Entente powers was only too apparent. It was a matter of paramount concern that the government take stronger surveillance measures, for a thousand ties of sentiment and interest would continue to draw such individuals into sympathy with the enemy cause:

> It is impossible that such people, whose families are suffering in their countries of origin as a result of the blockade we inflict on their commerce, that such people would not seek the means to alleviate this suffering.
>
> It is impossible that such people would not spread among us news from their home lands with the end of sowing panic and fear in our towns and in the countryside.
>
> Therefore, today more than ever, they are dangerous, and we must watch them closely.[36]

Malvy responded that counter-espionage efforts in the interior had produced 882 arrests, 12 death sentences, 44 sentences to confinement, detention or some form of hard labor, and 81 internments. Another 186 cases were still being processed.[37] Argument centered on the question of whether enough was being done. Yet the government's counter-espionage mechanisms, including the conseils de guerre, could not easily absorb the charge of overly lenient treatment of suspect foreigners. In January 1916, one Max Reissner, a German national arrested in the "entrenched camp" of Paris attempting to pass himself off as an American, received the maximum allowable penalty upon his conviction before the 2nd Conseil de Guerre (Paris): five years imprisonment with maximum bodily constraint and a 5,000 franc fine.[38] Insufficient evidence caused the government to drop the espionnage charge but Reissner was convicted of illegal residence in the entrenched camp of Paris. Reissner, who appeared to be enjoying a life of idleness with an annual income of 40,000 francs, had claimed to be an American commercial traveler. Lingering suspicions as to the sources of his comfortable income doubtless contributed to the harshness of the sentence.

The subject matter jurisdiction of the conseils de guerre was not limited to offenses that had occurred after the commencement of hostilities. Hermann Hochel, a German national who had been a long-time resident of Marseilles and director of a Hamburg-based international sulfur refining operation, had managed to escape the country with his family fourteen days before the declaration of war. A conseil de guerre sitting in Marseilles tried Hochel in absentia (*par contumace*) for conducting pre-war espionage activities on behalf of Germany, "with the effect of facilitating [the entry of enemy forces] into the territory of the Republic." Among other offenses, Hochel had used his position to impede the importation of sulfur products important for the manufacture of munitions. The Conseil de Guerre, presided over by a certain Lieutenant Colonel Kervela, found the absent defendant guilty of espionage and sentenced him to death.[39] In another espionage case, four vegetable wholesalers raised the suspicion of Sûreté personnel with their conduct in the markets of Dunkirk and the surrounding region. Tips that the four, a Belgian and three French nationals, were reconnoitering at the front with German soldiers led to their surprise and capture in East Flanders, at Herzele, on April 22, 1915, in the possession of signal flares. The trial was no simple summary affair. Forty-nine witnesses came forward to testify before the Conseil de Guerre convened at Dunkirk. Two of the four accused were found guilty and sentenced to death. The other two were acquitted.[40]

The harsh circumstances of war produced equally harsh applications of the laws. Article 5 of the espionage law of 1886 prohibited entry into a fortified area or other military facility by means of a false name or other disguise of identity.[41] A Parisian Conseil de Guerre had occasion late in the war to explore the limits of the statute as it applied to the conduct of a sixteen-year-old girl evidently *not* engaged in espionage activity of any sort. The girl had left her home in Héricourt, near Belfort in Alsace, under an assumed name as a means of escaping detection and followed her boyfriend, a deserter, to the "entrenched camp" of Paris. The issue before the tribunal was whether the girl's actions actually constituted an offense under the 1886 law. Did it matter that the false name had not been taken not with the intention of gaining entry into the *camp retranché* but for other, anterior reasons? The Conseil de Guerre, presided over by a Lieutenant Mornet, preferred an austere objective reading of the law, unalloyed by consideration of the extenuating circumstances. Disregarding the factor of intent, the tribunal returned a finding of guilty and sentenced the girl to three months in prison.[42]

Another grouping of cases dealt with a less tangible form of danger: the debilitating effects on morale posed by speech contrary to the war effort. Taking Abraham Lincoln's concerns regarding the potential dangers of unrestricted speech to a new level, the Conseil de Guerre of the 3rd region (Paris) sentenced a woman sixty-odd years old, Mme. Duthu-Sicard, to twenty days imprisonment for comments voiced while sitting on a park bench in the Jardin du Luxembourg. Her comments, charged as tending "to favor the enemy or exerting a detrimental effect on the population," amounted to assertions that "the Germans are better supplied than us"; that "we're in a bad situation; the winter will be hard for us; and, we don't have any munitions [to sustain the fight]."[43]

In perhaps a more provocative spirit, the German-born Karoline Arbruster, married to a French hairdresser of Levallois, had taken occasion in a tramway to proclaim, "We Germans will have the best of the dirty French. Germans are better than the French. All the French are———!" For uttering her "seditious cries," Mme. Arbruster received a sentence of one month's imprisonment and a 500 franc fine.[44] For his remarks "injuring and defaming the army," the baker's apprentice M. Turbotte received a sentence of three months imprisonment and a 250 franc fine. On July 7, 1915, Turbotte had indulged in some public sarcasm in a restaurant: "Only imbeciles go to fight in the war. Rich and poor, all have such great reason to subject themselves to [surprise] attack!"[45]

On other occasions, the connection to national security became more difficult to perceive. The Conseil de Guerre sitting in the Lyon-Rhône region heard a tragic case evidencing the extent to which the war had stirred up conflicting loyalties. A French industrial engineer at the Rhône Factories, André Barbier, and his German wife, Marie Seldmeier, had experienced an upsurge in marital friction with the outbreak of war. As the war continued, Barbier became increasingly irritated with his wife's constant mockery of his patriotic sentiments. After one contentious quarrel, in which Marie had been particularly difficult, Barbier took out his revolver and shot his wife dead. Unwilling, apparently, to countenance the possible applicability of Dr. Johnson's dictum locating "the last refuge of scoundrels," the Conseil de Guerre, having jurisdiction over the case by reason of the accused's military status, sympathized with its compatriot, the offended husband, and accepting his defense of provocation, returned a unanimous acquittal.[46]

As this brief sampling demonstrates, the adjudication of offenses committed by enemy combatants, spies, or prisoners made up only a portion of the work of the conseils de guerre. Moreover, as we shall see, supplemental adjustments intended to streamline the process entailed an unprecedented shrinkage of standard procedural safeguards in the provisions of the notorious special conseils de guerre (conseils de guerre *speciaux*)—the tenure of which endured for over a year after the Marne.

At their most severe, French security measures included the establishment of a system of some seventy concentration camps for the removal and internment of both suspect foreign nationals and "undesirable" French nationals.[47] Thus, Alsatian evacuees, suspect spies,[48] French prostitutes caught providing their wares to occupying forces, Hungarian artists, Polish migrant farmers, and German commercial travelers might potentially find themselves awaiting the conclusion of the war behind the barbed-wired confines of the French camps. Multiple espionage cases tried by the conseils de guerre originated from the internment camps, or *camps de triage*.[49] Vague suspicion on the part of police authorities was enough to render one subject to internment. Indeed, even an acquittal in the conseils de guerre might fail to remove suspicion and render an individual subject to further internment.[50]

It would of course be inaccurate and misleading to identify the camps with the Nazi extermination camps of the Second World War. It helps to keep in mind that the spectacle of total war precipitated massive, chaotic displacements of populations.[51] Moreover, with a significant swathe of its territory under occupation and serving as the theater of operations for the Western front, France faced a serious enemy alien problem,[52] outbreaks of xenophobic violence, and unprecedented threats to public health and safety. As Malvy argued, removal of these alien populations to camps located primarily in the west and south, away from the front, operated as an emergency public safety measure in the early weeks of the war. The bulk of the removals took place at this time, though internments continued throughout the war's duration. In establishing the camps, French authorities sought to remove suspect individuals and foreign subjects of the Entente powers from the Zone of the Armies and other militarily strategic locations in order to facilitate surveillance, protect troops, maintain order, and enhance security. Greater freedom of movement was allowed to internees from Alsace-Lorraine, Czech lands, Greece, Poland, and Armenia. Natives of the Entente powers, Germans, Austro-Hungarians, Turks, and Bulgarians, saw tighter restrictions.[53] The camps were further divided according to various categorizations: some camps were reserved for families or for the nobility; others for those under punitive discipline; one camp at the abbey of Langonnet was kept for ecclesiastics, and another at Kergroès was briefly opened to hold prostitutes and female criminal convicts. Many internees were released after the initial panic of August–September 1914 subsided. The government had no pre-existing systematic plan for the location of the camps. Thus convents, seminaries, abandoned churches, and schools, as well as island fortresses were chosen for their isolation and amenability to surveillance.[54] The camps and their occupants, numbering in the tens of thousands, figure as another tragic consequence, "collateral damage" emanating from the phenomenon of a total war characterized by the widespread breakdown of public order.[55] They prefigure too the repressions of the brutal years to come.

Theory and Crisis Response

Especially in France, the First World War marked a critical point of departure for a modern theoretical examination of the "state of necessity" and its accompanying institutions.[56] A diversity of theoretical perspectives reverberates from the basic question of the legality of the state of exception, *l'état d'éxception.*[57] Rossiter's oxymoronic title, "constitutional dictatorship," summarizes the attendant paradox. How could a constitution accommodate for the exercise of powers that run beyond (or contrary to) the authority granted by law? And if it fails to make such accommodation, does the constitution then become a form of "suicide pact," by which the polity implodes upon the emergence of conditions the response to which would require illegal action in order to preserve the safety and security of the polity? When the executive power takes exceptional powers upon itself in the name of self-preservation, how should such measures be evaluated? Three possible responses emerge. One is that the fundamental law is interpreted to positively provide for the *régime d'éxception.* Thus, in his own nuanced approval of the uses to which state of siege doctrine had recently been put, Joseph Barthélemy asserted in 1915 that modern constitutionalism had introduced a new branch of public law, one devoted to crisis response. The explicit *legality* of the state of exception brought with it the advantages of being adopted in an atmosphere of calm deliberation, not incipient panic, as well as an ability to alert the citizen in advance as to the sacrifices that might be required of him.[58] Alternatively, the silence of the laws is read circumstantially as prohibiting or sanctioning the use of extraordinary measures, depending on a given state of affairs. Or, finally, the constitution is deemed to place an explicit ban on the exceptional powers—which, when assumed by the executive become ipso facto illegal acts.[59] In this context the statutory provision for ongoing civilian control constituted the most important check on an otherwise unfettered discretion on the part of military authorities. As the Conseil d'Etat pronounced in August of 1915, the state of siege was a "*régime de legalité.*"[60] To attribute the designation of military dictatorship to the state of siege regime would here have been inaccurate and misleading: "military authority always remains effectually under the authority of the government, which is civilian."[61] Nevertheless, the effectiveness of this check in the form of civilian oversight would be severely tested with the use of the controversial conseils de guerre *spéciaux*.

In order to place these special tribunals in context, it is necessary first to examine further the schematic design of the French military juridical apparatus. The transition from the peacetime, permanent military tribunals to the wartime conseils de guerre *aux armées* (i.e., those attached to military units) varied according to the proximity of the theater of battle. The permanent conseils de guerre continued to function—their work was merely supplemented by the wartime tribunals adapted for the exigent conditions of the military front. With the mobilization of troops and the establishment of the Zone of the Armies, the powers of the conseils de guerre in the relevant areas transferred from the permanent territorial military courts to those established within the armies at the front. The organizing principle of the temporary wartime conseils de guerre had to do with the demands of military structure and operational movements rather than with territory and geography.[62]

The French code of military justice anticipated two varying sets of conditions within which the amplified jurisdiction of the wartime conseils de guerre could take effect. The first rule applied in the case of occupied territory. Just as General Winfield Scott had found it necessary to provide juridical tools in response to the U.S. Army's occupation of Mexican lands, the French *Code de Justice Militaire* of 1857 recognized the authority of the conseils de guerre in occupied territory, both as to French military troops and affiliated personnel and as to foreigners implicated in offenses against the order, safety, and security of the army and of the French nation. As we will have occasion to see, these provisions saw extensive application in the aftermath of hostilities in the occupied Rhineland.

The other situation matched more closely the predicament of the French armies throughout the course of the First World War. This provision secured the expanded wartime jurisdiction of the conseils de guerre to French territory wherever the armies found themselves "in the presence of the enemy."[63] The expanded jurisdiction of the military courts over foreign offenders was deemed necessary for reasons of state interest, military security, and maintaining public peace and order. Foreign offenders could be subject to the jurisdiction of the conseils de guerre for committing or assisting in the commission of any of the following offenses: treason, espionage, ambuscade; crimes or offenses against military duty (surrender, abandonment of post, etc.); mutiny, insubordination, or rebellion; abuse of authority; refusal to obey orders or desertion; sale, pledge, or theft of military equipment; pillaging; defacement or destruction of property; falsification, corruption, or forgery of military administrative materials; and the improper use of military uniforms, insignia, decorations, and medals.[64] The Cour de Cassation acknowledged the full extent of this catalogue by recognizing within the jurisdiction of the conseils de guerre any offenses threatening the peace and security of the armed forces or of French interests.[65]

Procedurally, the switch to wartime conditions entailed a significant streamlining of the trial process. Until a major revision of the law regarding the operation of the military tribunals was issued in April of 1916, the rights of the accused suffered serious curtailment as a direct consequence of the transition from peacetime conditions to war. In particular, four specific guarantees reserved to the accused as part of the process in time of peace were reduced or eliminated. First, the accused could not invoke important rights normally accorded at the preliminary investigation phase (*l'instruction préalable*)—e.g., discovery and assistance of counsel. Thus, the *défenseur* would not be present for the crucial interrogation of the accused—normally a requirement under a law of procedure dating from 1897. Nor could the *avocat* have communications with his client until after promulgation of the *mise en jugement* (the order convening the conseil de guerre). Furthermore, the *avocat* had no legal authority to obtain the *dossier* (discovery of government evidence) until after the *mise en jugement.* [66] Thus, from a practical standpoint, the reduction of the time (to twenty-four hours) allowed between *mise en jugement* and the formal appearance of the accused before the conseil de guerre (*l'audience*) meant that the accused would not have opportunity to consult with counsel or review the government's evidence against him until the actual *audience.* These adjustments had probably been adopted in acknowledgment of simple unavoidable realities: from a military standpoint, it would be impracticable and unwise to allow the investigation of each case to come to a standstill while awaiting arrival of defense counsel. Moreover, the very nature of attending circumstances would place a higher value on the alacrity with which the trials could be accomplished, as well as on removing a potentially limitless source of appeals.[67] Second, for offenses under the code of military justice, the accused was not allowed to introduce evidence of attenuating circumstances—unless specifically allowed by the Code.[68] In addition, the simplified procedure of the wartime tribunals barred the accused from the benefit of laws allowing in some cases for delay or reprieve in the execution of sentence. Finally, it barred appeals before the Cour de Cassation.[69]

Yet a limited form of appellate process applied to the judgments of the conseils de guerre. Paralleling the regular peacetime conseils de guerre *permanents* sat a smaller number of tribunals of review, the conseils de revision, the number of which was determined by presidential decree and apportioned according to the distribution of the military jurisdictional map. Enjoying no powers of factual appellate review, the authority of the conseils de revision was confined to a form of "due process" inquiry. Assessing the sufficiency of a limited number of legal and procedural matters, the conseils de revision could annul a judgment only for the following irregularities: defects in the composition or competence of the conseils de guerre; punishments failing to conform to legal restrictions; violations of certain prescribed procedural requirements; and the failure to accord legal rights afforded to the parties by law. After the passage of a law dated April 17, 1906, the peacetime review powers of the conseils de revision removed to the Cour de Cassation. The alteration probably occurred in order to effectively "civilianize" the military process, for the composition of the conseils de revision consisted entirely of military officers without legal training.

Notwithstanding these peacetime developments, after the decree imposing a state of siege at the beginning of the First World War, a subsequent executive decree, issued on August 11, established seven conseils de revision to cover the territory of France, and one for Algeria.[70] Military defendants seeking recourse from judgments of the conseils de guerre thus had the option of bringing their cases before the appropriate conseil de revision, though in time of war this privilege was susceptible to lawful suspension by executive decree.[71] In addition to the general right of appeal to the conseils de revision, non-military defendants appearing before the conseils de guerre received the benefit of an additional stage of subsequent, civilian review at the Cour de Cassation. At this level, the code of military justice stipulated a sole question for scrutiny—the competency of the military tribunal. Other types of cases could reach the high court through the power enjoyed by the Minister of Justice to seek redress before the Cour de Cassation on behalf of an adjudged accused, "in the interest both of the law and of the individual convicted of a crime" ("*tant dans l'intérêt de la loi que dans celui du condamné*"). In such cases, the high court's powers of review extended beyond the question of competence to embrace a wider array of legal and procedural issues. In the case of prisoners of war, such discretion on the part of the high court diminished to a vanishing point. Toward the end of the war, the Cour de Cassation addressed this question of the scope of its appellate review powers in the case of prisoners of war. One such prisoner, Beraha Haïm, sentenced to death by the Conseil de Guerre of Lyon on November 20, 1917, had appealed to the Conseil de Revision and, finding no success there, to the Cour de Cassation in January 1918. Apparently, this was the first time the court addressed the question in the course of the war; no such attempt had been entertained in the preceding years of the court's wartime jurisprudence. The high court flatly rejected Haïm's case: the strict letter of the applicable law of June 9, 1857, simply prohibited it from countenancing such appeals.[72]

With the passage of the new law promulgated April 27, 1916, the last major amendment of the provisions regarding the function and competence of military tribunals in time of war took effect. With regard to the issues surrounding the admission of matters in mitigation and extenuation, the legislature liberalized the rules for specifically military as well as regular "common law" offenses, allowing for the consideration of attenuating circumstances, in time of peace as well as in time of war—in both the territorial conseils de guerre and in the tribunals attached to military units (*aux armées*). Here, the legislature sought to ensure a judicial response more closely proportional to the offense and less likely, in the sympathetic case, to tend toward the drastic reaction of outright nullification. [73] The impact of the change was presently exhibited in a series of decisions of the high court, which quashed judgments on the part of the lower tribunals for failure to adequately address matters of extenuation and mitigation. Among the additional changes wrought by the law of April 27, 1916, several inured to the benefit of defendants before the military tribunals: the law restored the limited right of reprieve (*sursis a l'exécution de la peine*); rights of defendants with regard to the sequence and conditions of interrogation; and engagement and appearance of counsel at an earlier stage in the proceedings. Moreover, the new law altered the composition of the territorial conseils de revision, establishing a civilian-military mix, with two local civilian appellate magistrates joining three senior military officers. The law designated the chief magistrate of the relevant regional civilian court of appeal as the president of the territorial conseils de revision.

The competence of the tribunals *aux armées* extended to the armed forces and to all civilian individuals attached thereto in some capacity—"*réquisitionnés, employés volontaires, individus autorisés à suivre l'armée*"—as well as prisoners of war. As with the permanent tribunals, these wartime courts were composed of military members—non-jurists—who served in this necessary supplemental capacity, in a manner similar to civilian jury duty in the Anglo-American criminal system. With the passage of a law in 1875, in response to events of the Franco-Prussian War, the Assembly had reduced the statutory number of court members from seven—the requirement for the peacetime conseils *permanents*—to five. The same law had reduced the requirement for the finding of guilt and sentence in the wartime tribunals to a simple three-to-two majority, from the peacetime standard of five-to-two.

Judgments "sans délai": The Conseils de Guerre Spéciaux

The state of siege and the expanded jurisdiction of the military tribunals took effect within a wider network of government decrees designed to enhance public order and security. On repeated occasions, the government effectively "forced the hand" of the legislative Chambers, issuing extralegal decrees which eventually appeared for ratification in the Chambers as a fait accompli.[74] These *décrets-loi,* a new form of expedited legislation, suffered heavy criticism, and did not outlast the Third Republic—though political circumstances forced their resurrection, in modified form, under the 1958 Constitution.

Despite the prior legislative adjustments of the law of 1875, Joffre determined, less than a month after the commencement of hostilities, that the regular procedures of the conseils de guerre *aux armées* created obstacles diminishing the deterrent value of the military judicial process. In particular the regular statutory twenty-four-hour delay between *citation* (arraignment) of the accused and the convening of the tribunal functioned to undermine the exemplary impact of their decisions. Joffre urged and received, by decree dated September 6, 1914, the creation of conseils de guerre *spéciaux,* special tribunals, for use in the zone of battle, operating by a simplified and expedited form of procedure. Joffre's request evidenced the principal rationale underlying the demand for a streamlined procedure—internal troop discipline.[75] At the peak of the military and political crisis, in early September, the risk to national safety and security was deemed great enough to relax yet further the normal safeguards of criminal procedure in the individual case.[76]

As with the regular conseils de guerre *aux armées,* persons subject to the jurisdiction of the special tribunals included military members, any civilians affiliated with the armies, and prisoners of war. According to the terms of the September 6 executive decree, three-member panels could be appointed by the commanding officer of the relevant army, division, brigade, regiment, or unit. No rules existed for the selection of members: thus, it was legally possible for the officers immediately in command over the accused, or even for witnesses, to be called to sit in judgment of his case—the commander who ordered the investigation of the accused could be called to preside over his trial.[77] A two-to-one majority was sufficient to render judgment, from which there was no appeal. Judgments were subject to immediate execution. One important condition would serve to set limits on the jurisdictional power of the special tribunals—namely, their competence extended only to crimes in which the accused had been apprehended *en flagrant délit.*[78]

The special courts were not without precedent in French history. In an earlier dispensation, during the crisis of 1870, the government had resorted to similar tribunals (*cours martiales*) with expedited procedures—five members operating by simple majority vote—and stripping the defense of significant benefits such as the right to counsel. The harsh experience of these earlier tribunals had led the Assembly to adopt the simplified procedures of the law of 1875, discussed above, which were introduced as a compromise measure designed to foreclose the drastic extremities of the summary tribunals of the 1870 war.[79] Nearly from their inception, the extralegal special tribunals of the First World War incurred bitter criticism, mainly because the expedited nature of the process was perceived as being tantamount to doing away with process altogether. The unfettered discretion accorded the conseils de guerre *spéciaux* unsurprisingly produced some notable instances of appalling injustice.[80] The French lower house, the Chamber of Deputies, had ratified, without argument, the initial decree establishing the special courts in March 1915. By December of the same year, the Chamber voted unanimously to eliminate the much-despised institution. Article 7 of the law, dated April 27, 1916, served to reinforce what had already taken effect in practice, the abandonment of the summary special tribunals. The relatively swift revocation of the special courts, in practice and in law, probably helped to delay the "crisis of morale" which ultimately broke with the army mutinies of spring of 1917.[81] Moreover, the abrupt reversal on the part of the Deputies calls into question the effectiveness of the legislative oversight upon which the framework of extraordinary juridical response so heavily rested.[82]

Adjudication of War Crimes in the Conseils de Guerre

Controversy over the question of blame for causing the war, and over the atrocities of 1914 in Belgium and France, fed into the psychology of total war. In the aftermath of hostilities, vehement German resistance to charges of war guilt emanated in part from the sustained effort to justify the incidents of August–October 1914 according to the same terms under which they had been perpetrated, as a response to the unlawful and barbaric "attacks" of the mythical *Franktireurkrieg* on the part of Belgian and French civilians.[83] Moreover, the atrocities of 1914 served as the initial impetus behind the adoption of an allied plan to conduct war crimes trials.[84] The steady stream of accounts of war of law violations spawned currents of more fantastic fabrications, issuing in a sea of acrimonious nationalistic chauvinism and hatred. In the Allied nations, the war came to take on the form of a struggle of "civilization" against "barbarism"[85]—a rhetorical context which the Germans managed to abet on the Western front by, for instance, introducing chlorine gas at Ypres in 1915 and resuming the illegal use of unrestricted U-boat warfare in 1917. Thus, powerful psychological forces contributed to demands for the exaction of criminal punishment at war's end. Public discussions of the possibility of later retribution for war crimes continued throughout the conflict—though the controversy and debate over the matter surfaced with greater regularity in Britain than in France.[86]

It may be that the lower volume of discourse on potential post-war criminal sanctions in France was attributable to the greater amount of actual adjudication of such offenses during the war itself in the conseils de guerre. Indeed, the bulk of the war crimes cases brought before the conseils de guerre pending the duration of the conflict occurred while the memory of the violation of Belgium and the Meurthe-et-Moselle still freshly rankled. The decision to try enemy prisoners for the perpetration of war crimes stemmed from intelligence that "the Germans seemed to be continuing in France the deliberate use of terror that they had begun in Belgium."[87] Warrant under international law was clearly available. It was a well-recognized principle of international law that "the individual soldier who commits acts in violation of the laws of war when those acts are at the same time offenses against the general criminal law should be liable to trial and punishment by the courts of the injured adversary in case he falls into the hands of the authorities thereof."[88]

On the level of theory, French jurists engaged in extended discussions surrounding the authority of French courts (military or civilian) to try war crimes committed by the invading enemy.[89] The most elementary question, as to the justiciability of war crimes offenders, was a matter of international law. It seemed all too apparent that war crimes committed by German soldiers (and officers) were not being addressed by German courts—military or civilian. To argue for an army's exclusive jurisdiction over its own nationals would be tantamount to renouncing all prospect of criminal retribution—an objectionable and historically unwarranted result that would do nothing to prevent further atrocities and that could, indeed, easily accelerate them by the prospect of impunity.[90] Here, it was important to remember that the simple fact of invasion and occupation did not render French territorial laws a nullity. To recognize the juridical competence of an occupying power did not obviate the concurrent authority of the courts belonging to the occupied territory. Crimes committed on French soil remained justiciable in French courts, notwithstanding the fact of foreign occupation or invasion. By extension, French courts could try crimes committed in neutral or Allied territory, as in the case of Belgium, by operation of reciprocal treaty provisions. Moreover, the fact that murder, rape, theft, pillaging, and other offenses were committed during the course of war did not remove such conduct from the jurisdictional powers of the courts—however much it might render such adjudication a practical difficulty.

The next question concerned whether the offenses should fall within the province of the ordinary civilian courts or the military tribunals. Here, French statutory authority was clear. As we have seen, the conseils de guerre had competence to try *anyone* committing one of the scheduled offenses in the Zone of the Armies (Articles 204–208 of the *Code de Justice Militaire*) and, under Article 56, pertaining to prisoners of war. As to the *ratione loci* or geographic jurisdiction, practical considerations of proximity and opportunity prevailed: in the case of non-prisoners, the conseil de guerre of the army closest to the place of the offense should try it; for prisoners of war, the same rule, or proximity to the place of arrest, dictated, though any conseil de guerre could potentially try the case.[91]

The catalogue of offenses was long and comprehensive and included the crimes of murder and massacre, systematic terrorism, killing of hostages, torture of civilians, rape, pillaging, wanton destruction of property, and intentional bombardment of hospitals and other unlawful targets.[92] As we have seen, many such offenses on the part of the invading German armies had been alleged within the first five weeks of the war. The first of the trials by conseil de guerre appears to have been convened on October 2, 1914, in which three German prisoners were charged and convicted with the offense of pillaging.[93] In another case, a German reserve officer, Lieutenant Willi Erler, a teacher at the girls' school at Nordhausen in Saxon Prussia, was convicted of arson and condemned to twenty years of hard labor, as well as—perhaps surprisingly—a reduction in rank. Erler had set fire to a civilian home in Creil, near the Oise, on September 2, 1914. A shot had been taken from a window of the home and killed one of Erler's men as he led an advance guard in search of a means of crossing the river. Shortly afterward, the unit rejoined the batallion, whereupon Erler received the commander's order to set fire to the house; but on his return, found the house occupied by German soldiers. Erler carried out the order, though it appears certain the alleged *franc-tireur* had actually been a German sniper, who had fired the shot either in a state of intoxication or from a malicious interest in inciting criminal reprisal actions.[94]

Another French conseil de guerre found against a twenty-four-year-old Saxon soldier, Karl Vogelgesang, for acts of pillaging, arson, and assassination of wounded soldiers on the field of battle, acts committed in the critical early weeks of the war, in Allied Belgian territory. Vogelgesang was captured on September 15, 1915, at the Marne. Primary evidence used against him took the form of a personal diary, found on his person by hospital personnel treating him for injuries incurred during the battle. The diary, translated from the German in the report of the case, matter-of-factly states the young soldier's impressions and activities: "14 August.—Reveille at 0500. At 0945 the division is ready. Then we came to the village. *Then we robbed and pillaged, and set fire to the whole place.* A terrifying spectacle . . . " (italics in original). Again, on August 24, Vogelgesang reported: "In the afternoon, about 1400 hours, we discovered the enemy in a village. In the space of five minutes, the whole village was in flames. Anybody who escaped was slaughtered." The rest were taken as prisoners, about sixty altogether, most of whom were wounded: "Every step of the way, they would fall to their knees, but we gave no quarter to this scum." Two witnesses also appeared to testify before the military tribunal against Vogelgesang. Both had participated in his initial interrogation, and he had confessed to his participation in massacre and incendiarism.[95] The conseil de guerre condemned Vogelgesang to death.

By the close of 1915, the French Minister of the Interior, Malvy, reported that over 1,100 people had been arrested on espionage charges, though only fifty-five death sentences had been issued by the conseils de guerre.[96] Many war crimes had to await ostensible retribution with the cessation of hostilities. In the meantime, the record of violations mounted. Captured German notebooks and diaries provided some of the most damning evidence of war crimes, even if their discovery failed to produce criminal prosecutions, as it did in the case of Vogelgesang. To take a few examples at random, Private Hassemer of the German 8th Army Corps recorded his impressions of a massacre of French soldiers and civilians at Sommepy (Marne) thus: "September 3 . . . A fearful bloodbath. Village burned to the ground, the French thrown into the burning houses, civilians, everything burned."[97] Similar descriptions attended the attack on Saint-Moritz (Meurthe-et-Moselle): "In the night of the 18th, German troops . . . burned the entire village of St Moritz to the ground, as punishment for their having shot at German soldiers. The village was surrounded so that no one could get out, and then the fire was lit, house by house. Neither man, woman, or child could escape, only the animals were taken since we could make use of them. Whoever escaped was shot down. Every single inhabitant who was there burned in the flames."[98] Throughout the journal extracts compiled by the French Foreign Ministry in the first two years of the war, the term *standrecht* or *standrechtlich* surfaces, indicating that summary executions of British, French, and Belgian prisoners had been a recurring phenomenon.[99]

During the course of the war, the French government established commissions of inquiry for the purpose of assembling a record of German international law violations. French investigatory boards (*commissions d'enquête*), assisted by the conseils de guerre, took depositions and meticulously compiled the detailed reports, which ultimately covered multiple volumes. Much of the work of the commissions had to await the military recovery of French territory. To take one example: in October of 1918, the 127th French Infantry Division liberated Laon, a village of 6,000 inhabitants in the department of Aisne—which had been in German hands since September 2, 1914. Captain Facdouel, commissary-reporter for the Conseil de Guerre attached to the Division, compiled a report detailing acts of pillaging, vandalism, theft, violence, and brutality.[100] By this point, of course, many specific details were no longer recoverable.

Early in the war, the trial of law of war violations began to subside with the increase of reprisal actions. In January 1916, M. René Garraud, professor of criminal law at the University of Lyon, in his address before the General Society of Prisons, opined that too few prosecutions had so far taken place.[101] The threat of retaliation functioned to stifle what was perceived as one of the few viable and lawful sanctions available to address law of war violations: "It's true that there was a fear of provoking reprisals, which would have caused harm to our unfortunate fellow citizens imprisoned in Germany; it is for this reason that prosecution continued only in those cases where it was impossible to proceed otherwise."[102] Indeed, "a cycle of reprisal and counterreprisal began," with Germans holding French officers hostage until the release of convicted German offenders, and vice versa.[103] Nevertheless, considerable difference of opinion existed on the legal, moral, and military ramifications of reprisal actions.[104] Since the Land Warfare Regulations of 1907 did not in fact prohibit reprisals against prisoners of war—such a prohibition was not to be adopted until 1929—it is perhaps surprising that more such actions did not in fact occur.[105]

Nor should the effect of reprisals be allowed to obscure the sheer volume of juridical activity on the part of military authorities throughout the war. We have already discussed the wide-ranging jurisdictional powers of the French conseils de guerre with respect to civilians in the Zone of the Armies and more generally throughout the nation under the legal condition of the state of siege. It should be noted, if only in passing, that under the German occupation, military authorities dealt with similarly huge numbers of cases. This frequently occurred altogether outside of the workings of the military *court* system. Thus, in the calculation of the German judge Helmuth Mende, who analyzed juridical activity occurring during the course of one year of the German occupation of Belgium, "no less than 242,332 punishments were inflicted by the German authorities in Belgium from 1 January to 31 December 1917. Of this astonishing number, only 7,746 were inflicted by virtue of ordinary military court procedure; 4,796 were 'protective custodies,' and the remainder were inflicted outside the courts by military commanders and officials, under the authorization of the German Governor General."[106]

In Belgium, the Germans went well beyond the recognized international legal norm establishing the right of occupying powers to exercise jurisdiction over offenses against their own forces. In a fit, perhaps, of Prussian hubris, or, as the case may be, administrative thoroughness,[107] the Germans basically "supersed[ed] the great body of existing legislation of the country and [handed] over to the German military courts the larger part of the ordinary jurisdiction of the Belgian tribunals."[108] In just the year spanning from October 1, 1915, to September 20, 1916, German courts convicted 103,356 persons, of whom 19,857 were women.[109]

Perhaps the most infamous of the German military trials of civilians in Belgium involved the case of the British nurse Edith Cavell.[110] Cavell, aged forty-nine, had been supervising a nurses' training school and caring for the wounded in Brussels. In the previous year, she and other British nurses had refused a German offer of safe conduct to Holland. Arrested in August 1915, Cavell was charged essentially with aiding and abetting the enemy—by concealing, supplying, and returning British and French soldiers to the safety of neutral Holland. Cavell was one of several defendants to appear before a German court-martial conducted in secret from October 7–9, 1915. She confessed to having sheltered and assisted Allied prisoners, asserting that her purpose had been to save lives, rather than to aid Germany's enemies. Sentence was passed on October 9, and confirmed on the 10th by the military governor; Cavell was informed on the 11th, just a few hours before her execution. British and American authorities failed in their attempt to obtain a stay in her behalf—indeed, the business day ended before they were able to ascertain the status of her case—and a firing squad executed her in secret, at two-o'clock in the morning on October 12.[111] The story of her execution caught fire in the American and British presses and further ignited public sentiment against Germany.

Leipzig and the Failure of International Justice

It now appears incontrovertible that "the tragedy of the Treaty of Versailles was that it was neither conciliatory enough to remove the desire for change, even at the cost of war, nor harsh enough to make another war impossible."[112] The vigilance required for the preservation of the peace fizzled out, in some measure, in the Allies' fruitless search for an adequate resolution to the problem posed by the record of German war crimes.[113] Clauses 227–230 of the Versailles Treaty provided for the arraignment of Wilhelm II, as well as the establishment of military tribunals for the trial of violations of the customs and laws of war and other criminal acts.[114] These sections also required the assistance and cooperation of the German government in procuring the extradition of suspects and the production of evidence.[115] After the signing of the peace treaty, dissension prevailed among the Allied powers on the war crimes question. The early and vociferous cries for holding the Kaiser accountable for war crimes had faded when the Netherlands refused Allied demands for his extradition. German denial of war guilt and intransigence on extradition of suspected war criminals accompanied the general climate of exhaustion and revulsion at the carnage of the previous four years. With Britain moving steadily toward resuming normalized relations with Germany, France reluctantly conceded to a compromise arrangement whereby war crimes trials would take place before the German High Court (the *Reichsgericht*) in Leipzig.

After several months of foot-dragging on the part of German authorities, the trials opened in May of 1921. A compromise extradition list of some 1,590 names was eventually whittled down to 45, of which 11 cases were submitted by France. The Leipzig trials proved—for the Allies as well as the Germans—to be a deeply unsatisfactory attempt to address allied charges of German atrocities. Despite the court's independence from the Weimar government, the prosecution conducted its case with half-hearted reluctance, before a courtroom filled with hostile German spectators. Light sentences accompanied the few convictions handed down by the German high court. Only two defendants received substantial punishment—four-year imprisonment sentences for submarine officers who had "torpedoed an English hospital ship, raked and [sunk] the lifeboats full of nurses and wounded." Yet both these defendants managed to escape for good within a matter of weeks.[116] Many cases were abandoned because of the failure of the accused to appear. Perhaps the most critical of the cases submitted by France was that of Major General Karl Stenger—a case foreshadowing some of the command responsibility issues that would arise in another twenty years in the military commission proceedings against the Japanese general Yamashita. Stenger was charged with ordering the massacre of prisoners and wounded in the French Lorraine in August 1914.[117] At the conclusion of the trial, which lasted just over a week, the court acquitted Stenger, prompting the withdrawal of the

French delegation from Leipzig and the abandonment of the remaining French cases.

Leipzig posed an unpalatable combination for all concerned—to the extent it represented "victor's justice," it came only "on the terms of the vanquished."[118] For at least some of the Allies, the demands of justice acknowledged in 1919 had given way to a set of radically different requirements by 1921. The British now arrived at a willingness to put an end to the call for war crimes adjudication, while the French remained unsatisfied. With the advent of the government of Raymond Poincaré, who had come to view the Leipzig trials as "a *sinister comedy,*"[119] France began to prosecute German war criminals in absentia. The work of trying the cases fell to the conseils de guerre, which began processing through the cases of the 2,000-odd Germans given on the original extradition lists submitted in 1919. By December of 1924, the number of convictions exceeded 1,200. The Belgian contingent having walked out of the Leipzig proceedings after the outrage of an early acquittal, Belgian courts-martial also went about trying war crimes cases in absentia. The juridical incompleteness of the trials of absentee defendants was rendered absurd by the equally diligent work of the Reichsgericht, which rehabilitated the absentee defendants in separate series of *doppelgänger* proceedings. Since French and Belgian government officials provided no notice of the courts-martial to the German counterparts, the daily newspapers served as the source of names of those in need of German trial and exoneration. These parallel German proceedings almost invariably produced either a determination of *nolle prosequi* (a decision to cease with further prosecution of the case) or an acquittal.

The French prosecution of war criminals in absentia began to taper off only with Poincaré's removal from power in June of 1924. The succeeding center-left government, led by Herriot and then Briand, though it did not abandon the trials in absentia, substantially curtailed them as it followed the earlier course of Britain in pursuing normalized relations with Germany. Both Belgium and France allowed the prosecution of trials *par contumace* to lapse in 1926, after the passage of the Treaty of Locarno. In Germany, by contrast, the rehabilitative proceedings of the Reichsgericht continued apace until the ascent of Hitler and the Nazi Party in 1933, whereupon a prosecutorial quash order put a stop to further trials, and exonerated all putative defendants.

Yet "the honor of the German people, so frequently and so passionately invoked, would hardly have been stained by the just punishment of such criminals. The fuzzy thinking which manifested itself . . . showed all too well that, after the brief, sobering experience of November, large elements of the German nation had returned to the worship of their military gods."[120] While providing powerful evidence of the abiding animosity between the former belligerents, the juridical fiasco of the post-war trials further demonstrated that "political and diplomatic considerations [had] encroached upon impartial justice."[121] Or, perhaps more accurately, it showed the incongruence and ineffectiveness of what George Kennan would later criticize as the legalistic determination of international political affairs.[122]

Tribunals in the Armistice Period

Despite their decreased effectiveness as the conflict progressed, the work of the military tribunals was not finished until well after the conclusion of hostilities. Indeed, as would be the case to an even greater extent in the aftermath of the Second World War, the activity of military tribunals increased with the conclusion of the armistice of November 1918. The conseils de guerre, as well as comparable military courts of the other Allied nations, exercised jurisdiction over a variety of offenses in the occupied Rhineland.[123] Yet unlike the conclusion of the later war, the military courts of the Allies were not primarily set up to address war crimes, but rather to assist in the Allied mandate to provide legal process, order, and security throughout the region. In this sense, the better comparison is with the tribunals convened in the post-bellum South or with General Scott's tribunals in Mexico.

Though the local German courts continued to operate in the occupied region, their jurisdiction extended only to cases involving German nationals and had no connection to the occupation powers and their interests.[124] No international, inter-Allied tribunals were convened.

The military codes of justice of the Allied nations determined the substantive and procedural rules to govern the activity of the military courts, which were generally established in accordance with an instruction issued by Marshal Foch on November 15, 1918.[125] As was the case with the United States in Mexico, the Allies used the military tribunals not only to provide a check upon the conduct of the occupying forces, but as an effective means of addressing crimes committed by residents of the occupied territory as well. The generally commendable record of the military commissions in Mexico seems to have found emulation in the effectiveness and professionalism of the conseils de guerre operating in the Rhineland. For,

> there is no evidence whatever of extra-legal personal vengeance in the Rhineland for crimes committed during the war. Thousands of dismissed German soldiers and officers who had participated in the German occupation of Belgium and northern France resided in the territory which was now occupied by the soldiers of those nations. But not even German propaganda mentioned a single case in which members of the occupying forces took revenge for crimes committed in their own countries by German soldiers during the war. Since German propaganda against the Versailles treaty was for many years based to a considerable extent on the alleged crimes of occupation soldiers in the Rhineland, its failure to mention examples of lynch justice is ample indication that no such spontaneous revenge actions occurred.[126]

It is impossible to give precise figures as to the number of cases tried by the combined French, Belgian, British, and American military tribunals during the period of the Rhineland occupation, between 1920 and 1926. Based on the compilations given in his sources, Fraenkel provides a "conservative" estimate of ten thousand.

Postscript

The difficulties Alexander Hamilton had prognosticated for advance planning in response to future emergencies materialize in the history of development of the French catalogue of *régimes exceptionnels.* In addition to the state of siege, the oldest of French institutional crisis responses, the legislature of the twentieth century created a new adaptation, *l'état d'urgence,* or state of emergency, as a means of providing a vigorous response to modern forms of subversion and terror.[127] The French experience in Algeria in the 1950s led to the adoption of the state of emergency as a flexible tool for the containment of crisis situations not rising to the level of armed conflict. The statute provides that the state of emergency may be invoked throughout the nation, or in portions of it, or in overseas territories and departments, "in cases of imminent peril arising from grave threats to the public order and security," or in "public calamities" such as earthquakes, floods, explosions, etc. Although the Parliament had originally reserved the power to declare the state of emergency, as well as its scope and duration, a subsequent ordinance instituted a procedure mirroring that applicable to the state of siege: the Council of Ministers now has the power to order *l'état d'urgence,* with the Parliament alone reserving authority to extend emergency conditions beyond the initial twelve days.

The general category of *l'état d'urgence* further divides into two subcategories, "simple" (*état d'urgence simple*) and "grave" (*état d'urgence aggravé*). Many of the same extensions of the police power applicable to the state of siege apply to the state of emergency, the "grave" form entailing greater restrictions on the freedom of assembly and movement, as well as allowing for control over television, radio, press, cinema, and theater. In the case of an *état d'urgence aggravé,* additional powers to conduct searches at any time of day or night become available. The most significant difference remains that the civil authorities retain police power in the case of state of emergency, while in the state of siege, such powers transfer to the military. As noted above, as of 1982, the "shadow" jurisdiction of the permanent military courts has been abolished. Nevertheless, Article 700 of the Code of Criminal Procedure provides that "[i]n the event of a declared state of siege or emergency, a decree in the Council of Ministers . . . may establish territorial courts of the armed forces under the conditions provided for by the Code of Military Justice. The jurisdiction of these courts derives from the Code of Military Justice for time of war and specific provisions of the legislation on states of emergency and states of siege."[128]

Additional extraordinary powers were conferred by governmental decree after the expiration of the first state of emergency in December of 1955. The decree, promulgated on March 17, 1956, granted powers of internment to the government, powers hitherto unavailable under the regime of a state of emergency. Since the adoption of the law of April 3, 1955, the government has declared a "state of emergency" on a number of occasions during the Algerian crisis, and most recently during the riots and car-burnings of late 2005.[129]

A further provision for extraordinary juridical response takes the form of a constitutional safeguard, Article 16 of the 1958 Constitution. Article 16 is designed to address conditions in which "the institutions of the Republic, the nation's independence, the integrity of its territory, or the fulfillment of its international commitments come under grave and immediate threat, and where the proper functioning of the constitutional public authorities is interrupted."[130] In order to prevent an overly facile recourse to Article 16, the provision further requires a breakdown in the normal functioning of the civil authorities. In such cases, the article provides for an enhancement of the powers of the executive, placing at the disposition of the President all legislative, regulatory, and governmental power to the degree required by the circumstances at hand—an assessment left to the determination of the President himself. The Constitutional Council is to provide advice and consultation upon the presidential exercise of powers under Article 16. In 1961, during the Algerian conflict, President De Gaulle asserted Article 16 emergency powers in response to the military putsch attempt under General Challe. Though the rebellion had been quelled by the end of April, this sole instance of application of Article 16 remained in effect until September 29 of the same year.

In the nineteenth century, Adolphe Thiers had pronounced that "La République sera longtemps la liberté temperée par l'état de siège." ("For a long time to come, the Republic will be liberty, tempered by the state of siege.")[131] As a matter of historical record, the instability besetting governments and constitutions in France since 1789 contributed to form the conditions for a long succession of emergency measures. Geography, constitutional structure, history, military establishments, and politics together infused the French patterns of emergency response. Constraints of time and space limit our focus here to just one of the most severe crises in this turbulent history. As a basic, if sporadically discussed, feature of the French republican constitutional framework, the state of siege and its accompanying institutions, including military tribunals, have been widely exported. Indeed, much of the recent literature on states of exception, martial law and the state of siege emerged from the civil law nations of South America, where recourse to emergency conditions has been depressingly frequent in the twentieth century. Among the nations adopting and modifying the French state of siege mechanism have been Argentina, Bolivia, Chile, Colombia, Paraguay, and Venezuela.[132]

4

Trials by Military Commission in the Second World War

In a 1944 essay, George Orwell voiced the puzzling moral dilemma and failure of nerve presented by Leipzig and its ramifications for the current conflict. The seesaw of emotional responses had gone from vilification of all things German to an equally violent revulsion *against* anti-German sentiments. A state of moral exhaustion followed: "Ten million innocent men had been killed and no one wanted to follow it up by killing a few thousand guilty ones."[1] Lessons from the unsatisfactory outcome of the Leipzig trials no doubt contributed to significant changes in the official approach to war crimes when the need arose less than twenty-five years later. Timing, experience newly demonstrated, was everything. Leipzig's "colossal failure" pointed to the need to prosecute war criminals *before* rather than after the peace negotiations.[2] To be sure, the example of Leipzig fueled demands for a response to war crimes that might transcend the vagaries of international politics and diplomacy among sovereign nation-states.[3] Discussions over the appropriate course to take with regard to war criminals began early and continued throughout the duration of the war.

But the lesson of Leipzig did not necessarily lead everyone to the same conclusions. Winston Churchill, Anthony Eden, and other British government officials thought that Axis war criminals should be dealt with by summary execution. In America, too, prominent members of the Truman administration called for the administration of a summary form of "drumhead justice" for the trial and execution of war criminals. Yet the competing American plans all featured military commissions for the prosecution of alleged war criminals. Foremost among the "hard-liners" was Secretary of the Treasury Henry Morgenthau, whose post-war plan for Germany included military firing squads for a number of "archcriminals"—though lesser offenders were to be given the benefit of trial by UN military commissions. Addressing questions regarding war criminals formed only a portion of the larger task of securing the peace, which was to occur through democratic re-education and breaking up the German war-making industry.[4]

Seeking a less drastic approach to the related problems of post-war reconstruction and retribution for war crimes, the American Secretary of War, Henry Stimson, an opponent of "drumhead justice" for all levels of offenders, pressed a wider use of military commissions, "which would be empowered to expedite proceedings by making their own "bare bones" rules to avoid the legal technicalities that might arise in civilian courts or even in ordinary military courts martial."[5] Unlike the conclusion of the First World War, it was this American vision for addressing war crimes that overcame all of the objections in the international sphere as well. The flexible and decentralized process afforded by the military commission model, first adopted by General Scott in the peculiar circumstances of the Mexican War, offered needed balance in the context of new, equally unprecedented conditions and eventually formed an important component of the Allied plan.

Thus, the course of moderation that was eventually pursued did not by any means exclusively or necessarily lead to Nuremberg and Tokyo. The "progressive" narrative that proceeds from Leipzig to Nuremberg and beyond simply fails to provide a full and accurate accounting of the nature of war crimes adjudication over this period. A curious anomaly confronts the observer attempting to evaluate the practices of the Allies in conducting war crimes tribunals at the close of the Second World War. Conventional wisdom regards the international tribunals organized at Nuremberg and in the Far East as the most significant arenas for the adjudication of war-related crimes, while trials by military commission, or the corresponding equivalents in other nations, carry the aura of a rarer process of dubious legitimacy, feebly supported by U.S. Supreme Court decisions that recognized a limited role for the commissions in extreme circumstances.[6] The historical record reveals a radically different story. Though the international tribunals enjoyed greater attention due to the prominence of the defendants and the unprecedented nature of the undertaking, the sheer volume of cases processed by the national military tribunals of the Allies should assist in correcting the distorted picture that is usually presented.[7] The Nuremberg model misleads. The publicity and attention with which such proceedings were surrounded meant that criticisms lodged against the international tribunals also spread over to impugn the war crimes programs of the Allies more generally. It nonetheless remained the case that "the vast majority of cases in which sanctions are imposed on violators of the laws of war take place under military jurisdiction."[8]

Hawaii, Ex Parte Quirin, and the Military Commissions

The work of the American military commissions of the Second World War began almost simultaneously with the nation's engagement in the conflict itself. Immediately after the attack at Pearl Harbor, the territorial governor of Hawaii, Joseph Poindexter, under statutory authority,[9] issued an order placing the territory under martial law. *Habeas corpus* was suspended. Effective control over the territory was placed in the hands of the Commanding General of the Hawaiian Department. Army provost courts—a form of "police court" for the trial of misdemeanors and other lower-level offenses[10]—and military commissions took over judicial responsibilities for the same area. On December 8, President Roosevelt promptly dispatched his affirmation as to the rightness of the actions taken. Over the succeeding fourteen months, the Army provost courts tried the bulk of criminal prosecutions for the territory—with mixed results.[11] In light of the seriousness of the initial attack, as well as ongoing security threat, it was clear the Governor's emergency measures had been fully justified. Yet the urgency of martial rule subsided with the destruction of the Japanese fleet at Midway (June 1942). [12] As time went on, protests and criticism against the strict military regime mounted. The rule of martial law was relaxed with the return of eighteen governmental functions to civil control in February of 1943, but was not completely lifted from the area until October of 1944. [13]

Seven months after Pearl Harbor, the President promulgated a further order appointing a single military commission in response to the capture of eight Nazi saboteurs after clandestine landings on the East Coast. The defendants, German-born U.S. residents, had returned to Germany at various times between 1933 and 1941, with the aim of giving aid to Hitler's Reich. After training as saboteurs, the men had received navy U-boat transport to American shores in June of 1942 and landed in darkness at two separate locations, in Florida and Long Island, New York. The men quickly exchanged their German marine infantry uniforms for civilian clothing, burying the fatigues along with the explosives and incendiary devices they had transported from Germany for the purpose of destroying war industries and facilities. Shortly after the men dispersed, the leader of the Long Island contingent, George Dasch, stumbled into a Coast Guard patrol and eventually turned himself in to the FBI. His confession led to the discovery and apprehension of the rest of the conspirators. President Roosevelt's order authorized the trial of the men before a military commission composed of seven Army generals.[14] A pair of Army judge advocate colonels were appointed to represent the accused. Four charges comprised the government's case against the saboteurs: violation of the law of war; aiding the enemy (a violation of Article 81 of the American Articles of War); spying (Article 82, Articles of War); and conspiracy. The commission convened on July 8, 1942, and proceeded until August 3, with an interruption during which the Supreme Court in special session entertained the defendants' petition for *habeas corpus.* In *Ex parte Quirin,*[15] the defendants contested the legitimacy of the President's order for trial by military tribunal under the Articles of War. The defense raised the standard of *Milligan;* since the civilian courts were open and functioning, petitioners ought to be tried there and receive the full benefit of constitutional entitlements such as trial by jury.

On July 31, the Court issued a brief *per curiam* opinion affirming both that the order establishing a military commission was valid and that this military commission had been lawfully constituted, as well as rejecting the *habeas corpus* request for dismissal of the charges. The military commission resumed its sessions and issued its verdict on August 3. The record went directly to the President for review, and within the next five days, six of the prisoners were executed by electrocution, one received life imprisonment, and Dasch, the most cooperative of the defendants, received a thirty-year sentence.

The Court's full decision in the case was not released until October 29, 1942. In an unanimous opinion, the Court affirmed the validity of the military commission's jurisdiction over the case, articulating the legitimacy of the commission in terms of military necessity: "An important incident to the conduct of war is the adoption of measures by the military command not only to repel and defeat the enemy, but to seize and subject to disciplinary measures those enemies who in attempt to thwart or impede our military effort have violated the law of war."[16] The fact that a principle such as military necessity was subject to abuse did not obviate its occasional legitimate application. Moreover, unlawful combatants figured as a class of persons subject to the jurisdiction of military tribunals—for them the entitlement of prisoner of war status was unavailable: "The spy who secretly and without uniform passes the military lines of a belligerent in time of war, seeking to gather military information and communicate it to the enemy, or an enemy combatant who without uniform comes secretly through the lines for the purpose of waging war by destruction of life or property, are familiar examples of belligerents who are generally deemed not to be entitled to the status of prisoners of war, but to be offenders against the law of war subject to trial and punishment by military tribunals."[17] Drawing the parallels with the case of Major André in the time of the War of Independence and with numerous trials by military commission during the Mexican War and the Civil War and citing a wide range of international law authorities, the Court recognized "universal agreement and practice" under the law of war as establishing this fundamental distinction between lawful and unlawful combatants.[18] By passing behind military lines clothed as civilians, with hostile purpose, the defendants had forfeited lawful combatant status; with the removal of their uniforms, they had taken away those "fixed and distinctive emblems" designating them as combatants.[19] Even the privilege of citizenship could not erase this prior distinction, for citizens associating themselves "with the military arm of the enemy government, and with its aid, guidance and direction enter this country bent on hostile acts, are enemy belligerents within the meaning of the Hague Convention and the law of war."[20]

Since the petitioners' status as unlawful combatants rendered them subject to trial by military tribunal, the presidential order was correct to remove their cases from the domain of the civil courts. To begin with, the constitutional protections provided by the grand and petit jury were hardly absolute—the Constitution merely perpetuated the common law practice of affording jury trials in certain types of criminal cases, the Court said. Congress had not recognized such protections to apply to courts-martial of American servicemen, either before or after the adoption of the Constitution; *a fortiori* for the case of trials of *enemy* belligerents.[21] The *Milligan* Court itself had taken pains to make clear that it found the Indiana lawyer Lambden Milligan to be a *non*-belligerent.[22] The question of lawful or unlawful belligerency simply was not relevant to that case, a prosecution for conspiracy and incitement to rebellion. The *Quirin* defendants, on the other hand, acting on the basis of instructions from the German High Command, had received military training at a German sabotage school near Berlin and, in furtherance of those orders and that training, had been transported to American shores by a German

Navy submarine, wearing "German Marine Infantry uniforms or parts of uniforms." Upon reaching land, armed with explosives and incendiary devices with the purpose of destroying war facilities in the United States, the group had removed their uniforms, changed to civilian clothes, and dispersed in order to carry out their plan. Moreover, the saboteurs were being paid by the German government for their services.[23] The differences between these facts and the Milligan case were obvious and substantial.[24]

Perhaps an even more significant distinction lay with the fact that Milligan's case, by the time it reached the Supreme Court, could be heard from within the comfortable confines of safety and peace secured by the cessation of hostilities and the removal of the very threat that had necessitated the military tribunal in the first place. The *Quirin* Court, by contrast, sat during some of the darkest hours of the American military effort in the Second World War. It was hardly a matter of craven "deference to wartime attitudes"[25] on the part of the Court. Nor did it matter that these eight saboteurs were finally revealed to present less of a threat than might first have been evident. The reality of the national situation required the Court to proceed with due caution and prudence in its evaluations of executive action. The Court refrained from mentioning it, but *Milligan* had been rendered something of an "irrelevancy" upon its very promulgation, as the wide-reaching adjudication of the post-bellum military commissions of the South had quickly demonstrated. The Court noted that conditions of modern warfare—where systems of supply, production, and transportation operated as potential legitimate targets—had put the concept of front battle lines in a state of permanent flux.[26] As Charles Fairman noted one year later in a treatise on martial rule, Chief Justice Davis' dictum in *Milligan* had "at no time . . . been accepted as having settled the law for the future."[27] To say that until *Quirin, Milligan* "had been the beacon of wartime liberties"[28] neglects the fact that no war on or anywhere near U.S. soil had intervened to disturb or test that decision since its promulgation in the *aftermath* of the Civil War. As Lincoln had argued in the Corning letter, such critical temporal distinctions, too often quickly glossed over by self-appointed champions of civil liberty, actually made all the difference. Were the Court to produce another such ringing and impracticable paean to liberty, the result, however pleasing to the ear, would do little for the potency and integrity of the Court or even for the actual protection of civil liberties on the ground. It was not to be wondered at that little other Federal judicial guidance existed on the matter, since military commissions were, by definition, an extraordinary remedy, resorted to only in limited circumstances arising from the extreme conditions of war. The rightness and value of the *Milligan* decision simply could not be taken on absolute terms. Reality and necessity required that *Milligan's* strictures only be applied, to borrow the phrase of Edmund Burke, "in proportion and with reference" to current circumstances.

The Civil War had been the last war fought on American soil. But in the early summer of 1942 the constant, undeterred activity of German U-boats off the Atlantic coast had caused serious devastation up and down the Atlantic seaboard.[29] Even after the decisive naval victory at Midway Island turned the tide in the Pacific theater, much danger still lay ahead, on both fronts. And although the German U-boat campaign in the Atlantic "was to some extent weakened for the sake of competing attractions" after July, the autumn brought some of the fiercest attacks yet. Churchill spoke of the U-boat offensive as "our worst evil. It would have been wise for the Germans to stake all upon it."[30] The lesson was not lost upon Hitler, who viewed the U-boat war as one bright spot in the midst of expanding frustration and setback and, in January of 1943, promoted its architect, Admiral Karl Dönitz,[31] to Commander in Chief of the German Navy. Dönitz himself identified "the tonnage war" as "the chief task of the U-boats, perhaps the U-boats' decisive contribution to the outcome of the war."[32] Through much of the crucial year 1942, "the towns of the Atlantic shore . . . heard nightly the sounds of battle near the coast, saw the burning, sinking ships offshore, and rescued the survivors and wounded."[33] The attacks injured American morale. Churchill observed, "[t]here was bitter anger against the Administration, which was much embarrassed."[34] Notwithstanding some encouraging successes on the part of the Allies later in the year, the total inventory of operational U-boats doubled in number to nearly two hundred in the period from January to October 1942. Allied shipping losses in the month of November alone—i.e., *after* the Supreme Court promulgated its full opinion in *Ex Parte Quirin*—were the worst of any single month of the war. Both sides concurred in estimating losses of nearly a million tons of shipping for the month.[35] It was not unforeseeable that these devastating enemy attacks by sea could at some later point metastasize to produce even greater threats to the coastal mainland—perhaps even a more effective version of the Nazi saboteur mission, which itself had been launched from U-boats. Justice Frankfurter's subsequent misgivings notwithstanding, the decision represented a prudent exercise of judgment on the part of the Court: a standard promulgated within the relative safety of peacetime conditions could only enjoy limited applicability in the circumstances of ongoing total war. Acknowledging the rarity of recourse to the use of military tribunals did not obviate their occasional necessity.

Allied Military Tribunals in the Post-War Period

The *Quirin* decision did not issue in an avalanche (or even a trickle) of military prosecutions—specially conjured for the purpose of short-circuiting the Constitution—against German- or Japanese-American civilians. No one at the time believed it would.[36] Prior to the *Quirin* decision, military commissions had already been authorized with the implementation of martial rule in Hawaii, yet the majority of the martial law cases in that territory fell to the lower-level provost courts.[37] As it turned out, the greatest use of military commissions occurred, on a worldwide and international scale, after the conclusion of hostilities. As a means of addressing widespread violations of the laws of war committed throughout the course of the conflict, all of the Allies began trying vast numbers of Axis war criminals in their own military courts. Notwithstanding the unprecedented magnitude and scope of the undertaking, these Allied trials have remained "in relative darkness and obscurity"[38] under the shadows cast by Nuremberg and Tokyo.

This wider story of the Allied World War II military commissions dates to discussions and agreements among the Allies for the establishment of a United Nations Commission for the Investigation of War Crimes, publicly announced by the United States and Britain in October, 1942.[39] A year later, at a meeting of representatives of seventeen Allied Nations in London in October, 1943, the United Nations War Crimes Commission (UNWCC) was officially launched.[40] The Commission was organized with the goal of "putting teeth" into that branch of international law dealing with war crimes. Thus, it was authorized to "investigate and record the evidence of war crimes, identifying where possible the individuals responsible," and to provide feedback to the relevant governments as to those cases where sufficient evidence would be available and forthcoming.[41] Allied governments discussed a variety of forum options for the trial of war criminals, including the adoption of an international criminal court.[42]

The work of the UN Commission began slowly. Thinly staffed and lacking in resources, the UNWCC was forced to depend upon the endeavors of its constituent member states—many of which were governments-in-exile, enjoying no certain promise of return to power at the conclusion of the war. The Moscow Declaration of November 1943 made fair to further hamstring the powers of the Commission by effectively removing from the scope of its authority the disposition of the major war criminals. In the words of the final paragraph of the Declaration, produced by the foreign ministers of the Big Three Allied powers, the "major war criminals" would "be punished by a joint decision of the Governments of the Allies."[43] The primary impediment to the greater use of military tribunals in war crimes trials in the First World War—fear of reprisals—also dampened the immediate prospects for the work of the Commission and of the affiliated national adjudicative agencies.[44]

Yet the simple logistical difficulties brought about by the magnitude of the enterprise meant that significant work, both in terms of case volume and prominence of defendants, would necessarily devolve to the national military tribunals of the Allies. In addition to the indefinite reservation as to those major war criminals, "whose offenses have no particular location," the main emphasis of the Moscow Declaration was that the majority of war criminals were to be returned for trial to the *locus delicti;* in recognition of the jurisdictional principle of "passive personality," the nation in which crimes had been committed would be given authority to try the criminals. Though "the trial of Nazi [and Imperial Japanese] leaders . . . and the governing of Germany [and Japan] for a generation" were "distinct ideas," the two notions were regularly "linked together" for purposes of analysis.[45]

Thus, on all fronts, problems of scale were perceived to complicate the task of post-war reconstruction. In a memorandum on post-war policy in Europe, George Kennan would warn of the vexing magnitude and complexity of Allied undertakings designed to establish just and equitable administrative foundations for the new German government: "In the first place, it is impracticable. It presumes a degree of knowledge and of coordination in matters of personal intelligence which could never be achieved on a tripartite basis. There is no thornier problem or more thankless task in the field of foreign affairs than that of trying to probe into the political records and motives of masses of individuals in a foreign country. It is impossible to avoid injustices, errors, and resentment. It involves the maintenance of a huge, and necessarily unpopular, investigative apparatus."[46]

As Kennan himself observed, related problems of proportion and of limited knowledge attached to the post-war adjudication of war crimes. The achievement of justice both in individual cases and on the grand international scale, imposed by the very nature of the underlying conflict, presented a knot of difficulties. If it were necessary to adhere to strict domestic standards of procedural thoroughness as to each individual defendant, then the mere volume of war crimes cases would quickly and massively overwhelm any conceivable judicial arrangement set up to process them. Because the nature of the underlying context for adjudication was massive war on a worldwide scale, and not domestic crime, punctilious procedural rectitude in some few cases could indirectly if unintentionally produce blatant injustice in many others—either by postponing them indefinitely or precluding their effective prosecution altogether. Summary executions without trial, on the other hand, could potentially spill over in an anarchy of bloodletting that would undermine important principles undergirding the Allied cause. Moreover, these considerations had to be evaluated in light of the fact that a centralized, jointly administered world-wide "justice department" would quickly become an administrative and practical nightmare. Inundated with a sprawling and unwieldy mass of evidence and cases, such an international "war crimes prosecution agency" would invariably produce "injustices, errors, and resentment" of equal magnitude.

Such practical considerations led the Allied powers to reject the centralized approach; they resolved instead upon the creation of National Offices charged with the duty of investigation, apprehension, and trial of war criminals as a more practicable solution.[47] Because of the military nature of the crimes and the procedural and jurisdictional complexity of trying huge numbers of war criminals for offenses against victims from a wide variety of nationalities, responsibility and authority for carrying out the work of investigation, apprehending suspects, and prosecuting the actual cases devolved, in large part, to the military authorities of the Allied nations.

To take one example, almost at random, from the collection of documents presented in the course of the Nuremberg trials—it had fallen to the War Crimes Branch of the Judge Advocate's Section, 3rd U.S. Army, to ascertain the facts and details of some of the worst atrocities of the war from the Nazi death camp at Flossenburg. Third Army judge advocates and investigators gathered evidence in the form of letters, reports, photographs, and sworn deposition testimony from a variety of witnesses. In the final report, 2nd Lieutenant John J. Reid, U.S. Army, "investigator-examiner," summarized the body of accumulated evidence:

> Flossenburg and the branch camps under its control accounted for the death of 14,739 male inmates and 1,300 women. These figures represent the deaths as were obtained from the available records in the camp, however, they are in no way complete as many secret mass executions and deaths took place . . .
>
> Flossenburg concentration camp can be described as a factory dealing in death. Although this camp had in view the primary object of putting to work the mass slave labor, another of its primary objects was the elimination of human lives by the methods employed in handling the prisoners. Hunger and starvation rations, sadism, inadequate clothing, medical neglect, disease, beatings, hangings, freezing, forced suicides, shooting, etc., all played a major role in obtaining their object. Prisoners were murdered at random; spite killings against Jews were common; injections of poison and shooting in the neck were everyday occurrences; epidemics of typhus and spotted fever were permitted to run rampant as a means of eliminating prisoners; life in this camp meant nothing. Killing became a common thing, so common that a quick death was welcomed by the unfortunate ones."[48]

There followed a catalogue of the mass of exhibits gathered in evidence, documenting the unspeakable *totentanz:* hunger and starvation, freezing, medical neglect, torturous beatings and floggings, forced suicides, hangings, hand hangings, poison injections, typhus and spotted fever, and shooting.[49] In the turbulent conditions precipitated by war, military authorities already located in the field, uprooting the centers of destructive atrocity in their eastward push to liberate enemy-held territories, were often the only practicable agencies for the investigation, discovery, and, in many cases, adjudication of war crimes.

The U.S. war crimes apparatus in the Far East distinguished between three types of cases, and virtually identical categories applied everywhere: the so-called "Category A" offenses involved the major war criminals, whose offenses, in the words of the Moscow Declaration, had "no particular location." These were to be tried by the International Military Tribunals. This category comprised the high-level war criminals who had been responsible for war crimes on a global scale, such as genocide and crimes against humanity. "Category B and C" included the vastly greater number of offenders, who were accused of traditionally recognized violations of the law of armed conflict.

The volume of cases tried in this manner exceeded anything that had come before: "The enormous number of prosecutions, the conduct of which extended over the large part of the world must (like everything connected with the war) be almost or entirely unprecedented not only in aggregate numbers and in their complexity variety and geographical area, but also in the comparatively short space of time in which the programme was carried out."[50] In a much-cited work, published less than a decade after the conclusion of hostilities, John Alan Appleman tabulated "2,116 known hearings before military commissions or corresponding tribunals."[51] Though the United States conducted the greatest number of hearings, Appleman noted that Great Britain, Australia, France, the Netherlands, Poland, Norway, Canada, China, and Greece all conducted their own trials by military commissions or military tribunals.[52] At the time of his report, Appleman estimated the record was incomplete and that the true number of such trials would be much higher. Thus, in a document to which Appleman did not yet have access, dated the last day of April 1948, the Acting Political Adviser in Japan, W. J. Sebald, could report that over 2,200 Class B and Class C war criminals had been convicted and sentenced, so far, in the Far East alone.[53] Fuller details emerged later.

The European Theater

It still remains difficult to determine precise figures as to the total number of cases that appeared before military commissions. In 1993, Howard Levie reported the following tallies with regard to the European theater: the United States tried some 1,672 individuals, in approximately 489 separate cases, by military commission or military government courts; the United Kingdom, 1,085 persons charged, 348 acquitted, 240 sentenced to death, and 24 sentenced to life imprisonment; France, 2,107 persons charged, 404 acquitted, 104 sentenced to death, and 44 to life imprisonment; Belgium reported 75 convictions, with 10 sentenced to death; Denmark, 80 convictions, 4 death sentences; Luxembourg, 68 convictions, 5 death sentences; the Netherlands, 204 convictions, and 19 sentenced to death; and Norway, 80 convictions, and 16 death sentences. No reliable statistics could be obtained for the Soviet Union.[54]

National courts conducted some of these trials. In some cases, as occurred in Poland, a system of special criminal courts, and eventually a Supreme National Tribunal, were established for the purpose of trying war criminals. It was this Supreme National Tribunal, comprised of professional and lay judges applying modified and streamlined provisions of the 1928 Polish Code of Criminal Procedure, which tried Obersturmbannführer Rudolf Höss, the Commandant of the concentration camp at Auschwitz.[55] The majority of cases, however, were tried by military courts. These courts, established and convened according to the requirements of the several Allied military judicial systems, varied significantly among themselves. Testimony, arguments, and procedural matters are summarized in the reports of cases compiled by the UNWCC with discussion in a ten-volume collection.[56] More thorough and comprehensive reports of select cases appear in the British War Crimes Trials series edited by Sir David Maxwell Fyfe. These reports are in some cases verbatim transcripts (as, for example, in the record of the "Hadamar" trial, tried by American military commission); in other cases, (e.g., the Belsen trial, a British military court case), the summaries provided in the reports, though not verbatim, are quite elaborate and comprehensive.[57] The record of the Belsen trial alone runs to over seven hundred single-spaced pages.

American Military Commissions

The most common offense adjudicated in the Allied tribunals appears to have been the crime of unlawful killing of prisoners of war. For a prominent example, one of the earliest American UNWCC trials concerned the case of General Anton Dostler,[58] Commander of the 75th German Army Corps, who was charged with having ordered the shooting of fifteen American prisoners of war. The trial took place before a military commission composed of five U.S. military officers sitting in Rome, Italy, from October 8–12, 1945. The Dostler case presented a jurisdictional issue which persists in contemporary discussions as to the use of military tribunals. Given the streamlined process of the military tribunals convened for cases like Dostler's, how far should the safeguards supplied under international law actually be allowed to reach? In contesting the jurisdiction of the commission, the defense (a team of American Army judge advocates) argued for application of the provisions of Article 63 of the Geneva Prisoners of War Convention of 1929, which would provide to war criminals such as the accused the same statutory protections the laws of the capturing state made available to its own soldiers—in this case Fifth Amendment due process and the procedural safeguards enumerated in the Articles of War. Thus, they said, the proper tribunal for trying the accused should have been a court-martial; since this was the only forum available for the trial of American officers, the same procedural rigors must be extended to the accused, a German army officer, as well. Moreover, such an interpretation of Article 63 would have triggered the additional protections provided in Articles 60–66 of the Geneva Convention, regarding notice to the protecting power (in this case, Germany), its right of attendance, and right of appeal.[59]

The prosecution argued that a set of provisions focusing on offenses committed by prisoners of war in captivity had no application to these facts. As in the vast majority of "Category B" war crimes, the criminal act for which the accused was being tried had occurred before his capture and thus, Article 63 should not apply to his activities as a combatant. Since the defendant was being tried for an offense against the laws of war, committed as a combatant and not as a prisoner of war, a military commission was the proper method of trial, as it had been for over a hundred years. The distinction made sense. It is perfectly rational that international law should provide greater procedural safeguards to defendants being tried for crimes committed while in the status of prisoner, and thus committed while under the control and subject to the authority of the capturing state, than it would in the case of crimes committed at large, outside the control of the capturing state. Within the tighter restraints set for the adjudication of crimes committed while in captivity, international law was deemed to possess the capacity to exert greater controls. The context of Article 63 bore out this interpretation, which was also the conclusion of the majority of the U.S. Supreme Court in its *Yamashita* decision.[60] Though no explicit reasons were given in the *Dostler* record, this likely formed the basis for the military commission's rejection of the defense jurisdictional argument here as well.

In the records of the war crimes cases, such contests of jurisdiction were fairly common strategy on the part of American defense counsel. The resolution of the issue was by no means a matter of inconsequential legalistic hair-splitting. Had arguments like the defense's in *Dostler* been allowed to prevail, the ramifications for the UNWCC trials would have been considerable. Especially for nations such as the United States, Australia, Britain, and France, in whose hands fell the responsibility of trying the great bulk of war crimes cases, much of the value provided by the simplified procedures of the military commissions and other similar foreign military courts came through the ability of such courts to address a bewildering load of cases in a streamlined, yet principled and orderly manner. This ability would have been significantly hampered had the procedural rigors of Articles 60–66 been required in every case.

As to the determination of substantive issues, General Dostler relied on the defense of *Führerbefehl*—superior orders—and was unsuccessful. The victims, two officers and thirteen men from an American Army special reconnaissance battalion, had made an amphibious landing inside enemy lines on the Italian coast on March 22, 1944. The men were on a mission to destroy a railway tunnel. However, two days later, the group was captured by Italian and German troops, interrogated, and finally executed upon orders from General Dostler, early in the morning of the 26th. Before the commission, the defense argued for the legitimacy of the order, as adhering to the so-called *Führerbefehl*, which mandated the killing of "British saboteurs and their accomplices." The order was clear:

> Henceforth all enemy troops encountered by German troops during so-called commando operations, in Europe or in Africa, though they appear to be soldiers in uniform or demolition groups, armed or unarmed, are to be exterminated to the last man, either in combat or in pursuit. It matters not in the least whether they have been landed by ships or planes or dropped by parachute. If such men appear to be about to surrender, no quarter should be given them on general principle . . . If members of such commando units . . . fall into the hands of the Wehrmacht through different channels (for example, through the police in occupied territories), they are to be handed over to the *Sicherheitsdienst* [Security Service] without delay.[61]

Since the American mission had been a "commando operation" of the type contemplated in the *Führerbefehl*, it was argued, Dostler could not be faulted for obeying orders in carrying out reprisal measures as he had done.[62]

Justification for the *Führerbefehl*, or "Commando Order," had been based, ostensibly, on alleged violations of the Geneva Convention on the part of the Allies. Yet as Telford Taylor has observed, the motive behind the order was not, in fact, reprisal for Allied infractions, but rather an outworking of German *Kriegsraison* in response to damagingly effective Allied operations in 1942 up and down Europe's Atlantic coast:

> "If the German conduct of the war is not to suffer grievous damage through these incidents," Hitler wrote, "it must be made clear to the ad-

> versary that all sabotage troops will be exterminated, without exception, to the last man." That is why Hitler ordered that information of the killing of captured commandos should be publicized by printing the reports in Wehrmacht communiqués, while directing that the orders themselves "must not, under any circumstances, fall into enemy hands."[63]

The obvious response to the defense was that no refuge could be found in the false haven of an illegal order. "Whatever one might say about the action of a commander of a raid who orders a captured enemy killed on grounds of military necessity, that has little to do with an order for the execution of *all* commandos engaged in a perfectly legitimate raid, in uniform, innocent of any criminal conduct, who are captured, unarmed, helpless, and surrendering."[64] But the prosecution went on to point out that the actions of the defendant had exceeded even the broad limits of the *Führerbefehl* itself. In this case, the fifteen American victims had not been killed "either in combat or in pursuit"—rather, they had been kept in captivity for at least forty-five hours before the final execution took place. Under the terms of the "Commando Order," the men should have been turned over to the *Sicherheitsdienst* since they had not been killed during combat or taken in pursuit. The commission returned a guilty verdict and the defendant was sentenced to be shot to death by musketry.[65] Dostler appears to have been "the only German general executed on the sole authority of the United States."[66]

In the "Hadamar" trial, an American military commission sitting in Wiesbaden tried seven civilian defendants, six men and one woman, for the murder of over 400 inmates of a small sanatorium near the town of Hadamar, Germany. The evidence presented before the commission indicated that over 10,000 Germans had been brought to the institution, admitted ostensibly to receive treatment for mental illness, and had been put to death. The specific charges before the court, however, had to do with a particular group of approximately 476 Polish and Russian men, women, and children, who had been shipped to Hadamar from work camps or institutions throughout Nazi controlled territory at various times between the date of the D-Day invasion and the arrival of the American troops in Wiesbaden in March of 1945. Thus the defendants were being tried for violations of the laws of war against victims who had belonged to Allied and co-belligerent states. Most of these slave laborers were suffering from tuberculosis, at different stages, and, though no facilities for treating the disease were available at Hadamar, they had been sent there purportedly to receive medical treatment. Within two days of their arrival at the institution, all of the victims were given lethal doses of morphine or scopolamine. All died, and were promptly buried in mass graves at Hadamar. The accused included Alfons Klein, administrative head of the asylum; Adolf Wahlmann, a physician and a specialist in mental illness; the institution's chief male nurse, Heinrich Ruoff; two other nurses; and a caretaker, Philipp Blum.

The 250-page verbatim record provides a rich mine of material for examination, offering a detailed display of the thoroughness of the commission's procedures. As the prosecuting attorney, Colonel Leon Jaworski averred in his closing statement, "the Commission [had] accorded to the accused every right that they could possibly have expected or wanted, rights and privileges that were unknown to them under the government that was theirs for so long."[67] It also offers disturbing glimpses into the means by which "Hadamar drifted from a hospital to a human slaughterhouse."[68] Major Herman Bolker, a pathologist from the Medical Corps of the 7th Army's War Crimes Investigating Team testified that he had caused six of the bodies of the Russian and Polish victims to be disinterred. Of these, four had tuberculosis, one had been suffering from a non-tubercular pneumonia, and the other had "no evidence of bodily disease" whatsoever. None of the tubercular cases was determined to be of such severity "as to produce immediate death." In other words, none of the bodies examined by Bolker had even been terminal tuberculosis cases.[69] Dr. Wahlmann, the director of the institution had "found it necessary to write a letter suggesting that sicker people be sent there, [apparently, he] found it increasingly difficult to kill those well ones."[70]

The transcript follows weird twists in plumbing the depths of the monstrous machinery of what Hannah Arendt called "administrative massacre"—while noting at the same time the difficulty of grasping it "juridically."[71] One of the prosecution witnesses, Nurse Minna Zachow, testified on cross-examination that there had been many German mental patients killed at Hadamar before the arrival of the Russians and Poles at issue in the case. Upon the objection of the prosecution, that these facts were outside the scope of the charges, defense fought to have the evidence admitted, on the grounds that it showed the defendants did not distinguish between killing Germans and killing other nationalities: as defense counsel argued, "no distinction [was] made between the Russians and the Poles, and . . . thousands of Germans were killed at this same hospital by the prosecution's witnesses and they thought it perfectly proper . . . These people were carrying out the laws of the land."[72] The very fact that such arguments were even put forward by advocates clearly committed to the vigorous defense of their clients—in essence, that a prior uncharged atrocity could somehow merge with and thereby excuse liability for the charged offense—illuminates the moral and juridical quandary observed by Arendt.[73]

French Conseils de Guerre

In France, the trial of UN War Crimes Commission cases largely fell under the jurisdiction of the permanent military tribunals, the conseils de guerre *permanents*. Throughout the period of the occupation, the French population experienced what was ultimately discovered to be a systematic Nazi campaign of terrorization that formed part of a wider pattern extending across occupied Europe. Thus, the Nazis used arbitrary and indiscriminate arrests, detention without trial, and deportation as methods for maintaining control and snuffing out resistance and dissent. The UN War Crimes Commission had early determined that such offenses should be added to its list of war crimes—"Indiscriminate mass arrests for the purpose of terrorizing the population, whether described as taking of hostages or not"[74]—recognizing that "the principles of the laws of nations, derived from the usages established among civilized peoples, from the laws of humanity . . . and the dictates of the public conscience"[75] established such practices to be violations of the international law of war. Thus, the conseil de guerre *permanent* at Lyon tried twenty officers, NCOs, and other members of the former German Customs Commissariat stationed at Annemasse, French Savoy, for the illegal arrest and maltreatment of French citizens. Some of the victims had eventually been deported and died after subsequent maltreatment. Nineteen of the defendants received twenty-years' hard labor or imprisonment for a lesser length of time.[76]

At Metz, a Nazi government administrator in Sierck, Lorraine Pitz, was found guilty of complicity in the arrest and deportation of French local inhabitants, whom he had denounced for refusal to claim allegiance to the German government. Upon refusing to join the Wehrmacht, French youths were arrested and conscripted by force, and their families were deported to Germany. Pitz, who had drawn up the lists of names for Nazi authorities, received a sentence of five-years' confinement.[77]

The wider context provided by the character of a nation's encounter with the enemy logically often determined the nature of cases heard by the national military tribunals. In actions reminiscent of the *franc-tireur* hysteria in the opening months of the First World War, members of various German units in eastern France had committed murder, arson, torture, and other forms of maltreatment in an attempt to crack down on local French resistance efforts. The crimes had occurred in numerous locations in the region of Dijon over the course of several weeks in June 1944. In the subsequent military trial three years later, twenty-four defendants were accused of maltreatment and reprisal killings against civilians, as well as pillaging. The trial revealed that the German defendants, who consisted of Army officers and Gestapo and SD members and who claimed provocation by resistance fighters, had rounded up dozens of local inhabitants for massacre and indulged in wide-scale looting, burning, and pillaging. No evidence indicated that the victims belonged to the resistance movement or had committed any violation of the laws of war. Only two of the defendants were acquitted. All but two of the rest received death sentences.[78]

British Military Courts

British military tribunals tried some of the most serious and highly publicized cases in the European theater. Among the more conspicuous of these was one of the first cases tried by the British, the "Belsen trial," convened at Luneburg, Germany, between September 17 and November 17, 1945, a prosecution against forty-five defendants connected with the concentration camps at Auschwitz and Bergen-Belsen. The defendants, many of whom were civilians, were charged with war crimes in the killing and ill-treatment of Allied civilians and military personnel in the camps.[79]

As was the case with all the British military courts, a British Army lawyer, the judge advocate, served as an impartial observer to the proceedings and provided advice on substantive and procedural matters to the court, composed of five senior military officers. It was also the responsibility of the judge advocate to provide a summary of the evidence before the court entered the deliberation phase of the trial. British barristers and solicitors were qualified to appear as counsel on behalf of prosecution or defense; in addition to these, the accused could be represented "by advocates of their own nationality, or by British serving officers appointed by the Convening Officer"—these were not necessarily lawyers.[80] In the Belsen trial, Colonel H. A. Smith, a renowned professor of International Law at London University, was foremost among the counsel for the accused and delivered a closing argument on the behalf of all the defendants.

This was "an entirely different arrangement"[81] from the organization of the American commissions, where military lawyers (judge advocates) were appointed to serve in adversarial roles as prosecutors and as defense counsel. The difference reflected variations in the legal authorities that provided for the creation and organization of the military courts under the auspices of the UNWCC. Jurisdiction of the British military courts was sourced in the Royal Warrant, dated June 14, 1945, Army Order 81/45.[82] The Royal Warrant, in turn, was based on the ancient doctrine of the Royal Prerogative, which according to Dicey, is "nothing else than the residue of arbitrary authority which any given time is legally left in the hands of the Crown."[83] In contrast to the constitutional review of American military commissions provided in *Quirin* and *Yamashita,* no legislative or judicial challenges to the constitutionality and legality of the Royal Warrant occurred.[84] Jurisdiction under the Royal Warrant did not extend to crimes against peace or against humanity. It provided only for prosecution of war crimes committed against Allied nationals. Corresponding authorities regulating the establishment of military courts for Australia and Canada closely mirrored the provisions of the Royal Warrant.[85]

The Belsen military court heard thirty-one prosecution witnesses. Victims in the Belsen case represented ten different Allied countries; it was impossible to cover all their names and identities in the record, as their number came to millions in the camp at Auschwitz and to tens of thousands at Belsen. Apart from a few important exceptions, British military courts followed the general rules of evidence and procedure applicable in the English civil courts. The Royal Warrant did relax the rules of evidence; regulation 8(i) of the Royal Warrant provided for the admission of hearsay.[86] Accordingly, a mass of documentary evidence was introduced in the Belsen trial,[87] in addition to the testimony of the live witnesses. The record, which runs to over 700 pages, contains a harrowing, witness-by-witness account of the testimony and cross-examination, along with affidavit and deposition testimony heard by the court. Thus, the deposition provided by Lieutenant Colonel James Alexander Deans Johnston, R.A.M.C., who arrived at Belsen on the 17th of April, 1945, reported upon the condition of the camp and its inhabitants at the time of the cease-fire. Johnson's statement gives a sense of the near futility of words in conveying the horrors he encountered: "it is quite impossible to give any adequate description on paper of the atrocious, horrible and utterly inhuman condition of affairs."[88] As to Camp No. 1 at Belsen, he said,

> The prisoners were a dense mass of emaciated apathetic scarecrows huddled together in wooden huts, and in many cases without beds or blankets, and in some cases without any clothing whatsoever. The females were in worse condition than the men and their clothing generally, if they had any, only filthy rags.
>
> The dead lay all over the camp and in piles outside the blocks of huts which housed the worst of the sick and were miscalled hospitals. There were thousands of naked and emaciated corpses in various stages of decomposition lying about the camp. As far as can be ascertained there were some 13,000 dead lying unburied.
>
> Sanitation was to all practical purposes non-existent. Pits, with, in only a few instances, wooden perch rails, were available in totally inadequate numbers. The inmates, from starvation, apathy and weakness, defaecated and urinated where they sat or lay, even inside the living huts.[89]

Dora Szafran, a Jewess from Warsaw and inmate at Belsen and Auschwitz, testified to the conditions at Belsen: "In half a barracks there were 600 to 700 people. We were lying on the floor covered with lice and every other kind of vermin one could imagine . . . There was no bread for four weeks before the arrival of the British troops . . . Towards morning there were several hundred corpses in the blocks and around the blocks. When the Lager Kommandant or [Irma] Grese [a female defendant and an Aufseherin at both Auschwitz and Belsen] came along to inspect people, the corpses were cleared away from the front of the blocks, but inside they were full of corpses."[90]

Live witness testimony also included the wrenching account of the twenty-nine-year-old Sophia Litwinska, a Jewess from Lublin, Poland, and a survivor of the gas chambers at Auschwitz. On Christmas Eve, 1941, Litwinska and over three thousand other Jewish women had been paraded before Franz Hoessler, one of the Belsen defendants, and two doctors. She had been among those selected out:

> All those who could not leave their beds had their numbers taken, and it was clear to us that they were condemned to death. Those whose bodies were not very nice looking or were too thin, or whom those gentlemen disliked for some reason or other, had their numbers taken, and it was clear what that meant. My number was also taken . . .
>
> About half-past five in the evening trucks arrived and we were loaded into them, quite naked like animals, and were driven to the crematorium.

> [At the crematorium,] [t]he whole truck was tipped over in the way they do it sometimes with potatoes or coal loads, and we were led into a room which gave me the impression of a shower-bath. There were towels hanging round, and sprays, and even mirrors . . . People were in tears; people were shouting at each other; people were hitting each other. There were healthy people, strong people, weak people and sick people, and suddenly I saw fumes coming in through a very small window at the top. I had to cough very violently, tears were streaming from my eyes, and I had a sort of feeling in my throat as if I would be asphyxiated . . . At that moment I heard my name called. I had not the strength to answer it, but I raised my arm. Then I felt someone take me and throw me out from that room.[91]

Apparently, her provenance from a Lublin prison and her status as the wife of a Polish officer had made enough of a difference for her to be spared. The photos of the communal graves and of other scenes from the camps contained in the British record of the trial convey a similar sense of the incommensurability of the events under juridical examination.

On the nineteenth day of the trial, defense counsel began to present their case. Seventy-five witnesses appeared on behalf of the various defendants—more than double the number of witnesses for the prosecution. British lawyers—mostly army officers—represented the defendants. Their zealous advocacy brought the trial "a very bad press because the defense lawyers . . . made arguments supporting the legality of concentration camps under German law, leading to the conclusion that murder in concentration camps was not a crime, and referring to the Belsen victims as 'the dregs of the ghettos of Eastern Europe.'"[92] The closing statement of Major A. S. Munro, who represented Franz Hoessler, Juana Bormann, Elisabeth Volkenrath, and Herta Ehlert, argued from the silence of the response to the "parades" and "selections" endured by the likes of Litwinska. The passivity of the Jewish victims, a perplexing puzzle for anyone contemplating the monstrous efficiency of the camps, in Munro's eyes provided more than enough reason to doubt the guilty complicity of his clients. As Hannah Arendt would later suggest, justice might demand that some questions should better "be left in abeyance: 'How could the Jews through their own leaders cooperate in their own destruction?'" or, "'Why did they go to the death like lambs to the slaughter?'"[93] Yet in zealously putting these questions forward, the British defense counsel saw such passivity as the irrefutable argument for his client's exoneration:

> In any large camp people were continually being sorted out, paraded and detailed for all sorts of purposes, and in the absence of any positive proof that people could have known beforehand that any particular parade was for a gas chamber selection and no other, the accused must, at the very least, be given the benefit of the doubt. If a very large number of people were paraded knowing it was for a gas chamber selection, what was the behaviour and temper of that parade going to be? It was difficult indeed to keep order on even the morning or evening Appell [roll call]. How much more difficult would it have been to control large numbers of people who were perfectly well aware that if picked out they were going to be sent to a horrible death? . . . it would have been impossible. Would normal human beings stand there quietly and wait to be selected? Would they, after being selected, still remain quiet and orderly and wait to be sent to their death? Such an assumption was the height of absurdity. These people, who outnumbered their guards to a tremendous extent, would most certainly have panicked and stampeded if they had had no real doubt that they were going to be sent to the gas chamber. No evidence had been offered that any scenes of that kind had occurred, and this was conclusive proof that the people on these parades could not possibly have known what they were parading for.[94]

Thus, unlike the Eichmann trial some sixteen years later, this court received a cruel and sophistic answer "to this cruel and silly question."[95] The court found thirty of the accused guilty, and sentences in the case ranged from the death penalty to one year's imprisonment. Under the Royal Warrant, no right of appeal was allowed.[96] The fact that fifteen of the defendants were acquitted, though these were *Kapos*—lower level officials in the bureaucracy of the camps, and none of the S.S. zealots—produced a "flood of [international] criticism."[97]

The Pacific Theater

Statistics for the Pacific theater suffer from the same lack of clarity, though the obvious import of more recent accounts is to recognize a dramatic increase in the final tally of trials by military courts. To take one example, Appleman's figures noted only two Chinese trials by military commission. The later figure provided by Philip Piccigallo estimates that 883 accused were tried in 605 cases: "[Nationalist] China tried Japanese suspects before military tribunals convened and supervised by the Chinese

War Crimes Commission, following approval by the ministries of defense and justice." Beginning in April, 1946, and despite an escalating civil war between Nationalist and Communist forces, war-crimes trials were convened throughout the country, and remained in operation until March, 1949, with the collapse of Nationalist China spreading over the horizon. The Chinese statute allowed for a review process within military and defense channels:

> All convictions required confirmation by the ministry of defense. In cases involving death sentences or life imprisonment, the ministry further submitted all relevant information to the president of the Republic—Chiang Kai-shek—"for a fiat of execution." If for any reason the ministry or the president believed the judgment to be "faulty or improper," they returned the case for re-trial. An accused could appeal a conviction within ten days of the judgment. Finally, the Chinese—ever alert to see that no guilty Japanese went unpunished—permitted the ministry of defense to refer any case back for re-trial after further examination.

Despite the opportunities for abuse, Chinese military judges appear to have exercised considerable scruple in trying the Japanese accused. Of the 883 accused who were tried, there were only 504 convictions, for a rate of 56 percent and an acquittal rate of 39.6 percent.[98]

Approximately fifty military tribunals were established throughout the Far East. It was of course the United States that took the position at the tip of the spear of the Allied war-crimes effort. In the Pacific theater, U.S. military courts sat not only in Japan, but in the Philippines, China, and the Pacific Islands, conducting a total of 474 trials, adjudicating the cases of 1,409 accused. Perhaps the most prominent, and most controversial, of these trials was the first such case to be convened, that of General Tomoyuki Yamashita, the so-called "Tiger of Malaya," whose troops in the Philippines, forced into retreat by superior numbers of American forces, resorted to a systematic brutal reign of terror and murder against the Filipino population. Tens of thousands were butchered, including women, the elderly, children, and infants. Acts of rape and bestiality were committed on a massive scale.[99]

Upon his capture in September 1945, the Japanese general was brought to trial in October of that year on 128 specifications relating to a single charge, that of failure to discharge his duty to restrain his troops from committing these atrocities. The prosecution's case rested entirely on circumstantial evidence. General Yamashita adamantly denied knowledge of or the ability to foresee these acts. Yet, similarities among the crimes committed throughout the Philippines manifested a pattern, which prosecutors used to suggest a common plan. Yamashita's headquarters occupied a position in or near two prisoner of war camps where offenses had been committed. After Yamashita gave an order to suppress guerrilla activities, two thousand Filipinos imprisoned in Manila had been given summary trials, "none of which lasted more than five minutes, and none of which even conformed to Japanese legal requirements," and then had been beheaded. Furthermore, the evidence disclosed that Yamashita had given orders for the destruction of pro-American segments of the population. The military commission finally determined that, given the enormous scale of the vicious acts committed by troops under Yamashita's command, the Japanese general had made no effective attempt to "discover and control" the acts, and thereby incurred criminal liability for his troops' lawless actions.[100]

The case was appealed to the Supreme Court. Over a stirring dissent from Justices Murphy and Rutledge, the Court affirmed the decision of the military commission. It also affirmed the legitimacy of the military commission, as well as the commission's cognizance of a positive duty on the part of commanders to prevent war crimes by exerting control over their troops.

> *Yamashita* recognized the existence of an affirmative duty on the part of a commander to take such measures as are within his power and appropriate in the circumstances to wage war within the limitations of the laws of war, in particular exercising control over his subordinates; it established that the commander who disregards this duty has committed a violation of the law of war; and it affirmed the *summum jus* of subjecting an offending commander to trial by a properly constituted tribunal of a state other than his own. In the latter it became the foundation for all subsequent trials arising from World War II.[101]

The Allied national military courts almost uniformly followed the majority opinion. Yet in the intervening years, the weight of scholarly judgment has shifted to the dissenters, seemingly, for reasons that are not altogether clear.[102] This has occurred despite the fact that both Murphy and Rutledge transmitted several material factual misrepresentations in their opinions, including the "unjustified conclusion" that the military commission and Board of Review had not even attributed "knowledge of these crimes" to Yamashita.[103]

In another trial, convened at Shanghai between July 1 and July 25, 1946, Lieutenant General Harukei Isayama, along with seven other officers, was indicted for having "willfully, unlawfully and wrongfully commit[ted] cruel, inhuman and brutal atrocities and other offenses against certain [fourteen] American POWs, by permitting and participating in an illegal and false trial and unlawful killings of said POWs, in violation of the laws and customs of war." Numerous other trials, including one in Hong Kong involving General Hiskasu Tanaka and five other officers, focused on the same offense.[104] The accused had participated as prosecutors and judges in these illegal trials of American POWs. The cases are interesting for their supposition of both legitimate and illegitimate methods for conducting military trials of captured enemy combatants, while never calling into question the practice itself. In the Isayama trial, the evidence showed that "the American POWs had been denied the opportunity to obtain evidence or witnesses on their behalf; that no documents, besides the charges, had been interpreted to them; that they had not been provided defense counsel. Trials of all fourteen Americans had been completed in one day."[105]

Next to the United States and Britain, the nation with the largest number of military war crimes trials in the Far East was Australia. Australia based its jurisdictional authority and regulated the conduct of the trials on the War Crimes Act of 1945, which closely followed the pattern of the British Royal Warrant. Judge advocates took a neutral, non-voting, advisory position. Courts were not bound by the rules of evidence of regular military or civil courts; thus, they could hear "any oral statement" or "document appearing on the face of it to be authentic,"—in short, any evidence that appeared to the court "to be of assistance in proving or disproving the charge." Under the War Crimes Act, the death penalty could only be adjudged with the concurrence of all members in the case of three-member panels. For courts consisting of more than three members, the Act required at least a two-thirds concurrence of the voting members. The Australian military courts heard cases throughout Southeast Asia and the Southwest Pacific, trying offenses committed against Australian and Commonwealth nationals as well as Chinese, Dutch, and other European victims.[106] Piccigallo relates that one of the first Australian war crimes trials, at Wewak, New Guinea, involved cannibalism, a crime without precedent in modern international law. The offense, as it turned out, had been provided for by the extension of war crimes definitions under the statute, along with the crime of "mutilation of a dead body," with just such cases no doubt in view. In this case, the accused admitted to having eaten from the body of an Australian POW, pleading the excuse of starvation and temporary insanity in defense. At the end of two days' deliberation, the court returned a guilty verdict, and sentenced the officer to hang.[107] Another court found ten of eleven Japanese defendants guilty of the "crucifixion and murder" of Australian and American airmen on the Talaud Islands, northeast of Sulawesi in the Indonesian archipelago.[108] Though all of the Allied powers tried defendants en masse, Australian military tribunals conducted some of the largest mass trials, in cases involving up to ninety-three Japanese defendants.[109]

Piccigallo's final figures run as follows: For the United States, there were 474 total cases, 1,409 defendants tried, 1,229 convictions, 180 acquittals, and 163 death sentences.[110] Britain tried 306 cases, involving 920 accused, of whom 811 were convicted and 107 were acquitted; there were 279 death sentences, of which 265 were executed, and 55 sentences to life imprisonment.[111] Australia conducted 296 trials, with 924 accused, 644 convicted, and 280 were acquitted; of the 644 prisoners receiving a conviction, 148 were executed, and 496 were imprisoned; among the latter number, only 39 life sentences were adjudged.[112] China reported 605 cases tried, in which 883 accused were involved; 504 of these were convicted, and 350 were acquitted; there were 149 death sentences, and 83 life sentences.[113] For the Netherlands, there were 448 trials involving 1,038 accused; of this number 969 (or 93.4%) were convicted, and 55 (or 5.3%) were acquitted; there were 236 death sentences adjudged, and 226 of these were executed; 28 life sentences were also given.[114] The Philippines conducted 72 cases involving 169 defendants; there were 133 convictions and 11 acquittals, 17 death sentences and 87 life sentences.[115] After perhaps the Soviet Union, France tried the least number of cases in the Pacific. For the final count, French military tribunals tried 39 cases, involving 230 accused, of whom 198 were convicted and 31 acquitted; there were 63 death sentences, of which only 26 were carried out.[116] Each of the nations represented reported a small number of cases that were unaccounted for. The Soviet Union did not have accurate figures to report.

Given the wide extent of the practice, limitations of time and space prohibit anything like an exhaustive account of the cases tried before military courts in the aftermath of the Second World War.[117] Such a history remains to be written. I have provided only a miniscule sampling of cases[118] in order to give some sense of the range of offenses that were subject to the jurisdiction of the commissions, as well as the broad, international scope of the practice. Piccigallo's assessment at the end of an extensive survey of the cases from the Pacific theater deserves consideration:

> Minor trials featured, with admirable consistency in the various theaters, excellent and devoted defense counsel; sufficient procedural safeguards, subject, of course to military law; fair-minded judges; extraordinarily thorough and impartial review procedures in all theaters (save perhaps the Russian); adequate translation facilities; generally (with some exceptions) public hearings; and accessible, complete records of the proceedings. A considerable percentage of the accused, too, were acquitted; perhaps not as many as might have been expected received death sentences. Commutation of sentences was not uncommon.[119]

Comparative Assessments

The value of the Appleman, Levie, and Piccigallo studies consists in their effectiveness in placing the military commission in proper context. Given the vast scope in terms of sheer numbers of trials, and the breadth of the international dimensions of the practice of trials by the national military tribunals, it does in fact seem "egregiously unfair and inaccurate"[120] to evaluate the Allied adjudication of war crimes in terms of the IMTFE and Nuremberg alone. Moreover, given the tenor of the current debate over military commissions, the observation that "a good number of authorities who . . . criticized the [International Military Tribunals] . . . praised the conduct of [military commissions] . . . for their fairness and justness"[121] casts an ironic light. Yet the trials at Nuremberg and Tokyo represented "the cynosure of world attention to the great issues of war guilt."[122] With the zeal occasioned by the International Tribunals auguring the emergence of a new international legal order, George Kennan and other critics sought to maintain an important if misunderstood distinction regarding the *military* as opposed to *judicial* character of the tribunals.[123]

As the actual conflict receded into history, an emerging post-war political, psychological, and diplomatic paradigm, with new and urgent pressures and dangers, led to the conclusion that the war crimes trials "should be wound up within the shortest practicable period of time."[124] In the Far East, such warnings did not go unheeded. By Christmas of the same year, the work of the international military tribunals for the Far East came to a halt. The Acting Political Adviser in Japan, W. J. Sebald, communicated to the Secretary of State that nineteen suspects were being released by the Supreme Commander, Allied Powers (SCAP), Japan, "following intensive investigation," along with "the determination not to initiate any additional trials." This final release of suspects completed "the disposition of all former major war crimes suspects held in Japan."[125] Abstract and absolute requirements of justice had to yield to the political and diplomatic reality imposed by the unfolding of events in time in particular locations.

The specter of indefiniteness lingered in Europe as well. While the trials of the major war criminals had been completed by October of 1946, U.S. Army prosecutions continued, along with the so-called "subsequent Nuremberg tribunals" of over 180 additional defendants. The Army war crimes program in Germany, it now seems clear,

> did little to change German attitudes. Cries of foul play and "victor's justice" accompanied the proceedings of the Trial of the Major War Criminals and the subsequent tribunals. Already during the occupation, German legal scholars questioned the legality of the Nuremberg trials under international law. The constant attacks against the Allies, especially the United States as the main instigator of these proceedings, in the late 1940s by Germany's church leaders, politicians, veterans and refugee organizations demonstrated that the war crimes program had not reeducated and democratized the Germans. Ironically the War Department, not wanting the occupation to result in anti-Allied sentiment, achieved exactly the opposite on the problem of war criminals.[126]

A policy statement issued by the State Department in August 1948, addressing the subject of "denazification," argued that it had "become apparent, not only in the US zone but elsewhere in Germany, that indefinite prolongation of formal denazification procedures would be incompatible with the US aim to create an environment favorable to democratic political revival."[127] As the initial post-war furors began to cool and sentences issued by the tribunals became increasingly lenient, the Army War Crimes program introduced clemency and sentence reduction measures to overcome disparities among the results of earlier and later cases. As these measures came to function as an ersatz-appellate system, the process tended to "lead to wrong impressions, namely that American authorities themselves had lost faith in the war crimes program and were revising judgments and verdicts." With the passage of time, political issues such as the reintegration of West Germany into the defense structure of Western Europe eventually submerged the aims of the war crimes trials program. With the onset of new issues and concerns in the 1950s, it "ceased to be a priority, and became instead a political burden." Many convicted war criminals received clemency or drastic reductions of sentence. The aim behind the war crimes trials had been to adequately punish convicted war criminals and to reeducate the German public. Largely because of inadequate compensation for these complications wrought by the forward movement of time, the program fell short of the mark.[128]

Thus the national military tribunals were not immune from some of the defects decried by critics of Tokyo and Nuremberg.[129] The sheer magnitude of the undertaking meant that discrepancies and inconsistencies were inevitable. As the immediacy of events faded into memory, military and political objectives shifted and diverged. Yet there remained significant distinctions between the two categories of trials. The difference in reception among contemporaries closer to the scene makes sense when it is understood that the lower-level national tribunals, designated "military commissions" in U.S. practice, operated largely on the surer ground provided by certain and well-established principles of international law in defining the scope and application of war crimes charges. In this light, it must be acknowledged that the international war crimes tribunals were the exception—applying novel concepts of jurisdiction in holding individuals criminally responsible for acts of state, for waging a "war of aggression," for crimes against peace and crimes against humanity, etc.[130]—while the established, customary practice was represented by the thousands of military commissions applying more conventional war crimes concepts against lesser offenders. There was far less uncertainty as to the nature and purpose of the national military courts, which operated, for the most part, on the surer footing provided by centuries of military practice. The courts identified in the United States with the designation "military commissions," in France as "conseils de guerre," and in Britain simply as "military courts" had served generations of military commanders as a provision in case of military necessity.

The astonishing magnitude of the work of these lesser-known national military tribunals, completed in the aftermath of the war over the course of a short number of years, will probably never be ascertained in the fullest details. The success of the post-war reconstruction in the former Axis nations has not been attributed to the integrity and prudence of conduct of the national tribunals of the Allies. Perhaps this is just and fitting.[131] Conditions wrought by the Allied decision to carry out the war to the point of unconditional surrender may have been such that it would have mattered little for the rebirth of democratic Germany and Japan if all the defendants before the allied national military tribunals had been summarily executed without trial.

In his review of the war crimes sentences at Tokyo, General McArthur pointed to the need for humility in any attempt to assess the validity of the undertaking: "It is not my purpose, nor indeed would I have that transcendent wisdom which would be necessary, to assay the universal fundamentals involved in these epochal proceedings designed to formulate and codify standards of international morality by those charged with a nation's conduct. The problem indeed is basically one which man has struggled to solve since the beginning of time and which may well wait complete solution till the end of time."[132] From the perspective of other corners, "the whole of the war-crimes policy planning was shot through with excess and a failure to accept reasonable limits."[133] Justice Jackson himself had concluded his final report on Nuremberg with the admission that "many mistakes have been made and many inadequacies must be confessed."[134] The same could no doubt be said with regard to the thousands of lesser national military trials. Yet, since the military commissions and other associated national tribunals did not generally pretend to rise to the level of a supra-national form of absolute justice, their results proved to be less susceptible—though not immune—to the charge of "hubris." Here, the choice not to impose a Carthaginian peace—with regard to war crimes suspects, as with the other policies of the occupation powers—and to make use of the expedited procedures of the national military courts oriented itself around a limited, more modestly defined set of reference points.

Because these military courts largely kept within the bounds of their function as organs of the Allied military forces, expectations were different. With the military courts, engaged for the most part in the trial of lesser war criminals, there was little of the "odd" and "breathtaking" pretense "that the gigantic atrocity of Nazism and the Second World War" were being "moved before a court, examined, and judged"—with quickness and accuracy and "without excessive violence to customary principles of law."[135] Because the accused were not prominent state officials, but soldiers and officers accused of traditionally recognized war crimes, the added complexity of the international political dimension remained largely absent. These defendants were being held accountable not for the acts of the Japanese or German state governments, but for their own violations of the laws of armed conflict, a practice of ancient and long-standing custom. And though these trials did not carry all of the trappings attached to a domestic criminal forum, the privileges and rights provided often exceeded those on offer in the defeated nations themselves. Of course exceptions can be singled out; yet the painstaking procedural rigor exerted by the courts and by the officers responsible for preparing the cases quickly becomes evident to all who take the time to review the records beyond a selection of controversial standouts.

Competing interests tugged the process of war crimes adjudication in opposite directions. The pull of the world outside the ambit of law courts and procedures, represented most urgently by the goal of developing or restoring the rule of law and democratic political processes in Germany and Japan—but hardly limited to that—could ill afford the luxury of contemplating the pursuit of justice in the abstract. The realities imposed by the forward movement of time made tragic choices unavoidable. The same August 1948 Department of State policy pronouncement on "denazification" in Germany, quoted earlier, exposed this tension:

> The net result of denazification in the US zone will be that, of some 3 million persons found chargeable under the law, about 15 percent will have been subjected to penalties or placed on probationary status, and the remainder restored to normal German life. While experience has reaffirmed both the necessity and soundness of the US denazification policy, it cannot be claimed that there has been entire success in debarring Nazi activists from important posts in public and economic life, especially the latter where technical competence has been a factor to be considered. Only some two percent of all persons tried drew the more serious sanctions, and the procedure now accelerated with a view to early termination, will undoubtedly mean that some active Nazis will escape serious penalties . . . But it has become apparent, not only in the US zone but elsewhere in Germany, that indefinite prolongation of formal denazification procedures would be incompatible with the US aim to create an environment favorable to democratic political revival.[136]

To the greatest extent practicable, the Allied military tribunals allowed for a sustained equilibrium between the requirements of justice in the individual case and the extra-legal, yet equally important, international political concerns Kennan and others identified. By their very nature, as explicitly military organs, the lesser national tribunals could better remain in synch with the overall military, political, and diplomatic tasks of postwar reconstitution. Thousands of victims, their families, and survivors of war crimes were able to see justice accomplished, albeit expedited and foreshortened, in the thousands of cases that did not languish indefinitely for want of receiving a hearing.

The actual historical record does not bear out the presumption that Nuremberg and Tokyo rendered obsolete the "lesser" forms of justice, like the military commission.[137] While the evolution of international legal norms in the period since the convening of the last of the Second World War tribunals cannot be ignored, neither can the customary forms of adjudication generated on the ground, from long-standing military practice, in response to the specific needs and circumstances of war.[138]

5 Wartime Tribunals and the Future of Warfare

In her reflections on the nature of violence, Hannah Arendt emphasized the importance of distinguishing violence from power, identifying the former as a means and the latter as an end:

> Power springs up whenever people get together and act in concert, but it derives its legitimacy from the initial getting together rather than from any action that then may follow. Legitimacy, when challenged, bases itself on an appeal to the past, while justification relates to an end that lies in the future. Violence can be justifiable, but it never will be legitimate. Its justification loses in plausibility the farther its intended end recedes into the future. No one questions the use of violence in self-defense, because the danger is not only clear but also present, and the end justifying the means is immediate.[1]

The analogy to the instrumental character of the military tribunals—as implements of the commander in time of war—is instructive. As a concomitant to this instrumental feature, it must be recognized, as a matter of definition, that it is extremely difficult and even, in some cases, dangerous to isolate the work of adjudicating war crimes as an end in itself.[2] Rather, it is only possible to properly evaluate these secondary means when they are considered in the context of larger strategic and political ends. This means not only that the context for assessing the efficacy of military juridical processes must include consideration of the complex network of larger historical, institutional, political, strategic, and operational power structures within which these implements assume a subordinate place. The observation also contains important lessons about their usefulness over time, giving warning that "[their] justification loses plausibility the farther [their] intended ends recede into the future."

It is this relentless effect of the forward movement of time which renders the likelihood of domestic or international courts completely supplanting the national military courts an unrealistic prospect for the foreseeable future. To the extent that wars continue to occur, attended by significant, massive violations of the laws of war, there will remain a need for expedited procedures for their adjudication. In these circumstances, the political and military decision-maker finds himself in the grips of a tightening vice: on the one side accumulates the solid leaden reality of large numbers of law of war offenses; from the other pushes the inexorable onward drive of international political events, which, by an implicit, unavoidable interposition of temporal limits, compounds the urgency of the task. As the post-war events in Europe and Japan in the late 1940s and early 1950s demonstrate, only a fixed and limited supply of political capital exists to be expended on the punishment of such offenses. Such capital drains away with every day that the underlying conflict of arms recedes into history.

The juridical effort to punish war crimes diminishes in legitimacy, and the war criminal transforms into a kind of tragic victim. In a sense, this is what has happened with the events following September 11, 2001. The devastating attacks of that day have not been repeated, at least not against immediate U.S. national interests. The sense of urgency which attended the initial order for the establishment of the military commissions has dissipated with the subsequent apparent frustration of the threat to replicate itself—at least in America. Other parts of the world, London, Madrid, Jordan, Bali, have not been so fortunate. And of course, all of this stands subject to further change. Meanwhile, as memories of the 9/11 attacks fade, the continuing sequestration of detainees at Guantanamo Bay, Cuba, becomes the focus of media attention. Human rights groups come to the aid of the detainees, who are now widely seen as victims, suffering wrongs at the hands of the U.S. government. American defense lawyers step in to protest alleged abuses. The mood characterizes the opening sentences of Justice Stevens's majority opinion in *Hamdan v. Rumsfeld*: "Petitioner Salim Ahmed Hamdan, a Yemeni national, is in custody at an American prison in Guantanamo Bay, Cuba. In November 2001, during hostilities between the United States and the Taliban (which then governed Afghanistan), Hamdan was captured by militia forces and turned over to the U.S. military. In June 2002, he was transported to Guantanamo Bay. Over a year later, the President deemed him eligible for trial by military commission for then-unspecified crimes. After another year had passed, Hamdan was charged with one count of conspiracy to commit . . . offenses triable by military commission.'"[3] The implication is clear: such delays (though induced in part by the sustained criticism of the process, on multiple judicial and political fronts, from its very inception) give the lie to the purported need for expedited, truncated procedures.

The problem with such accounts is that no credit is given to the possibility of a real causal connection between such detentions and the absence of further acts of violence. Of course it is always difficult to prove a negative—these circumstances make it virtually impossible. But ultimately, the question is empirical in nature. When the lives of thousands of innocents potentially hang on the outcome of the experiment, where should the benefit of the doubt be placed? And who is constitutionally positioned to make such agonizing determinations?

The most significant contextual factor underlying the contemporary controversy over military commissions has to do with the understated yet obvious fact that President Bush's November 2001 order came in response to an unprecedented and unprovoked attack upon the sovereign territory of the United States and upon thousands of civilian non-combatants.[4] Critics argue that President Bush's order seeks to expand the meaning of "war" beyond the bounds of legitimacy. Thus, it is a smaller step of logic to move from this order to some future ukase arising from an executive-declared "war on drugs," or handguns, or rape, than to make the dangerous and irresponsible leap of logic that the President has already made here.[5] But surely, given the "disaster . . . of monstrous proportions,"[6] unleashed on 9/11—some 3,000 deaths in attacks targeting the financial, political, and military nerve centers of the nation—it requires no leap of logic to call the attacks acts of war, when the magnitude of the damages sustained exceeds anything in the nation's peacetime history.

It helps to begin by considering the explanations of the perpetrators themselves. Otherwise, we merely project our own interpretations on to the acts of people we would rather not listen to.[7] Those responsible do not view 9/11 as an isolated event, after the manner of a particularly brazen, one-off domestic crime. Nor is "war against the West" merely a colorful metaphor for the jihadists. Rather, the 9/11 attacks are celebrated as the most successful of a decade-long series of acts of war directed against the United States, its interests, and its allies.[8] Usama bin Ladin, the al-Qaeda chieftain, issued a formal declaration of war against United States in 1996, calling upon Muslims to make war against Americans for their "invasion" and "occupation" of Islamic holy lands.[9]

Throughout the 1990s, al-Qaeda and its operatives claimed victims in the World Trade Center bombing of 1993, the attacks on East African embassies in 1998, in the Khobar Towers bombing at the Dhahran military housing facility in Saudi Arabia, and on the USS Cole in 2000, to name only the most egregious assaults on American interests.[10]

The September 2001 attacks were appropriately identified as an act of war by the President, by a joint resolution of the U.S. Congress,[11] which, within a week, authorized "all necessary and appropriate force" in response, and by the Supreme Court in June 2004 in its *Hamdi* ruling.[12] Before the end of September 2001, the United Nations Security Council issued Resolution 1373 condemning the attacks, inter alia, as a threat to international peace and security, reaffirming the right of collective self-defense and "the need to combat by all means, in accordance with the Charter of the United Nations, threats to international peace and security caused by terrorist acts," and requiring that states "deny safe haven to those who finance, plan, support, or commit terrorist acts."[13]

The executive order of November 13, 2001, sought to reinstate the practice of military commissions after a fifty-year hiatus. The order itself amounted to little more than a skeleton instruction to Defense Department officials for the development of rules and procedures to establish military commissions for the trial of non-citizen enemy combatants.[14] Nevertheless, it prompted a barrage of criticism from left, right, and center. Some critics treated the order as if it were a bold attempt to set the broadest possible boundaries for adjudicating any number of criminal suspects via the streamlined process of the military commission, rather than in the terms the order itself set out: as a minimal framework for the extraordinary application of the tribunal method, in military necessity, to be fleshed out by the Secretary of Defense in further orders and regulations.[15] Thus, at the time of promulgation, by the order's own terms, "rules for the conduct of the proceedings of military commissions, including pretrial, trial, and post-trial procedures, modes of proof, issuance of process, and qualifications of attorneys"[16]—all such details remained to be developed. The elaborate framework outlining jurisdiction, personnel, procedure, evidence, post-trial process, and review established in subsequent regulations promulgated by Secretary of Defense Donald Rumsfeld helped to reduce some of the political tension.[17] The decision to prosecute the so-called "twentieth terrorist," Zacarias Moussaoui in Federal Criminal Court in Virginia, rather than in a military commission, itself not immune from criticism, further contributed to a temporary armistice. But only for a time. Subsequent developments in the media and in the courts exhibit the ambivalence which has characterized the Western and Anglo-American approach to the practice in the historical record chronicled here.

In the closing months of 2001, the United States and its allies delivered a series of devastating military strikes against Taliban forces in Afghanistan, a known sanctuary and training ground for Usama bin Laden's al-Qaeda terror networks. Over 7,000 terror suspects were captured and detained in mop-up operations. In January 2002, the detainment and interrogation center opened at the U.S. Naval Station, Guantanamo Bay, Cuba, for the purpose of detaining enemy combatants seized in the Afghanistan campaign. From the original number of seven thousand, approximately 600 enemy combatants were shipped for detention at the Guantanamo facility. The goal was to sift evidence, identify detainees for trial by military commission, draft charges, try the selected detainees, dismiss the rest, and finish with the tribunals by the end of 2004. As it turned out, by mid-2006, charges had been drafted and levied against only a handful of individual detainees, and no actual trials had been conducted. The reason for delay has much to do with the active oversight and intervention of the U.S. federal courts. Perhaps the greater degree of judicial intervention owes something to the compounded difficulties of determining definitive zones of engagement in an unconventional conflict with nebulous boundaries—a feature observed on a smaller scale in the Boer War. Perhaps it is an ironic consequence of the manifest success of the "war on terror" in knocking al-Qaeda and its adherents off balance. Whatever the reason, judges have shown an increasing willingness to step into the arena of decision.[18]

In June 2004, the Supreme Court issued two critical opinions on the subject of military commissions, both having to do with the question of the reach of constitutional *habeas corpus* protections. In *Rasul v. Bush*,[19] the defendants were two Australians and twelve Kuwaitis seeking *habeas* relief on the grounds that their detentions were illegal. Overruling district court and DC Circuit dismissals of the action, the Court in an opinion authored by Justice Stevens held that the writ of *habeas corpus* extends to foreign detainees at Guantanamo, rejecting long standing precedent represented by *Johnson v. Eisentrager*, and the government's position that the U.S. naval station in Cuba lay outside the jurisdictional reach of the U.S. courts. In the Court's view, the District Court's jurisdiction over the *custodians* of the petitioners was all that was required to allow it to hear the petitioners' *habeas* challenges.[20] As the dissent noted, the Court provided no explanation of its understanding as to the potential consequences flowing from the decision. With Guantanamo now for the first time subject to the oversight of the U.S. federal judiciary, it instantly became "a foolish place to have housed alien wartime detainees."[21] As Ruth Wedgwood commented, "[t]his was unfamiliar ground for the Supreme Court, for the capture and internment of prisoners of war and irregular combatants in overseas military operations has not generally engaged the attention of civilian judges." Despite a longstanding refusal on the part of the courts to issue the writ in the case of extraterritorial foreign actors, the *Rasul* Court boldly, if tacitly, held out the promise to "thrust the judiciary into the midst of controversies that extend far beyond the ordinary province of courts."[22] It would not be long before the Court would make good on this promise.

The companion case of *Hamdi v. Rumsfeld*[23] involved an American citizen captured and held as an enemy combatant during the course of U.S. operations against the Taliban in Afghanistan. The Court determined that Yaser Hamdi had a right to challenge the military designation of his status as an enemy combatant: "a citizen-detainee seeking to challenge his classification as an enemy combatant must receive notice of the factual basis for his classification, and a fair opportunity to rebut the Government's factual assertions before a neutral decision maker."[24] In the course of her opinion for a Court plurality, Justice O'Connor acknowledged that the September 18, 2001, Congressional Authorization for Use of Military Force (AUMF) included the power to hold enemy combatants in detention and suggested that military tribunals would be suitable forums for determining status questions raised by the *habeas* petitions of detainees. The Court recognized the long-standing principle that enemy combatants may be detained until the conclusion of hostilities. The plurality acknowledged the open-ended character of the "war on terror": "if the practical circumstances of a given conflict are entirely unlike those of the conflicts that informed the development of the law of war, that understanding may unravel." At the same time, it affirmed, "[b]ut that is not the situation we face as of this date."[25] As we shall see, the Supreme Court continued to hold this position on enemy combatant detention in the *Hamdan* opinion issued in June 2006.

A third important case, *Rumsfeld v. Padilla*, involved a U.S. citizen arrested in May of 2002 at O'Hare Airport in Chicago pursuant to a New York warrant related to the 9/11 investigation. The administration initially identified Jose Padilla, the so-called "dirty bomber," as an illegal enemy combatant and, without initiating charges, held him in a military detention facility in South Carolina. Padilla contested his indefinite detention without trial. The Supreme Court heard arguments in the case at the same time as *Hamdi* and *Rasul*. In June 2004, the Court ruled against the defendant on procedural grounds, requiring him to resubmit his case in the proper jurisdiction. In November 2005, after further litigation, the administration removed Padilla from "enemy combatant" status, and the government filed criminal conspiracy charges against him in Federal Court.

As an important immediate consequence of the Supreme Court's opinions in the summer of 2004, it was clear that the federal courts would be intervening with regularity into the process of the military commissions. Yet the halting, desultory character of recent efforts to use military tribunals in the case of the al-Qaeda and Taliban detainees at Guantanamo Bay derives at least in part from the sporadic nature of the practice in this tradition. Of course some of this delay is attributable to the additional layers introduced by supplementary procedural safeguards and by the intervention of appellate courts. But much is traceable to the fact that the entire machinery of the commissions had to be built from the ground up with the promulgation of the President's November 2001 order. Before then, precious little in the way of a preexisting framework, personnel, and process stood in place. The commissions convened in the aftermath of the Second World War had only become a dim and dusty memory. The inevitable inefficiencies that result from such haphazard practices feed into the stream of criticism, focused on dangers and gaps brought about in part by the vigorous critical tradition itself. Recognition that this ambivalence figures as a built-in feature of the Anglo-American history of the practice might have allowed for a more focused and even-tempered debate.

Nevertheless, the ongoing, apparently near-ubiquitous nature of the "war against terror" forces unpleasant prospects before the realistic observer. The asymmetrical character of a war against amorphous, sub-national underground networks leads us "to contemplate the scope and nature of armed struggle when neither nationality nor any other unit of local identity will count in distinguishing friends from enemies."[26] The prospect is not improved by considering the options of appeasement or acquiescence to the demands of al-Qaeda and its allies.[27] The incompatibility of such an option becomes evident when the statements of al-

Qaeda leaders are taken seriously, as their actions leading up to and following September 11, 2001, have required President Bush and other Western leaders to do.[28] The reality of an enemy demonstrably resolved to use all means for the killing of Americans, including even biological, chemical, and nuclear weapons, moves the debate from the criminal law enforcement context. The Blackstonian trope about preferring the freedom of ten guilty men over the conviction of one innocent loses some of its salience.

Such antagonists are hardly without precedent in the history of nations.[29] In his celebrated treatise on the *Law of Nations,* the Swiss international lawyer Emmerich de Vattel emphasized the importance of distinguishing between lawful and irregular operations, or

> marauding expeditions, which are carried on either without lawful authority or without apparent cause, as likewise without the proper formalities . . . Of that character were the expeditions of the *Grandes-Compagnies* which were formed in France during the wars with the English and which were mere armies of brigands, who overran Europe to pillage and destroy. Such were the cruises of the buccaneers, who had no commission, and who fought in a time of peace; and such, in general, are the depredations of pirates.[30]

War on the part of pirates, the likes of al-Qaeda, did not partake of the privileges and duties bestowed by the law of nations, and as such, must be characterized as "brigandage":

> Undertaken without any right, and even without apparent grounds, it can give rise to no lawful effects, nor confer any rights upon the author of it. A Nation that is attacked by enemies of this sort is not under any obligation to observe towards them the rules belonging to formal war; it may treat them as outlaws. When the town of Geneva escaped from capture at the time of the famous escalade [in the year 1602] it caused the prisoners taken from the Savoyards to be hanged like robbers in that they had attacked it without cause and without a declaration of war; nor was it blamed for doing so, although the act would have been reprobated in a formal war.[31]

The belligerent actions of pirates and marauders removed them from the protections bestowed by the laws of war.

Vattel's predecessor Hugo Grotius recognized the same need for careful distinction between the nation-state—notwithstanding the fact that "it commits some Acts of Injustice, even by publick Deliberation"—and "a Company of Pirates and Robbers . . . [who are] associated on the account of their Crimes."[32] Profound changes in the technology and methods of warfare tend to obscure the larger reality of an intransigent human nature that remains remarkably resistant to ideal visions of moral improvement, however well-intended. The intervening passage of time has done nothing to vitiate the perception of Vattel and Grotius; subsequent examples remain available to the observer willing to examine the historical record. "Outlaws" and "brigands" of the order of al-Qaeda have posed threats to civilized order for a very long time.

Modern international treaty law continues to respect the distinctions identified by these early international law theorists, and for the same reasons—containment of violence and protection of innocents. Article 4(2) of the Third Geneva Convention (GPW) affords protection and privileged POW status to regular combatants as well as members of militias and of "organized resistance movements" as long as such irregular belligerents meet four conditions: they must a) answer to a discernible command structure; b) wear distinctive insignia visible at a distance; c) carry arms openly; and d) conduct their operations according to the laws and customs of war.[33] The same treaty makes provision as to where the benefit of the doubt should rest:

> Should any doubt arise as to whether persons, having committed a belligerent act and having fallen into the hands of the enemy, belong to any of the categories enumerated in Article 4 such persons shall enjoy the protection of the present Convention until such time as their status has been determined by a competent tribunal.[34]

Out of deference to the varied forms of adjudication among nation-states, the GPW gives no further guidance on the question of what constitutes such a "competent tribunal."

Where any of the four criteria have not been met, combatants forfeit the privileges attached to the "lawful" status under international law. Yet the drafters of the GPW perhaps underestimated the difficulties that would attend future determinations of combatant status. As a standard operating procedure, irregular combatants like the members of al-Qaeda exploit a non-military appearance, slipping into crowded civilian areas, dropping a bomb, killing some of the "enemy"—civilian or otherwise—and either dying in the effort as "martyrs" or slipping away to "fight" another day. The safeguards established by international law for the benefit and protection of innocents become shields behind which deadly surprise attacks can be launched. It should come as no surprise that ambiguity and, at least in some cases, continuing deception would attend the best-designed process of combatant status identification. No more than the basic international rules distinguishing lawful from unlawful targets, Article 4(2) is not immune from manipulation by the desperate and unscrupulous.[35]

As a response to the *Hamdi* ruling, military authorities sought to address some of these difficulties, instituting an additional layer of administrative oversight, the so-called "Combatant Status Review Tribunals" (CSRT), for the purpose of hearing challenges on the question of enemy combatant status. The CSRT process itself followed a fairly elaborate set of instructions delineating the personnel and structure of the hearings, the handling of classified information, and the detainee's participation, including the right to silence, to testify, present evidence, and question witnesses, to review unclassified government evidence, and to assistance by a government-appointed personal representative (a non-lawyer). The tribunals were not bound by the rules of evidence and could consider hearsay evidence, ruling according to a "preponderance of the evidence" standard of proof. The government enjoyed a rebuttable presumption that its evidence supporting the classification of the detainee as an enemy combatant is authentic and accurate.[36] The hearings commenced on July 30, 2004, and by the end of the process, March 29, 2005, nearly 600 such hearings had been held. Over 200 detainees refused to participate in the proceedings. The CSRT panels released four of the detainees after determining that they had been wrongly classified as enemy combatants. A further 200 individuals were released under other circumstances—some being given outright freedom, others turned over to the custody of their home states.

In addition to the CSRT process, a further level of administrative oversight was introduced with the establishment of an Administrative Review Board, (ARB), which allowed for the annual review of the potential threat posed by those detainees initially identified and adjudicated as combatants. Petitioners to the ARB were allowed to present evidence and witness testimony to substantiate their claim that they no longer pose a threat.

Congress was not inactive during the same period, bringing into law the Detainee Treatment Act (DTA) on December 30, 2005. Designed as a mechanism for supplying legislative oversight for the detention, treatment, and determination of status of detainees at the Cuban U.S. naval base, the statute provides uniform standards of interrogation, as well as protections for U.S. interrogators, and prohibits cruel, inhuman, or degrading treatment of detainees. For our purposes the most important section of the DTA removes *habeas* petitions arising out of Guantanamo from the oversight of Article III courts—pursuant to the powers of Congress found in Article III, Section 2 of the Constitution, which grants legislative power to limit the appellate jurisdiction of the Supreme Court. This section of the statute provides that "no court, justice, or judge shall have jurisdiction to hear or consider an application for a writ of habeas corpus filed by or on behalf of an alien detained by the Department of Defense at Guantanamo Bay, Cuba." In another section, this provision is stated to "take effect on the date of the enactment of the Act." The same holds true for "any other action against the United States or its agents relating to any aspect of the detention by the Department of Defense of an alien at Guantanamo Bay, Cuba, who is currently in military custody."[37]

The statute channels exclusive jurisdiction over the determinations of the Combatant Status Review Tribunals regarding enemy combatant status to the U.S. Court of Appeals for the District of Columbia Circuit. In addition, the statute limits the types of reviewable claims and the scope of such review. The same exclusive jurisdiction in the DC Court of Appeals is to apply to the determinations of military commissions organized under the President's order. Further provisions address the training of Iraqi personnel for the treatment of detainees. The focus of the legislation is clear: in the wake of controversies over the treatment of detainees, and over the entire military commission process, Congress sought to exercise its supervisory responsibility over the facility and over all activities surrounding the detainees.

In the meantime, the proceedings of the handful of six military commission cases slated for trial in 2003 had sputtered and choked through the next two years, as review status procedures and appeals wound their way through the courts before finally grinding to a halt in 2006.

Hamdan v. Rumsfeld

Salim Ahmed Hamdan, a former driver and bodyguard for Usama bin Laden, from Yemen, was captured during operations in Afghanistan by forces allied with the United States and was transported to the facility at Guantanamo in 2002. Hamdan's trial by military commission began in August 2004, but in November of the same year, a District of Columbia U.S. district court put a stop to the trial, ruling that the military commission violated military law and Article 5 of the GPW, and requiring that a separate "competent tribunal" must be convened in order to determine the status of detainees under the Geneva Conventions.[38] In spelling out what it deemed to be the critical differences between military commissions and Uniform Code of Military Justice (UCMJ) courts-martial, the District Judge acknowledged an extensive array of rights available to defendants in military commissions:

> [Rules established for the commissions] provide that the defendant shall have appointed military counsel, that he may within reason choose to replace "detailed" counsel with another military officer who is a judge advocate if such officer is available, that he may retain a civilian attorney if he can afford it, that he must receive a copy of the charges in a language that he understands, that he will be presumed innocent until proven guilty, that proof of guilt must be beyond a reasonable doubt, that he must be provided with the evidence the prosecution intends to introduce at trial and with any exculpatory evidence known to the prosecution [with some important exceptions having do with national security], that he is not required to testify at trial and that the Commission may not draw an adverse inference from his silence, that he may obtain witnesses and documents for his defense to the extent necessary and reasonably available, that he may present evidence at trial and cross-examine prosecution witnesses, and that he may not be placed in jeopardy twice for any charge as to which a finding has become final.[39]

Furthermore, as Judge Robertson observed, the President had appointed a review panel to provide oversight for the commissions that includes luminaries of the legal community such as former Attorney General Griffin Bell, former Secretary of Transportation William T. Coleman, and Frank J. Williams, Chief Justice of the Rhode Island Supreme Court—"some of the most distinguished civilian lawyers in the country."[40]

Nonetheless, the sum total of these protections did not measure up to the standard required by the GPW, since the military commission had the potential power to convict the accused on the basis of undisclosed evidence. Further, because the CSRT process had only determined that Hamdan was properly detained as an enemy combatant, and not the legality of his status under the GPW, a separate "competent tribunal" had to be convened for this purpose.[41] Until such time, he must be accorded the full privileges of prisoner of war status.

A three judge panel of the DC Circuit overruled, finding, significantly, that the Geneva Conventions are not "judicially enforceable," since enforcement powers over the provisions of treaties like the GPW rest with the political and military authorities of signatory nations, and not with the courts in the context of litigation on the part of individual defendants.[42]

The Supreme Court granted certiorari, asserting "that trial by military commission is an extraordinary measure raising important questions about the balance of powers in our constitutional structure."[43] On the last day of the Spring 2006 term, a five-member Supreme Court majority issued its negative judgment on the military commissions, by way of a curious reading of the DTA. For detractors of the military tribunal process, a lingering complaint had always circulated in the air. Notwithstanding the post–9/11 legislative grant sanctioning the use of "all necessary and appropriate force," Congress had never explicitly declared war, and thus, it was argued, had never given authorization for the kind of unilateral assertion of power that the President had displayed in initiating the tribunals. The commission process had been established in November 2001, rules had been promulgated, debated, and refined—and Congress never acted to curtail or assert control over the process. As John Yoo has observed, Congress's most effective tool of oversight remains its control over the purse strings. This restraining power had not been exercised to curb the administration's military tribunal plans. But for opponents of the commissions, mere silence from Congress provided insufficient warrant. Objection fixed on the notion of a system of courts established by the executive, operating according to rules developed in the same branch. Agents of the same branch of government had acted and sought to function as legislator, judge, and executive, and thus, by definition, the military tribunals could not possibly enjoy legitimacy under a constitutional system fundamentally organized around the principle of the separation of the powers of government. Congress therefore must act, since the promulgation of rules for trial is inherently a legislative function.

Interest awaited the Supreme Court's application of the DTA. Congress had in fact taken action: it had unequivocally stripped the courts of their *habeas* powers as to Guantanamo detainees and severely curtailed the judicial power of intervention in the military commission and status review procedures. Nevertheless, the Court evaded these roadblocks by finding the statute to apply only to prospective, not pending cases. This interpretation had the curious effect of transforming "a provision abolishing jurisdiction over all Guantanamo-related habeas petitions into a provision that retains jurisdiction over cases sufficiently numerous to keep the courts busy for years to come."[44] It is particularly strange that the Court should have read legislative intent in this way, since the practical effect of the opinion is to call into question the entire military commission process itself. It is true, the Court in *Hamdan* did not abolish the practice of military commissions per se. It merely rejected the administration's current plan. The administration was free now, and indeed was invited by four of the justices to seek further legislative guidance from Congress. The Court acknowledged that "the DTA obviously 'recognize[s]' the existence of the Guantanamo Bay commissions," but only, it said, "in the weakest sense."

But under a plain, straightforward reading of the DTA statute, the military commission process and the subsidiary CSRT procedures it addresses pertain not to some hypothetical, prospective commission process yet to be established once the hurdle of judicial approval is finally crossed. Indeed, there was no such thing as a "CSRT" process until the developments set in motion by the President's military commission order made it necessary. It is only too clear that the December 2005 statute addresses actual processes as currently established under the executive order. Under the Court's reading, it is as if Congress had intended to curb judicial interference in Guantanamo-related activities, including the military commission process, but still wanted to give the courts a last opportunity, by means of pending cases, to turn the entire statutory exercise represented by the DTA into an anachronous irrelevancy.

Moreover, the Court found that because the alleged conspiracy with which the defendant was charged pre-dated the attacks of 9/11, it therefore could not be considered as an act of war subject to the jurisdiction of a military commission. For reasons that should be apparent by now, it is difficult, both as a matter of constitutional principle and of practical reality, to see how a five-member Court majority's determination as to the nature, timing, and extent of hostilities should command the settled authority it denies to the executive power's interpretations. Though they may take a personal interest as concerned citizens, judges have no professional expertise or constitutional mandate to make such determinations, nor does their mandate include securing a stable and lasting peace, the ends of a just war, in the most effective manner and with the fewest possible casualties.

Alexander Hamilton's reasoning in favor of a vigorous executive bears repeating: "The circumstances that endanger the safety of nations are infinite; and for this reason no constitutional shackles can wisely be imposed on the power to which the care of it is committed. This power ought to be co-extensive with all the possible combinations of such circumstances."[45] As the history of this case demonstrates, the judicial ends of pursuing justice in the individual case do not necessarily move in synch with these other tasks.

Probably the most far-reaching effect of the opinion was to elevate members of al-Qaeda into the protections afforded by the Geneva Prisoner of War Convention. The Court interpreted the relevant applicable provision of international law to be Common Article 3 of the Geneva Conventions. The complete text of Common Article 3 (so-called because the same provision is included in all of the Geneva Conventions) provides:

> In the case of armed conflict not of an international character occurring in the territory of one of the High Contracting Parties, each Party to the conflict shall be bound to apply, as a minimum, the following provisions:
>
> (1) Persons taking no active part in the hostilities, including members of armed forces who have laid down their arms and those placed 'hors de combat' by sickness, wounds, detention, or any other cause, shall in all circumstances be treated humanely, without any adverse distinction founded on race, colour, religion or faith, sex, birth or wealth, or any other similar criteria.
>
> To this end, the following acts are and shall remain prohibited at any time and in any place whatsoever with respect to the above-mentioned persons:
>
> (a) violence to life and person, in particular murder of all kinds, mutilation, cruel treatment and torture;
> (b) taking of hostages;
> (c) outrages upon personal dignity, in particular humiliating and degrading treatment;
> (d) the passing of sentences and the carrying out of executions without previous judgment pronounced by a regularly constituted

court, affording all the judicial guarantees which are recognized as indispensable by civilized peoples.

(2) The wounded and sick shall be collected and cared for.

An impartial humanitarian body, such as the International Committee of the Red Cross, may offer its services to the Parties to the conflict.
The Parties to the conflict should further endeavour to bring into force, by means of special agreements, all or part of the other provisions of the present Convention.
The application of the preceding provisions shall not affect the legal status of the Parties to the conflict.[46]

As the opening clause indicates, this is a provision mainly applicable to internal conflicts such as civil wars—i.e., conflicts occurring "in the territory" of one of the contracting parties—but the Court found it to be pertinent here because of the non-state status of al-Qaeda. Thus, while finding that the defendant violated none of the laws of war, since his conspiracy predated what it deems to be the start date of the conflict, the Court still manages to find international law to be applicable to a conflict it defines as "not of an international character." Granting the questionable premise that the conflict with al-Qaeda cannot be characterized as "international," on the basis of a literal understanding of that term, the Court's reading seems to be that Common Article 3 would apply to everything else but a "conflict between nations," since the commentaries to the GPW suggest that the Common Article should be given as wide a scope as possible.

For the most part this would not prove problematic for the administration or for its plans for the military commissions. In February of 2002, the Bush administration made it an official policy to provide humane treatment to detainees and to apply the GPW as far as possible to detainees belonging to al-Qaeda.[47] The problem comes with interpretation of some of the fine print of Common Article 3. What does vague language such as "regularly constituted court" or "all the judicial guarantees . . . recognized as indispensable by civilized peoples" actually require? And who will decide? Of course, it is the courts who will decide these questions of legal interpretation. There is much scope for litigation here among the undefined, aspirational cadences; "it is not uncommon for legal aspiration to outstrip political reach."[48] How is it possible to avoid the inference that since Common Article 3 applies to any conflict that is not a conflict between nations, its strictures as to "regularly constituted courts" will effectively airbrush the category of military tribunals from legitimate existence? After all, according to Justice Kennedy's interpretation—and the rest of the Court majority agreed—the "regularly constituted courts" of the American system are UCMJ courts-martial. In the Court's view, no "evident practical need" justified deviation from the procedures governing courts-martial, and "for that reason, [the procedures of the military commissions] fail to afford the requisite guarantees of the GPW."

As we observed in the previous chapter, the Third Geneva Convention does limit the potential scope of application of military commissions. Actors qualifying as lawful combatants receive the benefit of trial according to procedures applicable to the detaining nation's own troops. Protocol I, a later treaty provision, further expands the protections afforded to irregular combatants. The United States has refused to join—in large part for this very reason. Protocol I, if ever widely accepted, would impose even greater limitations on the use of commissions. Nevertheless, even if the GPW were (wrongly) interpreted to mean that a government trying all enemy detainees must follow the same procedure used for the trial of its own military members from beginning to final disposition, this still should not rule out the use of military commissions, which the Manual for Courts-Martial (MCM) designates as a valid method for trying U.S. servicemembers. Indeed, the MCM explicitly provides for such use of military commissions in at least two categories of offenses: spying and espionage.[49] But the Court has spoken: this does not make them "regularly constituted courts." It is always difficult to speculate, but it appears that the only time that "evident practical need" will ever justify "deviation" from the full-blown court-martial model will be if the defendant makes an up-front admission to being an illegal enemy combatant. But given the success that recent denials of this very point have obtained in the federal court system, why would any defendant pursue such a strategy of acquiescence?

The argument of many international law specialists is that in the recognition it gives to protection of traditionally unrecognized irregular combatants, Protocol I has become widely accepted as a form of "customary international law." Justice Stevens's opinion tacitly draws on this understanding. But in terms of international law these dubious interpretations of the widespread customary acceptance of a controversial provision of treaty law must be balanced against the abundant, far-reaching evidence of customary practice as evidenced in these studies. The District Court recognized another important principle within this framework of custom and international practice in finding the GPW to be judicially unenforceable. This basic principle of treaty construction is founded not on disregard of international law for individual persons, but on its recognition of the primary importance of nation-states for the responsibility of maintaining international order and security.

As we have seen, international law always distinguished between lawful combatants and bands of terror-raising outlaws. To effectively obliterate such distinctions in the name of humanity, on a "rising tide lifts all boats" theory, might give off the appearance of moral progress. But this blurring of categories simply ignores the well-considered reasons behind making the distinctions in the first place—and the real benefits they afford. Again, strictures requiring the use of discernible uniforms and insignia, command responsibility, open display of arms, and most importantly the conduct of operations according to the customs and laws of war exist to limit and contain the violence, to protect innocents, and to preserve lives. The expansive gesture of apparent magnanimity, in sweeping away such distinctions, inspired perhaps by the model of the heroic criminal defense lawyer, carries heavy consequences in its train. While it may give greater protection to a number of "marauders," it threatens to withdraw protections from whole populations of innocent civilians, for it removes the most potent incentive for compliance with the standards traditionally set for lawful combatants. Orwell's dictum that "every war suffers a kind of progressive degradation with every month that it continues, because such things as individual liberty . . . are simply not compatible with military efficiency" applies here as well. When long-standing distinctions established for the protection of innocents may be flaunted with impunity, it is not just the "individual liberty" of the Hamdans and Rasuls that falls into jeopardy.

As the judges who continue to insist on further legal fine-tuning are well aware, the very reasons for having a special form of wartime adjudication, organized and administered by military forces, are vitiated of sense as the entire process submits to slow dissection on its meander through the courts, as well as being forced into a mold that approximates ever nearer to the domestic criminal trial process.[50] In his opinion for the five-member *Hamdan* majority, Justice Stevens asserted that the very existence of a delay between arrest and formal charging in this case gave the lie to "any urgent need for imposition or execution of judgment." Time has passed, nothing has happened, *ipso facto,* where is the urgent need for expedited tribunals? The mere passage of time skillfully comes to function as a judicially managed referendum on the wisdom of executive decision-making.

Ironically, despite the Court's rejection of the military commission process developed by the Bush administration, Justice Stevens stated near the end of his opinion that the Court did not dispute the government's characterization of Salim Ahmed Hamdan as "a dangerous individual whose beliefs, if acted upon, would cause great harm and even death to innocent civilians, and who would act upon those beliefs if given the opportunity." Nor, significantly, did the Court call into question "the Government's power to detain him for the duration of active hostilities in order to prevent such harm." At the time this work was in its final stages of preparation, the controversy over the military tribunals continued. So did the belligerent activities of the jihadists. Proposals for additional legislation, including amendments to the UCMJ, followed quickly upon the Court's decision, as did fall-back plans for the use of regular courts-martial. On July 13, 2006, apparently in response to the *Hamdan* decision, the Bush administration issued an announcement that it now regards Common Article 3 as applicable to al-Qaeda detainees.[51] Widely viewed as a major shift in policy, a concession in response to the *Hamdan* Court's judicial rebuke, the measure nevertheless failed to win respect for the administration from its critics.

With the passage of the Military commissions Act of 2006, President Bush and Congress together issued a compendious response to the putative deficiencies identified in the *Hamdan* opinion. After some internal congressional squabbles over the precise extent of protections afforded to unlawful combatants under various versions of the proposed legislation, the President signed the act into law on October 17, 2006. The statute seeks to answer, in greater detail than the DTA had done, the Court's concerns about the lack of specific legislative directives for the military commissions.[52]

The Act makes unlawful enemy combatants subject to the jurisdiction of the commissions, which have authority to try offenses committed before, on, or after September 11, 2001.[53] It recognizes the jurisdiction of regular UCMJ courts-martial over lawful combatants.[54] As to the crucial distinction of status, the Act identifies lawful enemy combatant status in terms of long-standing international law criteria: members of regular forces of hostile parties, either recognized or unrecognized by the United States; or members of militia or organized resistance movements, a) under responsible command, b) wearing fixed distinctive signs recognizable at a distance, c) carrying their arms openly, and, d) abiding by the law of war. "Unlawful enemy combatants," then, are those persons engaged in hostilities against the United States, who fail to meet these traditional criteria—including members of the Taliban, al-Qaeda and associates—or who already have been identified as such, prior to the passage of the new Act, by the Combatant Status Review Tribunals.[55] Authority for convening the tribunals rests with the Secretary of Defense or his designates.[56] All commissioned active duty military officers are eligible to serve as members of the commissions. As with regular courts-martial, convening authorities are required to choose those officers who are "best qualified for the duty by reason of age, education, training, experience, length of service, and judicial temperament." Officers with prior involvement in the case of the accused, either as an accuser, investigator, counsel or as a witness, are ineligible for this duty.[57]

The qualifications for military judges, who are non-voting members, mirror the requirements of regular general courts-martial.[58] The same requirements obtain for counsel, both prosecution and defense. The statute also requires verbatim transcripts of the court proceedings, by qualified court reporters, as with general courts-martial. The minimum number of members for the commissions is five, while cases in which the government seeks the death penalty require at least 12 members.[59] The statute prohibits compulsory self-incrimination, grants the accused a right to silence, and excludes statements obtained under torture. Statements obtained under lesser forms of coercion not amounting to "cruel, inhuman or degrading treatment" as prohibited by the DTA, are admissible subject to a totality of the circumstances assessment that measures the statement's reliability, probative value and the interests of justice.[60] The accused also has the right to receive prior notice of the charges, sufficiently far enough in advance of trial to allow for the preparation of the defense's case.[61]

Additional provisions afford the right to present evidence and witnesses, to examine and respond to government evidence, to cross-examine government witnesses, a right to military and, if desired, civilian counsel, and a right to be present at all military commission sessions.[62] Disruptive behavior on the part of the accused may lead to dismissal from the courtroom. With regard to the critical question of hearsay evidence, the law imposes special advance notice requirements on the government, requires that it pass threshold tests of reliability, relevance, probative value, and fairness, and subjects such evidence to the criteria of admissibility applicable in cases of classified information.[63] The statute balances the right of the defense to procure witnesses and evidence with the government's need to protect classified information.[64] Such information sensitive to national security may be privileged from disclosure, in which case the statute allows for practicable substitutes to disclosure. Upon proper motion, demonstration of reliability and suitable justification, the law also allows for evidence to be introduced without revealing classified "sources, methods or activities." [65]

Significantly, the rules impose the highest "beyond reasonable doubt" standard of proof upon the government.[66] A two-thirds majority is required to sustain a conviction, while death penalty cases require unanimity on both findings and sentencing. To impose a penalty of 10 years confinement or more, a concurrence of three-fourths of the voting members is required.[67] Cruel and unusual punishments such as "flogging, branding, marking or tattooing on the body" are prohibited.

Congressional oversight of the process is maintained through a requirement for annual reporting to the Armed Services Committees of both houses of Congress. Reports are to address any trials by military commission in the given reporting year.[68] Additionally, the Congressional committees must be notified of any changes to the military commission process sixty days before the proposed modification goes into effect.[69] Other provisions address the accountability issues that have concerned critics of the process. As with the regular court-martial process, unlawful command influence is expressly prohibited. In addition, the law requires that service on the commission panels must in no way affect officer fitness reports.[70] Detractors might object that these safeguards offer slight guarantee of enforcement. To be sure, those who insist on making such violations perhaps may not be deterred, but as with any preventive law of this type, these violators will be on notice that they are in breach of the law, and subject themselves to scrutiny and sanctions if caught. The larger point to keep in mind is that no further safeguards would be made available if the military commissions were scrapped and replaced with UCMJ general courts-martial.

Moreover, the new statute provides for an extensive appellate review process, in which each case is eligible for review and revision of findings or sentence from the level of the convening authority all the way to the Supreme Court. Convening authority revision of findings or sentence is limited to the reduction or set-aside of a charge or specification, or a suspension, commutation, or reduction of the sentence.[71] Limited interlocutory appeals are allowed to the government in case of judicial termination of proceedings, exclusion of evidence, or on matters relating to classified information. Provision is made in some circumstances for a rehearing, which requires the empanelling of a new board of officers. The law establishes a new appellate layer in the Court of Military Commission Review, panels of which will be comprised of three or more appellate military judges.[72] Exclusive appellate review from the Military Commission Review Courts is vested in the United States Court of Appeals for the District of Columbia Circuit. Writ of Certiorari is obtainable from the D.C. Court of Appeals to the Supreme Court.[73] Accused will be appointed appellate counsel for representation throughout the appellate process. Presidential approval is required for every death sentence, and execution of the sentence may only occur after final judgment is entered and the appellate process is finally exhausted.[74]

The statute contains a list of offenses triable by the military commissions, which aligns closely with earlier renderings: enumerated crimes include the murder of protected persons; murder or inflicting serious bodily injury in violation of the laws of war; destruction of property in violation of the laws of war; attacking civilians, civilian objects, and/or protected property; pillaging; denying quarter; taking hostages; employing poison or similar weapons; using protected persons or property as a shield; torture; cruel or inhuman treatment; use of treachery or perfidy; improper use of a flag of truce or other distinctive emblems [like the symbol of the International Red Cross]; intentional mistreatment of a dead body; rape; sexual assault or abuse; hijacking or hazarding a vessel or aircraft; terrorism and providing material support for terrorism;[75] wrongfully aiding the enemy; spying and conspiracy.[76]

With the exception of the provisions on hearsay admissibility and protection of classified sources, virtually every level of this process emulates the full array of protections of the regular courts-martial process.

The statute addresses critical questions of treaty interpretation raised by *Hamdan*. As mentioned above, a basic long-standing international law principle of treaty construction recognizes that the primary parties to an international treaty are the signatory states, and not private individuals. Thus, unless they contain express language to the contrary, international treaties do not vest individual persons with claims of right or causes of action against governments. The new statute reinvigorates this fundamental principle, destabilized by the *Hamdan* majority: "No person may invoke the Geneva Conventions or any protocols thereto in any habeas corpus or other civil action or proceeding [involving the United States or its representatives as a party] as a source of rights" in any U.S. court.[77] A further provision of the statute seals off U.S. courts from the judicial introduction of extraneous readings (i.e. the interpretations of foreign or international courts) in determining the extent of U.S. compliance with its obligations under Common Article 3 of the Third Geneva Convention: "No foreign or international source of law shall supply a basis for a rule of decision in the courts of the United States in interpreting the [enumerated] prohibitions [of the War Crimes Act]."[78] Further, the statute reinvests interpretative authority in the president as to the meaning and application of the Geneva Conventions.[79] As we have previously noted, such corrections simply recognize the importance and priority of nation-states for the maintenance of peace, order, and security in a dangerous, often unstable world. Moreover, the changes acknowledge basic constitutional division of labor principles: that international affairs, such as the conduct of war and diplomacy, the punishment of violations of the law of war, and the scope and tenor of the nation's adherence to its treaty obligations, are the special province of the political branches.[80]

Controversy over the new statute has centered on its *habeas corpus* provisions, which appear toward the end of the statute. Significantly, these provisions amend the Federal *Habeas* Statute, which provides a separate track for *habeas* petitions apart from the provisions of the U.S. Constitution. Thus, Constitutional *habeas* provisions remain in full force, and are not affected by the adaptations of the Military Commissions Act. Since the *habeas* guarantees of the U.S. Constitution have been interpreted to pertain to citizens and resident aliens, and never to alien enemy combatants, petitioners in this category necessarily have to follow the tracks provided by the Federal statute, which is always subject to further legislative revision. As it did here with Section 2241 of Title 28 of the United States Code, i.e., Federal statutory habeas corpus, Congress is free to amend its own legislative acts. Unlawful enemy combatants have never had a right to *habeas corpus* petition under the United States Constitution. Therefore no such right is being denied to them. Critics of the Act fail to make this important distinction.

As we have seen, it was the *Rasul* decision which was the innovation, for it recognized for the first time, a *statutory* habeas right in foreign nationals captured and held overseas in the course of enemy combat operations. Significantly, in passing the Military Commissions Act, Congress did not purport to reverse the Court's ruling in *Rasul*. In its revision of statutory *habeas corpus* provisions, the new statute simply reinforces the mechanism, previously established and recognized for addressing such petitions under the DTA of 2005—that is to say, the Combatant Status Review Tribunal process. As we have seen, the DTA does not foreclose detainees from appeals beyond the CSRT panels. It simply channels such appeals to the D.C. Circuit, and beyond through writ of certiorari to the Supreme Court.

Such a narrowing of detainee options was well within the purview of Congressional authority. This is the effective meaning of the new law's pronouncement curtailing judicial intervention in the war against terror: "No court, justice, or judge shall have jurisdiction to hear or consider an application for a writ of habeas corpus filed by or on behalf of an alien detained by the United States who has been determined by the United States to have been properly detained as an enemy combatant or is awaiting such determination."[81] A similar provision addresses judicial intervention into questions regarding "detention, transfer, treatment, trial, or conditions of confinement" of such alien combatants.[82]

Together these new provisions seek to wrest the supervision of the conduct of war away from judges, and put it back with the political branches. The message and language of the previous Detainee Treatment Act, which the Court had deemed insufficiently precise, is now bolstered and amplified. Although the measure may appear controversial, it surely comports with the long-recognized constitutional distribution of powers. As we have seen, the characteristic judicial focus on private, individual claims of right ill suits members of the judiciary to levels of oversight that have direct bearing on the tactical and strategic dimensions of military decision-making in war and on international relations in time of peace. It has been the argument throughout this book that the forms and practices of military tribunals developed out of just such a recognition. Whether this insight survives the internal attacks and litigation of domestic critics will have serious implications for the success of the nation's efforts in time of war—both in the current actions against jihadist terror and in any future conflicts.

The qualities identified by Alexander Hamilton as critical to a well-functioning executive—"decision, activity, secrecy, and dispatch"—mirror the occasional needs to which, in time of extremity, military tribunals have been traditionally suited. In his *Hamdan* dissent, Justice Thomas put the question of the compatibility of these qualities with the habits and practices of legalistic casuistry in some perspective: "Those Justices who today disregard the commander-in-chief's wartime determinations, only 10 days ago deferred to the judgment of the Corps of Engineers with regard to a matter much more within the competence of lawyers, upholding that agency's wildly implausible conclusion that a storm drain is a tributary of the waters of the United States. [Citations omitted.] It goes without saying that there is much more at stake here than storm drains."[83]

These developments have brought the future of military commissions in American practice very much into doubt. This much appears certain: it will be impossible to seal off the final resolution of the matter from the political and military circumstances prevailing at the time of decision. The current debate over military commissions is not finally over whether the order and rules promulgated for their use meet certain technical requirements of international or domestic law. It is really over whether the onward progressive march of international legal institutions has rendered such nationally constituted tribunals an anachronism, in the words of one critic, a relic of "the dark days of history when the fate of the captive rested on the whim of their captors."[84]

The Future of Military Commissions

Principles of *jus in bello* recognize that the first-order agents of its implementation are military commanders, officers, and other personnel themselves.[85] The tradition acknowledges military forces as the front-line custodians of the tablets of law of war principles. This requires a certain modicum of cooperative effort on the part of warring opponents. Both sides have an interest in ensuring the fair treatment of their own prisoners; both have a stake in insuring against the downward spiral of accelerated violent reprisal actions; and so forth. In this regard, the military tribunals function as a version of the classic of game theory, the Prisoner's Dilemma. Within the circle of the military professional caste, incentives exist for the "cooperative" maintenance of a practice that ensures the application of rational, predetermined, neutral procedures (albeit streamlined), to the adjudication of enemy war crimes. These studies trace the contours of a customary law of intra-conflict war crimes adjudication, with the military tribunals functioning as a critical node of "communication," in Lon Fuller's sense, between hostile parties.[86]

Yet the specter of "defection" can never be eradicated. Especially in the brutal twentieth century, the cooperative outcome has faltered, as in the First World War, when the French use of military tribunals to address law of war violations by German combatants led to retaliatory measures against French prisoners-of-war. The German retaliation was so severe that it finally caused the usage of French conseils-de-guerre—for this purpose at least—to dry up altogether. In this intra-European context, presumably, the French move was meant to prompt a corresponding relaxation of stringent responses on the part of the adversary. Although the "Boche" enemy was proving to be unscrupulous in regard to long-standing military practices, Germany remained an adversary with whom the French shared a long history of common tradition and culture. The French and their Allies still deemed it possible to influence the opposition, to prompt a rational, calculated response that would inure to the Allies' benefit through the discontinuation of a specific practice. The same cannot be said with regard to opponents who routinely violate fundamental law of war principles for the ostensible purpose of wearing down their enemies' will to resist, as al-Qaeda have done in the current war on terror.[87] In such conditions, the explanatory powers of the "rational actor" model, upon which game theorists rely in predicting human behavior, breaks down.[88] For all the insistence, from certain observers, on the medieval quality of radical jihadist terror, the irony is that the medieval model of the chivalric code is too "rational," too "civilized" to fit.[89]

The practices examined in these studies appear to confirm the thesis of Jack Goldsmith and Eric Posner that "the payoffs from cooperation or deviation are the sole determinants of whether states engage in the cooperative behaviors that are labeled customary international law," and thus that customary international law, while it does exist, "is not an exogenous influence on state behavior."[90] As we have seen, one historian of the Mexican War concluded that General Scott's order establishing the American military commissions was drawing upon an "unwritten Martial Law," partaking of a "natural law as applied within the military sphere."[91] In a case arising out of occupied Germany after the Second World War, the Supreme Court made a similar determination, identifying the military commissions as "our common law war courts."[92]

This custom has been a "law" that the participants to conflict have routinely developed and modified according to circumstance, often as a form of "bilateral cooperation" and attended by occasional breakdowns. The asymmetrical character of guerrilla warfare we noted in the Boer War—the conflict that proved an ominous harbinger of things to come in so many different ways—is heightened and amplified in the current war on terror.[93] This asymmetry extends to the manner in which the two sides administer "justice" toward captured enemy adherents. America and its Western allies wrangle over the sufficiency of procedural and substantive safeguards for the trial and treatment of enemy detainees, even those identified as illegal combatants under the traditional understanding of the laws of war. Their opponents, illegally organized underground non-state actors, take captive American and allied troops, civilian journalists, aid workers, and other non-combatants without discrimination, subject them to torture, and then execute them without trial as part of a standard operational strategy.[94] A perceived asymmetry, which effectively shut down the French utilization of the conseils de guerre for the trial of German combatants in the First World War, now resurfaces in grotesque magnification. The calculated reduction in reprisal actions anticipated by the French in 1915 could not be expected from a similar exercise of self-restraint today.

What this potential for breakdown portends for the future of the law of war remains to be seen. Much of the force of international law—its "bite"—customarily derives from a recognition on the part of state actors that acceptance of its precepts invites and encourages a reciprocal response from other nations. This recognition has formed the basis of arguments in favor of U.S. ratification of and adherence to a whole variety of international treaties.[95] Indeed, it undergirds many of the arguments against the use of anything short of UCMJ courts-martial against captured al-Qaeda combatants.[96] The effect of such arguments, to draw a rough line of equivalence between the "procedures" used, e.g., by the Somali warlord Mohammed Aidid against U.S. Warrant Officer Michael Durant in 1993, and those of the new U.S. military commissions, does not bear up under scrutiny.[97] According to this argument, the United States exhibits a lack of good faith in seeking protections under the GPW for its soldier Durant, while it parsimoniously denies similar protections to detainees like Hamdan. The unspoken assumptions underlying the argument are that the treatment of the two captives was essentially similar and that no legal or moral justification exists for making any distinction between the two cases.

The prevalence of just these kinds of arguments within the professional class of military lawyers evinces the conclusions of Kenneth Anderson that "US military lawyers need to move beyond the practice of conducting pragmatic, realist negotiations while seeking approval from the moral arbiters among the NGOs [non-governmental organizations] and Europeans . . . US military lawyers need to understand that they will never be counted as part of the 'good guys' whenever their views diverge—as, of necessity, they will—from what NGOs and demilitarized European states think the law is and should be. It is a profound mistake for the representatives of the US to hold a sort of emotional torch, hoping to be let into a church from which they will always be, in some way, excommunicated, because they represent an actor who must deal with power and not merely abstract morality."[98] Given a situation in which one's chief opponent is not a nation-state at all, but an international terror network, exhibiting no inclination to adhere to law of war principles, the argument from reciprocity loses its persuasive punch.

This conclusion does not necessarily project us outside the orbit of international law. Sobriety as to the likelihood of exerting ameliorative pressure on the adversary's conduct does not militate against use of the same measures as a means to other ends not immediately cashing out in terms of influence upon the opposition. It is on the basis of such arguments, e.g., that the rule of law means nothing unless it is strictly adhered to even against those who are most ruthless in their efforts to undermine it—that critics mount their arguments against a contemporary reinstatement of national military tribunals.[99] But neither does the non-state status of al-Qaeda justify forcing juridical questions arising out of this conflict into the Procrustean bed of the domestic criminal trial model. The false antithesis lurking behind such choices ignores the elastic nature of the well-developed concept of "due process" in American jurisprudence. There exists a whole range of approaches, depending for instance on the nature of the proceeding, the status of the accused, whether or not there is a victim, and if so, the status of the victim, the severity and location of the offense, and the extent of harm. The "present contours" of the rights conferred by the Constitution, "having been shaped far more by judicial interpretation than by the literal text (which doesn't define such critical terms as 'due process of law' and 'unreasonable' arrests and searches), are alterable in response to changing threats to national security."[100]

Given the "communication" problems posed by the specter of reprisals, evidence of customary practice has assisted in setting acceptable boundaries. As we have seen, a fairly common charge levied by the Allied military tribunals of the Second World War had to do with the violation of accepted standards of process for the trial of prisoners of war. More cases in the UNWCC reports from the Eastern theater dealt with the offense of illegal trials and unlawful killings than any other single charge.

In these trials, the defendants themselves routinely argued in their defense not in terms of the non-existence of such common standards of practice, but, contrary to the contention of Allied charging authorities, on their own adherence to them. All sides to these litigated disputes presupposed the existence of a standard of procedural fairness, with which earlier Japanese trials of Allied POWs had or had not complied. None disputed the legitimacy of the practice itself. All gave tacit support to the notion of a customary standard of procedure in time of war.

There were significant variations in the process applied by the allied military courts, and there may not have been 100 percent agreement as to all the procedural elements of a fair trial, but the characteristics of an unfair one were plain and obvious. In a manner analogous to the *jus in bello* principle of proportionality, the differences came to be seen as a matter of scale. When the enormity of the injustice of Axis "trials" was in view, the relatively minor procedural differences among the Allied tribunals fell into perspective. Moreover, the flaws, such as they were, tended to arise not as the arbitrary abuse of power, but as the tragic result of a necessary pragmatic calculus of ends fitted to limited knowledge, means, and resources. In a case like the Belsen trial, to do away with hearsay evidence or restrict its admission in order to bring the tribunals into greater conformity with civilian procedure would have meant the loss of invaluable testimony through the silencing of hundreds, even thousands of victims. In the extraordinary conditions of war, this too would have worked an egregious wrong—a wrong as to innocents, the very people the laws of war exist primarily to protect.

Careful, conscientious distinctions are possible, and they must be made in the course of making responsible judgments. Little is gained by setting in abstraction the discrete category labeled "military tribunals" as a subject for analysis across national, historical, and cultural boundaries. These studies have identified profound differences even within the experience of the Western democracies. Most striking, of course, is the French record, linked to larger distinctive features of its legal and military culture. As we have noted in chapter three, long before the advent of the German declaration of war in August 1914, the rudiments of organization for a French military governmental system were set in place. The rare, but constitutionally-sanctioned declaration of a "state of siege" functioned as a switch, producing a radical and instantaneous change in which the military exercised largely unfettered discretionary authority at all levels of government. This model, we have seen, went well beyond the phenomenon of military courts running parallel to the normal civil system. Rather, the "switch" brought about military control over law enforcement, policing, and a variety of local government functions. Recall René David's statement, issued in the early days of the Fifth French Republic, that "a Frenchman will allow the government a degree of discretion, and even arbitrariness, that is hard to reconcile with the certainty characteristic of legal principles. The assumption predominates that society's interest requires that one trust the police."[101] It helps to explain a transformation that is much more difficult to achieve in countries that follow the Anglo-American common law tradition. The difference hinges, in part, on the relatively greater authority, prestige, and power enjoyed by the courts in this tradition; and partly on the fundamental nature of the public-private distinction in nations adhering to the Napoleonic tradition of the *Droit Civile.*

Along these same lines, notwithstanding the existence of localized temporary and partial precedents such as martial rule in Hawaii after Pearl Harbor, it is very difficult to imagine American military forces ever being equipped to take over state and local government, police, and court functions across the United States—the military simply isn't configured that way. Indeed, since its adoption by Congress in 1878, the statutory doctrine of *posse comitatus* exists to prevent the military usurpation of civil police functions.[102] Large sections of the United States—New England, for instance—contain very little military presence whatsoever. To be sure, the National Guard does provide some of this militia structure at the state level, but it would require a huge overhaul and a vast, politically infeasible expansion of military resources in order to accomplish the military take-over of regional, state, and local civil government functions that French authorities deemed prudent to build into their strategic planning in the years leading up to the Great War.[103] The psychological and sociological significance of shared borders alongside a large, powerful, and perennially hostile nation cannot be underestimated. Largely because of the blessings of geography and of geopolitical circumstance, it has never been necessary in the United States to think along the lines of a "shadow" parallel military government—a phenomenon which appears to have been more of the norm in civil law nations. All of this contextual background, critical for making important distinctions, is lost in the chorus of criticisms equating recent American attempts to utilize military commissions in the war against al-Qaeda with the experiences of military tribunals in Latin America and other nations of the developing world.[104]

The observation evinces Montesquieu's assertions on the differences in laws generated by climate, geography, economic conditions, and social circumstances.[105]

These differences mix into a complex blend generated by the corporate experience of the military itself. The point is made with force by Alistair Horne in examining France's eight-year ordeal in the Algerian conflict. The "shocking disaffection within the French army" which eventually culminated in a "full-scale revolt" becomes more understandable in the light of a turbulent and at times humiliating institutional history: "Since the execution of Louis XVI in 1793, the French army had been subject to the First Republic, the Directory, the Consulate, the First Empire, the First and Second Restorations, the 'Bourgeois Monarchy' of Louis-Philippe, the Second Republic, the Second Empire, the Commune, the Third Republic, Petain's Vichy and de Gaulle's Free French Committee, the Fourth Republic and now the Fifth Republic. Each change of regime had contributed fresh schisms within the army, and added new confusion as to where loyalties were ultimately due—a compound of experience shared by no other army in the world (outside, perhaps, Latin America)."[106]

The difference traced here discloses a further irony—rooted in the fact that war is not a permanent, unbroken condition. Methods recognized as legitimate only on rare and extraordinary occasions are more likely to become rusty, unwieldy, inefficient, even dangerous—not to mention, a more difficult political sell—in the event that, after long disuse, they are finally retrieved and implemented. Whatever its faults, the systematic, constitutionally recognized model represented by the *état de siège* could not fairly be criticized as a clumsy, makeshift arrangement.

While the "state of siege" existed as a legal arrangement provided for by statute in France, Anglo-American use of military tribunals functioned as the result of ad hoc adaptation to the particular circumstances of time and place. In the Mexican War, it was the need to have a means of exercising control over U.S. army troops occupying a foreign territory that led to the adoption of military commissions. In the American Civil War, it was the lawless conditions in the border states. In the Second World War, it was the huge unprecedented volume of war crimes offenders, the thousands of cases that needed to be dealt with. All of these situations presented unprecedented and unusual circumstances, which the normal civil and military court systems were ill-equipped to address. Nor did these examples present an exhaustive list of possible uses. The military commissions served in such conditions as a flexible tool, "adapted in each instance to the need that called it forth"[107]—an extralegal, emergency military stop gap, to be assessed and evaluated within the general terms of the category of military necessity.

At least some of the confusion surrounding the amorphous "war on terror" results from a perceived need for politic indirection in identifying the opposition in the current war. Perhaps a better and more accurate characterization would acknowledge what amounts to a new and virulent resurgence of fascism, now wearing the face of an aberrant militant Islam.[108] It must be acknowledged that while "[m]ost Muslims are not fundamentalists, and most fundamentalists are not terrorists," nevertheless, "most present-day terrorists are Muslims and proudly identify themselves as such."[109] Problems of classification are compounded by the fact that the religious character of the war aims of al-Qaeda and its supporters tends to escape the comprehension of Western elites,[110] who minimize the relevance or significance of religion in public life generally and insist the "root causes" motivating militant radical Islamic groups must be sought elsewhere, perhaps in terms of structural economic inequality or poverty.[111] As we have suggested, a close historical analogy does exist, in the wars on piracy of the nineteenth century. In any event, contemporaneous disclosures surrounding the United Nations' mismanagement of the "oil for food" program in Iraq—the "colossal swindle in which Saddam Hussein embezzled some $21 billion in oil money over a dozen years"—bureaucratic corruption in the secretariat, and sex-trafficking, rape, and abuse on the part of UN peacekeepers in the Congo and elsewhere,[112] together give scope for skepticism on whether the dangers and problems associated with the use of military tribunals would dissolve with their displacement by international substitutes. The problem of accountability does not disappear with the simple transfer of authority from commanders in the field to supranational institutions. As Goldsmith and Posner suggest, "international law is a real phenomenon, but international law scholars exaggerate its power and significance."[113] The same holds for supra-national institutions.

Those who would disparage the continuing relevance of nation-states in confronting the phenomenon of international terror neglect to the peril of the civilized world the important function states and organized military forces exercise in containing and limiting violence. As Michael Ignatieff has observed: "In the Western antiwar tradition, we are so used to thinking of the state as an agent of violence, as the instigator of war, that we forget the state's other historical role in our own development, which was to confiscate weaponry from the militias and retinues of the medieval warrior barons and to secure to a single authority the monopoly over the legitimate use of force. However paradoxical it may sound, the police and armies of the nation-state remain the only available institutions we have ever developed with the capacity to control and channel large-scale human violence."[114] The Supreme Court's determination to make Common Article 3 a basis for litigation on the part of individuals in the courts of foreign nation-states tends to disparage this important role by providing individual litigants a ready avenue for side-stepping the entire apparatus of the state system. It is an experiment fraught with uncertain and potentially dangerous consequences.

Presuppositions and Consequences

As Aristotle long ago remarked, the initial trajectory determined by one's starting points exerts momentous impact on all that follows. The period under consideration in this book saw a series of "revolutions in military affairs"—revolutions wrought by technological, social, and institutional change, attended by corresponding changes in attitudes and perceptions on the nature of human warfare.[115] We have examined a small slice of the operational decision-making landscape faced by a wide variety of Western commanders, civilian and military leaders, courts, and other participants. Leaders such as Lincoln and Kitchener, Joffre and Roosevelt characteristically worked from a tragic conception of the intransigence of human conflict and violence and maintained a corresponding modesty as to the possibilities for achieving justice at the international and individual level amidst the carnage of modern warfare. The context provided by these studies amply demonstrates the salience of this tragic element. At every turn, with the passing of every moment, the actors in this account run up against limits—limits imposed by the uncertainty and insufficiency of information (or perhaps by its surfeit); by the spatial, physical circumstances of terrain, logistics, and manpower; by the ongoing counter-activities of the opponent; by domestic and international political considerations; by the moral and intellectual character of opponents; by their own. Perhaps more unyielding than any of these, indeed super-adding a dimension of complexity to the whole, are the limits imposed by the incessant forward movement of time itself. It was the sheer passage of time, in the midst of a psychologically wearing guerrilla struggle, compressing the decisional matrix of the commander Kitchener, that led to stern measures against Gideon Scheepers. Time, and the healing brought by a prudentially orchestrated peace, allowed the *Milligan* court a luxury it probably could not have countenanced in 1863.

The furniture of judicial procedure invariably produces a time lag between a given offense and its punishment—"the law's delay." Whatever the extent to which human justice could ever approach absolute proportions, the inescapable human element of time introduces a factor of depreciation into the calculus of its attainment in any given case. Justice must also be perceived as such. With nations as with individuals, an important value attached to the punishment of atrocities or war crimes lies in what George Kennan in the aftermath of the Second World War emphasized as its "swift and incisive [and] . . . immediate" character.[116] If justice is to have exemplary effect, the causal connection between offense and punishment must not be allowed to dissolve in the minds of those intended to benefit from the lesson. When the punishment of a war crime lags indefinitely behind the triggering event, the actual crime itself, the potential for a curious inversion of categories increases profoundly. The perpetrator of atrocities slowly and steadily metamorphoses into a kind of victim. The war criminal's erstwhile victims, at least those still alive, and those who try him, face either the prospect of oblivion or of reconstitution as a type of "aggressor" themselves. The spectacle of long, elaborate trials—expanded indefinitely, as at the end of the Second World War, by the volume of potential cases—can invoke a perverse whipsaw effect, by which the end goal, justice, comes to be viewed almost in inverse proportion to the expenditure of time and procedural energy exerted for the purpose of bringing it about. In such an event, both victims and the greater public are ill served by a proceeding which by its very nature tends to the dissolution of the very presuppositional link between act and consequence that had brought it into being in the first place. The problem resurfaced in recent years with the trial of the former leader of the Federal Republic of Yugoslavia, Slobodan Milošević, in the Hague International War Crimes Tribunal. The achievement represented by the capture and indictment of the former Serb leader before the ad hoc international tribunal led some to call the event "a triumph for the new world order." After Milošević's arrest in April 2001 and initial entries of pleas, his trial began in February, 2002. The prosecution took 296 days to present its case. Milošević's defense opened on August 31, 2004. Over a year later, he claimed to have presented only ten percent of his case. Of course, the whole process came to an abrupt end when Milošević was found dead in his cell at the Hague, on March 11, 2006. Over the years, the never-completed trial "had the effect [while the defendant was still alive] of once again making Milošević a popular figure where once he was thoroughly discredited." Moreover, the international justice approach of singling out individual war criminals for trial altogether left to the side "those who need to be held accountable and to build up a domestic culture of the rule of law . . . —the states in the Balkans, including Serbia."[117]

In this brief space I do not necessarily mean to weigh in on one side or the other as to the merits or relative fairness of the proceedings against Milošević, or on the question of the relative culpability of the Serbian state; nor do I mean to argue that a national (Bosnian?) military tribunal should have been the forum of choice for a trial. The case, however, does point rather effectively to the problems involved in converting matters of international relations, politics, and diplomacy into the stuff of a protracted criminal litigation. Even if one posits a litigation scenario in which unlimited time and resources could be given to both sides so that each were able to present its "perfect" case—in the patois of law and economics, the condition in which there are zero "transaction costs"—this would in no way guarantee that its outcome would achieve the right balance in the larger context of politics and international relations that exists and continues to function outside the walls of the courtroom—i.e., the balance of comprehensive justice. Indeed, given the forward movement of time *outside* the courtroom, there is every reason to believe that the opposite is just as likely to be the case.

Consider also the trial of Saddam Hussein, in process during the preparation of this book. A propos of the trial of the former Baathist dictator of Iraq, Charles Krauthammer sharply criticized the "bungling" of the Bush administration: "Instead of Hussein's crimes being on trial, he has succeeded in putting the new regime on trial. The lead story of every court session has been his demeanor, his defiance, his imperiousness . . . he struts. And we are witness to a political test of wills between the new Iraq represented by an as-yet incompetent judicial system and the would-be tyrant-for-life defiantly raising once again the banner of Baathism, on a world-wide stage afforded him *by us.*"[118]

All of these problems are compounded by the facility with which the defendant is able to exploit the channels of modern communications to his own advantage, regardless of the forum chosen. Full-blown international tribunals, like Milošević's, serve as a stage for garnering world attention to the cause. Civil trials in national courts, like Saddam's, though in some ways a better solution, still can be indefinitely prolonged, transmogrifying into a mockery of justice. As Orwell observed in 1943, "the trial of war criminals, with all the slow cruel pageantry of the law, . . . after a lapse of time has so strange a way of focusing a romantic light on the accused and turning a scoundrel into a hero."

Enlisting the aid of a vigorous tradition of critique that forms such a significant part of the Western liberal democracies' practice and experience, the savvy enemy can subject any form of military tribunals, no matter how elaborate, to a withering war of attrition, rhetorically applying the skirmishing tactics that the Boers found so effective against the British army in the veld, calling the world's attention to the stings of an injustice here, a procedural shortcoming there. The continuation of war by means of litigation tends to equalize disparately endowed opponents and assists in bringing publicity and even sympathy to the cause of the defendant. Justice Jackson's warnings from the 1940's remain applicable today: "There are many appeals these days to liberty, often by those who are working for an opportunity to taunt democracy with its stupidity in furnishing them the weapons to destroy it . . . "[119] A well-developed rhetoric of "social justice," developed over decades of American constitutional criminal procedure litigation, becomes available for exploitation by the creative litigant-combatant.

The observation, reiterated throughout this work, that the activities of war do not readily transpose to the idiom of the courtroom points to another less tangible element. Military strategists and historians from Clausewitz to Liddell Hart to Keegan, Davis Hanson, and Worden in the contemporary era, emphasize the psychological dimension of war, the indirect, yet powerful manner in which "the psychological permeates and dominates the physical sphere."[120] Of course there is a psychology of trial that affects everything from jury selection to trial strategy and tactics. But a domestic court system, by definition, enjoys a relative position of sealed separation, defining the parameters and meting out justice within a self-contained sphere. Jury members are sequestered from news media and all outside sources of information about the case. Cameras and recorders are prohibited from the courtroom. In the pursuit of the ideal of impartial justice, the deliberations of law courts adhere to the demands of an internal logic, immunized as much as possible from the interference of exogenous influences. In an important sense, the normal passage of time is suspended in the civil courtroom. Such a luxury never obtains for the operational commander in the midst of war—porous as he is against the onslaught of circumstances, over many of which he has little control.[121] The psychology of battle extends in all directions. Outside events affect the tenor and shape of a campaign, and the influence is reciprocal.

The spectacle of trials of enemy combatants cannot be somehow sequestered as an anomalous exception. It was awareness of this reality that prompted the *Quirin* Court to rule in the manner it did. As odious as the thought may be to some well-meaning pacifists and legalists, a unanimous and instant opinion—only to be followed at a later time by an elaboration of the rationale—was deemed valuable for preserving and delivering a unified response. This gesture on the part of the Court is often characterized as an unsavory, limp obsequiousness before the wartime executive. But it is possible to view it differently. For it contained a recognition that the Court's opinion was not to affect merely these defendants, but that, as a development in time of war, it could exert psychological repercussions—a ripple effect, subtle, indirect, yet real, though at far remove from the immediate participants. No one on the Court would have presumed to consider the opinion as a belligerent act in support of the nation's war-fighting effort. It was not. But the opinion exhibited a sense of modesty about the limits of judicial vision, as well as a candid acknowledgment of the fundamental irresponsibility animating the old maxim *fiat justitia, ruat coelum.*[122] Moreover, by virtue of the relative speed and unanimity with which the case was resolved, the morale of a nation involved in a two-front war against formidable and ruthless adversaries was not slowly and imperceptibly drained away through endless internal squabbling over the fate of a handful of hapless enemy spies.

The incommensurability of an opponent's capacity for rational action, evident in the current conflict, applies along the full range of options. The difficulty of achieving the required balance between the demands imposed by military and political circumstances, and the demands of justice and procedural fairness, like the difficulty of evaluating the proportionality of a military action under the strictures of the laws of armed conflict, must not be underestimated. Yet the difficulty of assessment in no way removes the obligation. That Western military commanders and political leaders, operating within a long-standing tradition and climate of critical self-appraisal, military legal process, and civilian oversight, have been largely successful in maintaining the balance in the midst of war and in its aftermath is the deposit left by the substance of these studies.

But there is another point of departure, opening from the supposition of the essentially aberrational character of warfare. From this "progressive" and "optimistic" standpoint, recognition of the place of the military tribunal in the toolkits of military and political leaders ignores greater possibilities for a world—borrowing from the domestic sphere—in which disputes are no longer settled by resort to violence, but by the orderly processes of courts of law—or to put it more bluntly, of a world in which law swallows up war, and renders it progressively obsolete. It is not hard to see how this view would nourish skepticism and even hostility toward attempts to "dust off" the record of usage of military tribunals, for acknowledgment of their legitimacy, even in strictly limited circumstances, seems to provide justification to a whole chain of suppositions that begins with the objectionable assertion of the constancy and inevitability of human warfare.

It is the "progressive" vision that characterizes much of the *Hamdan* decision, where the Court found the military commission structure established by President Bush to be illegitimate, despite a fairly elaborate formal trial process, numerous privileges and protections to defendants, its provision for multi-level administrative review, and the opportunity for appellate and Supreme Court review. The full effect of *Hamdan*, and of subsequent statutory responses, remains to be seen, but the Court's practical suspicion as to the existence of a category of offenders and offenses that would require truncating the full protections of internal domestic courts-martial calls into question the very reason for the existence of military tribunals as traditionally constituted in prior conflicts.

This conflict between what I have called the "tragic" and "progressive" visions[123] promises to continue to shape the ongoing dialogue over specific methods for adjudicating offenses against the laws of war.

Contrasts with Civilian Justice

As this study has shown, the nature of the wartime adjudicative enterprise, as a matter of international political and military import, requires a different set of skills and expertise than are available to most lawyers. Expertise in the domestic legal arena is only of limited value here. Because these cases involve specifically military offenses, violations of the laws of armed conflict, tribunals that are military in nature are uniquely suited to address such offenses. The military officers who sit on the panels receive regular training in the laws of armed conflict, have experience with the nature and scope of military operations, and live and move within the world of customary practices, habits, attitudes, and convictions that inform the lives of those serving in the army, the navy, and the air force. It is naive to expect civilians untutored in the laws of war, unfamiliar with and immune from the unique stresses and vicissitudes of the military life, and foreign to the practices of warfare nevertheless somehow to exercise sound judgment in assessing transgressions of these customs and practices. The presumption that civilian tribunals, simply by virtue of their non-military character, would operate at a higher level of equity and fairness lacks warrant.[124] Indeed, it is interesting to note the frequency with which contemporary criticisms of the military juridical processes examined in these pages tended to center not on their harshness, but on their excessive leniency or on the insufficiency of their attentiveness to the military realities on the ground. Apart from a handful of notable exceptions, the distance and comfort allowed by the passage of time alone allowed for the isolated consideration of the circumstances of individuals who appeared before the tribunals. Yet the benefit realized by the concentrated focus on specific defendants runs the danger of ignoring the specific limits that formed the reality of the decision-makers at the time. Appeals to a handful of cases in which the tool suffered abuse do not thereby render it useless.

The crux of the problem is that jurists trained to measure the value of a trial in the technical terms of its adherence to procedural standards are ill equipped to see beyond the limits of narrow legalistic categories. The yardstick of procedural correctness simply fails to provide a sufficient index of the worth and value of a given proceeding, as an historical phenomenon taking place within, and itself shaping, the unfolding international political and military matrix.

For the foreseeable future, the commander who voices skepticism as to the reality of law's triumph over war may be forgiven his incredulity.[125] Gary Bass tacitly connects to the same point in his summary of recent legalistic efforts to address the major international crises of the 1990s: "In the last analysis, the two international war crimes tribunals in The Hague and Arusha stand largely as testaments to the failure of America and the West. Had the West managed to summon the political will to stop the slaughters in Rwanda and Bosnia, there would have been no need for these two fragile experiments in international justice."[126] The very fact of the need for *ex post facto* adjudication has frequently arisen in the aftermath of political failure. This side of the political calculus seldom receives a hearing in the advocacy for a new internationalized criminal system. Yet as subsequent events in Afghanistan and Iraq have shown, the prior active exercise of political will carries in its train a different and equally complex knot of problems. The decision to respond proactively, to prevent atrocities before they happen, means that commanders, and their political superiors, get dirt and blood on their hands. No simple solutions exist.[127]

It may remain difficult to ascertain with certitude the reason why the belligerents who masterminded the September 2001 massacres have failed to mount further subsequent attacks on U.S. soil. Still, the chosen method of dealing with terrorists throughout the 1990s, *viz.*, the domestic criminal trial system, resulted in only a handful of terrorists being brought to account, at considerable expense, measured in terms of time and resources. More importantly, the terrorist trials of the 1990s demonstrably failed to deter the escalating chain of attacks on U.S. interests leading up to the calamity of September 11, 2001. The means of the occasional domestic criminal trial could not secure the just ends of lasting peace and a stable international order, ends that help to legitimize the resort to war. Even without an airtight cause-effect explanation sufficient to satisfy the rigors of the beyond reasonable doubt standard, the political or military decision-maker, as always having to *act*, and to do so on the basis of incomplete knowledge, would be irresponsible to disregard these connections.

We have already mentioned Aristotle in another context. The foregoing observations bring to mind his characterization of the justice process of the courts. For it is in the very nature of a criminal trial to be retrospective in its focus. Precedents might be established for application in future cases, but the primary function of a trial is to dispense justice with respect to some prior series of actions on the part of a limited number of individuals, according to predetermined clearly defined standards of criminal conduct.[128] This backward-looking perspective, perfectly appropriate and even necessary in the arena of the domestic criminal trial, shrinks—when transferred to the context of large scale armed conflict—to one monochrome bandwidth the spectrum of information the political decision-maker has to consider in determining a course of action in the midst of war. This is why it was traditionally considered to be a prudent and efficacious compromise to allow for quasi-judicial mechanisms for the punishment of war crimes. The military tribunals could provide a forum for dispensing justice according to set procedural and substantive principles that would never leave out of vision the exigencies of the rapidly changing military situation.

Thus, faced with the damaging indeterminate continuation of the guerrilla phase of the war, haunted by the specter of insurrection in the Afrikaner-populated Cape, British authorities deemed it necessary to scale back on the earlier leniency afforded enemy combatant prisoners. It is virtually certain that injustices occurred when the amnesty grants issued after the first Cape invasion of early 1900 are compared to, e.g., the case of Gideon Scheepers, tried and executed in the waning days of the following year. But to argue against the tradition of the national military tribunals on the grounds that it risks the perpetration of injustices in individual cases is to ignore the countervailing, and for the policy-maker, ever-present and magnified risks attached to ignoring the consequential impact of neatly transposing the courtroom paradigm onto the battlefield. Of course it is impossible to define with certainty the extent to which such actions as the decision to try Gideon Scheepers for war crimes functioned as a preventive measure against greater future blood-letting. But this does not mean that commanders are thereby immunized from the responsibility of taking such prospective and potential consequences into account in making their decisions.

For the resolution of any contentious contemporary political dispute, it is always helpful to consider the position of key figures of the American framing. In this regard it is interesting to consider that when Alexander Hamilton did have opportunity to voice an opinion concerning a concrete example of a controversial military court, i.e., the trial of Major André, he did not question in any way the legitimacy of the hastily assembled military court or its actions in the case. The letter to John Laurens demonstrates throughout that in Hamilton's view, the procedure is assumed to be legitimate and necessary, "agreeable to the laws and usages of nations," despite the recognition that, in this case, it leads to tragic results. It is mere speculation, of course, but one gets the sense, from Hamilton's sympathetic rendering of the events, that if it were possible to find some legal means of exonerating the unfortunate André, Hamilton, an accomplished trial lawyer, might well have sought it. But he was simply not thinking in those terms. The contention of this book is that there is a plain, common sense reason for this: that is to say, he was not assessing the facts at an abstract distance, from the peaceful groves of an academy rendered safe by other men's blood, but as an officer charged with defending and protecting lives in a perilous war. In these conditions, he recognized, tragic choices have to be made.

As a tool of military commanders, as appendages of the war-fighting machinery, manned and operated by military officers, the tribunals and the martial rule they apply may be regarded in a sense as implements of violence. Yet the term's descriptive power breaks down under further consideration. A closer look at the practices of the military juridical measures outlined in these historical examples provides illumination on the volatile nature of contemporary debate on the subject. If it were simply a matter of wreaking vengeance for an opponent's wrongdoing, there would be no need for the greater complexity of quasi-judicial procedures. A bullet in the back of the head will suffice. The recognition of the forms and requirements of due process, the acknowledgement that some—albeit streamlined—process is due in such cases, bespeaks a purposiveness that sets limits on the descriptive usefulness of the "tool" analogy. The irony of the attempt to bring rational principles of order, justice, and fairness to bear on an activity that so often appears to epitomize brutality and disorder clings to the notion of a *law* governing armed conflict. Yet this is the very mandate of the tribunals charged with adjudicating violations of the laws of war, and points to their greatest potential value as checks, or brakes against the descent into random cruelty and bloodletting that always looms in war. This curious twilight amalgamation of features has rendered the implementation of martial rule, and of military tribunals, a subject of contention on every occasion of armed conflict in which they are exercised. The current controversy should have come as no surprise.

From the longer view provided by the history of the practice, it becomes clear that the use of military commissions resists the formulaic suggestion of a pattern of gradual desuetude and eventual abandonment. The fact that fifty years had elapsed between President Roosevelt's order for the establishment of commissions for the trial of the Nazi saboteurs and President Bush's order of November 2001 means little, even when adjustment is made for intervening developments in international law. An even longer hiatus marked the period between the last significant American usage in the Reconstruction period, and 1942, a period which witnessed equally expansive legal changes. Resort to the military commission or its rough equivalent in other national settings has proved a function of the confluence of time, the exigencies of military circumstance, and the quality and character of political and military command. The context within which such measures were implemented demonstrates a connection between the very nature of the activity of warfare and the need for expeditious legal procedures, in some limited circumstances, as a feature of the commander's panoply of resources.

It would be fruitless to deny that errors and injustices have resulted from the practice. Nevertheless, more difficult questions concern whether the net effect of abandoning the practice of the national military tribunals would prove a net gain in justice or fairness. The answer depends in part on whether sufficient checks inform these quasi-juridical structures such as to ensure their operation by rule of law, rather than by the arbitrary caprice of military or civilian adjudicators. Of course, it would depend too on the situations in which the resort to such tribunals occurs. For, as we have seen, and as the Supreme Court has amply demonstrated in a vast and growing body of jurisprudence, the "rule of law" is a flexible concept, not an abstract charter of fixed principles applicable to all times, places, and persons.

The "calm perspective of hindsight" casts a different light on conditions appearing to pose any number of imminent dangers in the present. In a not-unrelated opinion on a similarly controversial subject, the Supreme Court in *Korematsu*, the famous (or infamous) Second World War case that upheld the wartime internment of Japanese-Americans, reckoned that the relevant perspective to take was to view the order of exclusion in question "as of the time it was made and when the petitioner violated it."[129] Of course, many view *Korematsu* as a tragically wrong opinion. Yet it is difficult to fault the Court in this particular, its determination to adopt the frame of reference that it did. To paraphrase Edmund Burke, no executive or judicial determination is good, but in proportion, and with reference.

The passage of time renders the sought after balance between liberty and order a matter for continuous recalibration. Much of what has been identified as the "irrelevance" of the *Milligan* decision emanates from the ironies cast by the forward movement of time. The same Supreme Court hearing the same case in the conditions that had surrounded the initial trial by military commission in Indianapolis could not have allowed itself the luxury of the *Milligan* Court's stirring defense of civil liberty. By the time of the actual decision, events had transpired in such a way as to make such pronouncements politically convenient and palatable. The lag of the law's delay means far less in the context of the conditions normally attending the peacetime civil adjudicative process. Such lags produce strange anomalies in the vicissitudes of war. As President Lincoln wrote a month before Gettysburg, in the famous Corning letter, "Civil courts are organized chiefly for trials of individuals, or, at most, a few individuals acting in concert; and this in quiet times, and on charges of crimes well defined in the law. Even in times of peace, bands of horse-thieves and robbers frequently grow too numerous and powerful for the ordinary courts of justice. But what comparison, in numbers have such bands ever borne to the insurgent sympathizers, even in many of the loyal States?"[130] The same potential for an inundation of offenders that the civil court system cannot withstand continues to beset the current war on jihadist terror.

The developments represented by *Hamdan* and the 2006 Military Commissions Act point in the direction of a more comprehensive process, modeled after the civilian criminal trial or military domestic court-martial models. In the event that the number of defendants subject to this scenario multiplies to any significant degree, the prospect for a just, fair, and timely disposition of such cases diminishes significantly. The elaborate trial and appellate process embraced by those who would disparage the military commissions as an unworkable relic of the primitive past means as a practical consequence that the volume of war crimes cases processed at the end of the Second World War would simply rot on the vine. This, too, is an option fraught with moral and political consequences. The fate of the *Milligan* case ought to warn against the imposition of abstract legal solutions.

In the midst of war, open trial process is not an absolute end in itself. Conventional criminal court procedures do not set much store upon the value of secrecy—excepting, perhaps, the potentially self-incriminating secrets of the defendant. Yet sometimes governments have valid, legitimate, critically important reasons for maintaining secrecy. In the Federal District trial of the embassy bombings, the al-Qaeda training manual was introduced into evidence. It is doubtful that subsequent al-Qaeda operations continued along the same grooves after this disclosure. Valuable intelligence, information that may have been and would continue to be critical in the successful prevention of subsequent attacks, loses all its potency when publicized before the world in federal criminal court.

The institutions and safeguards represented under the rubric "the rule of law" are not self-sustaining or impervious to the destructive forces of war. Just as the rule of law requires vigilance against internal (perhaps unwitting) agents of erosion, so a different kind of vigilance must ensure against its wholesale destruction from the dangers posed by external sources. The ambivalence evident in the record of the Western tradition derives from the complex problem, arising in times of crisis, of discerning the source, trajectory, and magnitude of the greater danger.

The decision to try Zacarias Moussaoui, the so-called replacement "twentieth hijacker," in Federal Court meant the elongation of his trial, punctuated by a steady cross-fire of pre-trial motions and appeals—over a course of years, with no end in apparent sight—before the advent of a guilty plea. Still, the eventual life sentence handed to Moussaoui after four-and-one-half years of trial might lead some to the conclusion that the civil trial process "worked" in this case, and so demonstrated its perfect capacity for addressing such problems. But this is to presume that individuals like Moussaoui willingly limit their subversive energies to the outcome, and not the process of their trials—that for such defendants, the trial process itself is simply a neutral framework to which they submit and within which they agree to work, once inside it; that this neutral framework remains somehow impervious to the lethal maneuverings of fanatical jihadists. But given the capacity of minds set on transforming passenger jetliners into weapons for the mass destruction of innocents, it is dangerously naive to think that the tools of the trial process remain immune from similar manipulation. The shape of future potential problems is indicated in the recent criminal trial of Lynne Stewart, a self-styled "civil rights" lawyer, convicted of funneling information for her client, Sheik Omar Abdel-Rahman. Rahman himself continues to serve a life sentence after his 1995 conviction for plotting terror attacks in New York City. The 67-year-old Stewart was convicted of passing information from her incarcerated client to members of the Egyptian terrorist group al-Gama'a al-Islamiyya, in violation of court orders. Interestingly, Stewart, celebrating her relatively light 28-month sentence—(the government had asked for thirty years)—called it "a great victory against an overreaching government."[131]

There is no lingering quality of resilience that makes the rule of law itself the one thing to rest invulnerable against malevolent forces. It too needs to satisfy basic conditions of security in order to function and thrive. The idea that its greatest and only necessary protection consists in the mere expansion of its orbit of usage rests on premises that have never held true for any human society.

Conclusion

> Invocation of constitutional liberties as part of a strategy for overthrowing them presents a dilemma to a free people which may not be soluble by constitutional logic alone.
>
> —Justice Robert Jackson

In the aftermath of the First World War, a French commentator criticized the very idea of military courts in terms that now recirculate in the contemporary West: "Military men are men of action and vitality, they care little for formalities. In their hands, the tasks of investigating and adjudicating the facts proceed like an assault with bayonets. The key is to reach the objective—it doesn't matter how—the objective being, so to speak, execution."[1] The character of the military professional, it is said, is inimical by nature to the exercise of reflective judgment, and thus the very idea of a military tribunal administering justice calls forth the hackneyed analogy with military music.[2] Yet a long-standing tradition of custom and practice in developing and applying the *jus in bello* gives the lie to these facile dismissals. The cases give little support to the oft-repeated contention that the military commission functions as a reflexive "rubber stamp" of executive will.

As a matter of daily routine, military commanders participate in complex hierarchical networks of decision-making by which they hold one another to account according to public, clearly defined standards of general application. To increasing degree they are themselves accountable for their adherence to the customary international legal strictures that include but extend beyond the *jus in bello*.[3] These standards of practical judgment form a critical component of the training and education of the modern commander. The *jus in bello* principles of military necessity, proportion, and discrimination all require the application of critical judgment, the balancing of elements across a complex spectrum of rapidly changing information.[4]

The historical array of examples gathered here suggests the close affinity between the legitimacy of the usage of the military tribunals and the application of these fundamental law of war principles. Conditions of war where the use of force is most justified will often also, mutatis mutandis, justify resort to military tribunals. When the use of military tribunals is contemplated during the course of ongoing hostilities, even as the tribunals issue their decisions, such determinations simply cannot be abstracted from the larger context of the commander's operational, strategic, and tactical decision matrix. This does not require the abandonment of the process to the unfettered discretion of military decision-makers accountable only to the executive authority. It is to insist that there remain undeniable, lasting distinctions between the courtroom and the field of battle.

To be sure, the record points to other historical contexts for the use of the quasi-judicial procedure of the tribunals, brought about by the extraordinary consequences of war. In all of the conflicts examined here, military commissions functioned as a means of maintaining civil order in the face of the potential anarchy of wartime and/or post-war conditions—for this use the jurisdiction of the military courts often extended to civilians, largely for the trial of violations of the laws of war and of specified military offenses tangential to the actual conduct of hostilities. The national tribunals convened in the aftermath of the Second World War facilitated the worldwide adjudication of war crimes on a bewilderingly massive scale.

The approach exemplified in the foregoing brief survey of Western military history provides a helpful rubric for understanding more than just the fierceness of internal opposition to the tribunals. It is part and parcel of this tradition that the military tribunal was viewed as an emergency provision, to be appealed to by means of an application analogous to the law of war principle of military necessity. Extraordinary threats required the use of extraordinary protections for the safeguarding of the nation and its institutions—indeed, of the rule of law itself. Once the threat occasioning an invocation of emergency measures has subsided, those extraordinary remedies should inexorably give way to the abiding gravitational pull of normal legal processes as soon as practicable.

In this series of studies I have sought to provide a contextual account of the manner in which military tribunals have formed a regular part of the military commander's operational landscape. The fierce and bloody twilight of the border territories of Missouri and Maryland in the American Civil War; the depressing prospect of unending guerrilla warfare and the ever-looming danger of insurrection by Boer sympathizers in the South African war; the waxing and waning of the threat of total submersion in a tidal German onslaught faced by the France of 1914; the daunting magnitude of military aggression and atrocities on a world-wide scale faced by the Allies in the Second World War—in all of these conflicts, military commanders and their civilian overseers found it necessary to employ tribunals as a means of restraining and containing real threats of potentially catastrophic proportions. The instrument, as all tools associated with warfare, tended, necessarily, to be somewhat bluntly fashioned and crude in execution.

As with all actions pursued and justified on grounds of military necessity, it is possible with the benefit of hindsight, and in the comfort and security provided by a costly peace, to discover injustices or to dispute the processes and decisions attending individual cases. It is much more difficult to speculate upon the reconfigured, hypothetical contours of the result in the absence of the disputed measures. In a recent set of thoughtful studies illuminating the complex relationship between civilian leaders and military commanders in modern Western democracies, Eliot Cohen observed: "The moods of peace and contemplation [characteristic of the scholarly observer] differ in the most fundamental way from the crucible of wartime leadership. The difficulty writers have in putting themselves in the place of a wartime political leader, who bears manifold responsibilities and carries stresses that they have never borne, is the greatest obstacle to sound historical judgment on wartime statesmanship. Indeed, even the immediate subordinates of the man at the top only dimly understand, much less share, the acute pressures or the perspective of a prime minister or a president."[5]

It may be that history will determine that President Bush overestimated "the magnitude of the potential deaths, injuries, and property destruction that would result from potential acts of terrorism against the United States," as well as "the probability that such acts will occur," in judging that an "extraordinary emergency" exists.[6] At least five members of the Supreme Court have demonstrated their own willingness to call this characterization into question and thereby refashion the contours of the American response. The emergency may already have been overcome by developments in Afghanistan, Iraq, or elsewhere. Yet events thus far do not give warrant to such an interpretation. The July 7, 2005, terror bombings in London or the Canadian "sting" arrest of seventeen terror suspects in southern Ontario in the same month as the *Hamdan* opinion, to give just two recent examples, suggest otherwise.[7]

The omniscience we desire continues to elude us. This simply means that careful, conscientious exercise of critical judgment must be brought to bear in assessing threat levels and appropriate responses. That such dangers have been overstated in the past in no way obviates the need for continuous vigilance. The most serious threats have all too frequently materialized upon the shores of unsuspecting and unprepared nations. As Richard Posner observed in the wake of September 11, 2001, "It is because officials have repeatedly and disastrously underestimated these dangers that our history is as violent as it is."[8] Candid acknowledgment of this history gives no warrant for rejecting a policy, such as the use of military commissions, that must nonetheless be pursued with caution and circumspection.

The problems confronting the statesman seeking to sustain the right balance of liberty and order persist through a long and tumultuous history of warfare and politics in the West: "Careful and accurate calculation is essential in order to maintain freedom in a world where power is [still] so important."[9] The unsatisfactory legacy of the response of the "international community" to humanitarian crisis and genocide in the 1990s, acknowledged by Gary Bass, Michael Ignatieff, and others, points to the limits of a legalism that runs the risk of falling out of step with the time and circumstances of actual international political events. The greatest threats to peace and security in the world do not come from the potential for arbitrary abuses of power on the part of Western military and political leaders. The long history of vigorous, open political debate and dissent, undergirded by relatively stable institutions of accountable political and military leadership, on evidence in all of the conflicts surveyed here, demonstrates as much.

These studies should make it clear that a discussion of military tribunals as a legal abstraction cannot be particularly helpful. The appropriateness of the practice can be evaluated best when considered within the unfolding context of particular, time- and circumstance-dependent responses to particular acts. No showing has yet been advanced to indicate that law-trained civilian judges are especially well suited for making determinations of this order.

Too often the debate over military tribunals comes to rest on the horns of a false dilemma, wrought by this very type of abstraction. In the view of many critics, the issue comes down to a simple choice: *either* meticulous adherence to the exacting procedural rigor of the criminal law *or* blind acquiescence to the caprice of unaccountable military and political leaders; *either* the wide open process and disclosure of democracy *or* the secrecy and violence of arbitrary rule. The option is put in such a way as to force the conclusion that the successful establishment of the domestic criminal trial model would obviate the necessity for political decision-making, for practical wisdom on the part of political and military leaders—at least when it comes to the matter of addressing war crimes. But the historical survey presented here amply demonstrates this to be a false hope. The exigencies surging with the forward press of time reveal the inescapability of political judgment.

The greater danger arises from a willingness on the part of governmental leaders to acquiesce in a responsibility that is purely retroactive, a passive contentment that the burden of international order is met with the construction of supra-national mechanisms of justice patterned after the model of domestic criminal adjudication, with the relief that the responsibility of moral judgment now rests in other, perhaps less compromised hands.[10] Some would actually argue that Western efforts in the use of force to achieve security, a better peace, and justice, albeit imperfect, are no better than the savageries of the terrorists. Acquiescence in such exercises in moral equivalence, this failure to make critical distinctions, imperils a nation's very will to go on existing.

Academic pundits have not been immune from the error of underestimating the potency of the threat of international terror. Take this representative statement, from a South African scholar, published in the year 1995, which attempts to diagnose, among other things, "the absence of a sense of proportion to the West's reaction to the onset of the age of terrorism."[11] This lack of balance leads more sensible observers, it is said, to

> comparison with other periods when public opinion has been in the grip of a great fear. R. J. Vincent has drawn parallels between the reaction of the guardians of order to terrorism and their reaction in previous periods to communism, liberal nationalism, and Jacobinism. The alarmist nature of the response to terrorism was somewhat akin to the

> fear of domestic communism that arose in the United States in the late 1940s and early 1950s.

The only difference being, according to this author, that "McCarthyism's enemies were largely imaginary" while, it has to be admitted, "the emergence of small groups engaged in clandestine violence across national boundaries" cannot be denied.[12]

To be sure, the contrast between such "calls to reason" and any random sampling of jihadist advocacy could hardly be greater. Yet one must question the logic that insists that the eventual demise of any enemy means that such a result was inevitable and, therefore, that alternative outcomes should never have been seriously considered. Nor is it reasonable to dismiss as irrational fear and hysteria the response of "the guardians of order" to earlier menaces to the civilized world.

To trust that sufficiently "robust" international institutions such as the International Criminal Court will somehow manage to eliminate the wrongs to which the twentieth century was a recurrent witness, miscalculates the retrograde, unrelenting brutality of the most immediate and pressing threats to international security and stability. The fact that the ruthless methods and strategies of a sub-national terror network bid fair to occupy the collective might and resources of the world's most powerful nation for years to come indicates that there does remain a place for the greater severity and flexibility of the customary, quasi-judicial military tribunals.

This is not to disparage the often noble aspirations of those who strive for a better world.[13] But its approaches only come into reach when the threats to its fulfillment are faced squarely, with no illusions as to the difficulties that lie ahead.

Notes

Introduction

1. Detention, Treatment, and Trial of Certain Non-Citizens in the War Against Terrorism §§ 3(a), 4(b), 66 Fed. Reg. 57,833 (Nov. 13, 2001) [hereinafter, Military Order].

2. The observation appeared early enough in the history of the American republic: "Safety from external danger is the most powerful director of national conduct. Even the ardent love of liberty will after a time, give way to its dictates. The violent destruction of life and property incident to war, the continual effort and alarm attendant on a state of continual danger, will compel nations the most attached to liberty to resort for repose and security to institutions which have a tendency to destroy their civil and political rights. To be more safe, they at length become willing to run the risk of being less free." Alexander Hamilton, *The Federalist*, Jacob E. Cooke, ed., No. 8, p. 45 [hereinafter, *Federalist*].

3. Franklin, *Extraordinary Measures*, 3.

4. I use the term "juridical measures" to distinguish these emergency proceedings from the activities of the normal domestic civilian courts and from the normal workings of the military justice systems of the various nations under examination here.

5. These advantages are summarized and discussed in Solis, "Military Commissions and Terrorists," in Fidell and Sullivan, eds., *Evolving Military Justice*, 195–205. See also Neal Richardson and Spencer Crona, "Detention of Terrorists as Unlawful Combatants and Their Trial by American Military Commissions," and Robert Hardaway, Christopher Hardaway and James Siegesmund, "Military Tribunals and Civil Liberties in Time of National Peril: A Legal and Historical Perspective" in Nanda, ed., *Law in the War on International Terrorism*, 123ff., 169ff.

6. This is changing rapidly. The list of post–9/11 works on these matters continues to experience a steady growth rate. See, e.g., Berkowitz, ed., *Terrorism, the laws of war, and the constitution*; *Cases;* Fisher, *Military Tribunals and Presidential Power;* Nanda, ed., *Law in the War on International Terrorism;* Tushnet, ed. *The Constitution in Wartime.*

7. Some notable exceptions include Neely, *The Fate of Liberty;* Fisher, *Nazi Saboteurs on Trial;* and most recently, Fisher, *Military Tribunals and Presidential Power.* For all their strengths, Professor Fisher's contributions can hardly be classified as works of military history. Rather, his focus on constitutional separation of powers issues limits the scope of inquiry to the appellate cases in which courts have addressed military tribunals. Though this "legalistic" approach can be helpful, I believe it also runs the risk of presenting an incomplete picture while giving the impression of comprehensiveness.

8. Perhaps, too, the pronouncements in the Charter of the United Nations to the effect that war is now illegal as a matter of international law could have assisted in creating such an atmosphere of scholarly sequestration as well. See, Jovan Babic, "War Crimes, Moral, Legal or Simply Political?" in Jokić, ed., *War Crimes and Collective Wrongdoing,* 57, 64 (2001). Yet, as Alfred P. Rubin has recently noted, "the United States has acted militarily under the laws of war for over 200 years without declarations." Rubin, "The New World Disorder: Applying the Geneva Conventions: Military Commissions, Armed Conflict, and Al-Qaeda," 26 Fletcher F. World Aff. 79 (2002).

9. William K. Suter, forward to *Evolving Military Justice,* Fidell and Sullivan, eds., ix. This issue takes shape within the wider context of a perennial debate over the nature of civil and military relations in American society. The literature on this subject is large and growing. As in so many other areas, Tocqueville's famous account offers an analysis of ongoing percipience and relevance, see Tocqueville, *Democracy in America,* 617–35; the modern *locus classicus* is Huntington, *The Soldier and the State.*

10. Gone, apparently, are the days when a Charles Fairman could write a treatise on martial law while serving as a Lieutenant Colonel in the Army Judge Advocate General's Department and as Professor of Political Science at Stanford University (see Charles Fairman, *The Law of Martial Rule*); when a Felix Frankfurter, an Edmund Morgan, a Eugene Wambaugh, or a John Henry Wigmore would interrupt distinguished civilian careers for military service experience as JAGs—as all of these Harvard men did after America became involved in World War I. Before joining the JAG corps during the First World War, the renowned evidence scholar Wigmore had already served as Dean of Northwestern University Law School (see Lurie, *Arming Military Justice,* 1: 46). Needless to say, it would strain the bounds of credulity to imagine a prominent law school dean making similar moves today, under any such circumstances. The phenomenon of American lawyers stepping in to defend alleged terror suspects confined at Guantanamo falls into a different category.

11. "The definition [only] shifts the problem of meaning back to the defining terms . . . But these, for many reasons, are likely to be just as vague and confusing as the terms we started with; and in any case, we should have to go on to define them in turn; which leads to new terms which too must be defined. And so

on, to infinity." Popper, *The Open Society and Its Enemies,* 2: 9–21, 17. But as soon as this is asserted, it must be heavily qualified, with the recognition that in history "there is no such thing as an entirely independent, isolated, or unchanging fact. Any 'fact' is inseparable from our association of it with another 'fact' (and in our minds this association is an association with a preceding fact) . . . Every 'fact' is not only dependent on but inseparable from our statement of it." Lukacs, *At the End of an Age,* 136. In the field of history at least, this calls for a certain level of definitional clarification, exercised, hopefully, with due humility, and with the acknowledgment that different interpretive angles of approach can yield different conclusions, but that even when our understanding of an historical event is partial, incomplete, and contingent, our knowledge of it retains validity as true and accurate knowledge.

12. Sean D. Murphy, "Terrorism and the Concept of 'Armed Attack' in Article 51 of the U.N. Charter," 43 Harv. Int'l L. J. 41 (2002).

13. To be sure, in the context of criminal defense, the form of argumentation can have great utility, for it tends to require the government to meet its burden of proof as to each and every element of a charged offense. It will come then, perhaps, as no surprise that Murphy's conclusion in the article referenced above is to determine that the attacks of September 11, 2001, were not "armed attacks" but "uses of force or intervention below the threshold of armed attack, which is perhaps better characterized as a conventional (albeit heinous) criminal act." Ibid., 46. But the world of policy and military decision-making is not the same as a courtroom. Confusing the two spheres carries potentially serious consequences.

14. Baudrillard, *The Spirit of Terrorism,* 28–31. Baudrillard earlier achieved notoriety for his contention that the Persian Gulf War of 1990–1991 was a "fictional" event that did not "really" occur. It comes as no surprise that he takes a similar view of the current conflict.

15. The term also covers the rarer trials of civilians not subject to the Uniform Code of Military Justice. See *Johnson v. Eisentrager,* 339 U.S. 763 (1950).

16. Fisher, *Military Tribunals and Presidential Power,* xiii. I use the term with some reluctance, aware as I am that the term "tribunal" when qualified with the adjective "military," may carry an unavoidable whiff of opprobrium and disdain.

17. Pollock and Maitland, *The History of English Law,* 1: 1.

18. Timothy McCormack, "From Sun Tzu to the Sixth Committee," in McCormack and Simpson, eds., *Law of War Crimes,* 33–34, citing Maridakis, "*Un précédent du procès de Nuremberg tiré de l'histoire de la Grèce ancienne,*" 5 Revue Hellénique de Droit Internationale 1 (1952).

19. Ibid.

20. Ibid.

21. See Keen, *The Laws of War in the Late Middle Ages,* 47.

22. Ibid, 53.

23. Dunn, *The Political Thought of John Locke,* 7.

24. Locke, *Two Treatises of Government,* 2, 374–80.

25. See, e.g., Yoo, *The Powers of War and Peace,* and Tushnet, ed., *The Constitution in Wartime.* See also Yoo, "The Continuation of Politics by Other Means: The Original Understanding of War Powers," 84 California Law Review 167 (1996); Turner, *The War Powers Resolution;* and Turner, *Repealing the War Powers Resolution.*

26. *Youngstown Sheet & Tube Co. v. Sawyer,* 343 US 579 (1952), J. Jackson, concurring, at 635.

27. *Federalist* No. 8, p. 46 (Hamilton).

28. The extensive record of widespread executive recourse to these emergency juridical mechanisms in time of war, regularly attended by vigorous policy debate and sometimes controversial judicial opinion, evinces the theory of John Yoo that "the unsettled nature of foreign affairs does not arise from a systematic defect in the constitutional regime. The conflict among the branches of government over foreign affairs . . . is not a flaw in the constitutional design, but is instead its conscious product. In the area of foreign affairs, the Constitution does not establish a strict, legalized process for decisionmaking. Instead it establishes a flexible system permitting a variety of procedures. This not only gives the nation more flexibility in reaching foreign affairs decisions, it gives each of the three branches of government the ability to check the initiatives of the others in foreign affairs. The deepest questions of American foreign relations law remain open because the Constitution wants it that way." Yoo, *The Powers of War and Peace,* 11–12.

29. Authorization for Use of Military Force, Pub. L. No. 107–40, 115 Stat. 224 (2001) (codified at 50 USC § 1541 note). This "explicit or implied authorization of Congress" would place it under the first of the three categories identified by Justice Jackson in *Youngstown Sheet & Tube,* and thereby give it the support of "the strongest of presumptions and the widest latitude of judicial interpretation, and the burden of persuasion would rest heavily upon any who might attack it." *Youngstown Sheet & Tube,* 343 US at 637.

30. George Orwell, "Who are the War Criminals?" in *Collected Essays,* 2: 319, 325.

Chapter 1

1. *Federalist* No. 8, p. 49 (Hamilton). These observations comport with the assertions of Montesquieu regarding the influence of climate, geography, economics, and culture upon the legal ordering of a given society. Such differences, Montesquieu argued, make for a view of law that emphasizes its contingent, empirical, and pragmatic nature, rather than its universality and rational construction. Montesquieu, *The Spirit of the Laws,* Parts 3, 4, and 5.

2. Rossiter, *Constitutional Dictatorship,* 209–10.

3. Ibid.

4. *Federalist* No. 23, p. 147 (Hamilton).

5. The eventual fate of the newly born French Republic only two decades later.

6. See, e.g., George Coil, "War Crimes of the American Revolution," 82 Mil. L. Rev. 171 [hereinafter, Coil] (1978).

7. Washington, *Writings,* 7: 443, quoted in Harold E. Selesky, "Colonial America," in Howard et al., eds., *The Laws of War,* 74–85 [hereinafter, Selesky].

8. *Ex parte Quirin,* 317 U.S. 1, 20, note 14 (1942), provides a list of cases tried by military tribunals during the Revolutionary War. Ramsay, *The History of the American Revolution,* 518–24, contains a detailed contemporary account of the case of Major André.

9. Hamilton to John Laurens, c. October 11, 1780, in Rhodehamel, ed., *The American Revolution,* 600, 604 [hereinafter, Hamilton Letter].

10. Ramsay, *History,* 521.

11. Ibid.

12. Ibid, 523.

13. Hamilton Letter, 605.

14. Articles of War, June 30, 1775, revised, September 20, 1776, in 2 *Journals of the Continental Congress, 1774–1779,* pp. 111–23; available at http://www.yale.edu/lawweb/avalon/contcong/09-20-76.htm#b1.

15. For a helpful discussion of the general treatment of prisoners of war during the War of Independence, and especially of Thomas Jefferson's initiatives for humanizing the practices of warfare, the treatment of prisoners of war and non-combatants, see Coil; see also Burrus M. Carnahan, "Reason, Retaliation and Rhetoric: Jefferson and the Quest for Humanity in War," 139 Mil. L. Rev. 83 (1993); and Ramsay, *History,* 598–606.

16. Selesky, 74–85.

17. Martin and Lender, *A Respectable Army,* 42, 193–94.

18. Hickey, *The War of 1812,* 213.

19. James, *The Life of Andrew Jackson,* 259–60.

20. Ibid., 261.

21. Ibid.

22. Ibid., 262.

23. Hickey, *The War of 1812,* 213.

24. Ibid.

25. Lincoln to Erastus Corning and Others, June 12, 1863, in Lincoln, *Speeches and Writings,* 454, 460, 461–62.

26. James, *The Life of Andrew Jackson,* 287.

27. Ibid., 289.

28. Winthrop, *Military Law and Precedents,* 464.

29. Ibid., 465.

30. Peterson, *The Great Triumvirate,* 55.

31. Ibid.

32. Ibid., 56. Jackson never forgave Clay for this performance. Ibid.

33. Richard Rush, minister at London, to John Quincy Adams, Secretary of State, Jan. 12, 1819, MSS. Dispatches, Gr. Brit., quoted in Wharton, *Digest of International Law,* 3: 328. On another occasion Rush wrote, "In the midst of all this passion, the ministry stood firm. Better informed, more just, they had made up their minds not to risk the peace of the two countries on grounds so untenable." "Rush's Residence at Court of London," 304 ff, 338, quoted in ibid., 329.

34. The importance of the incident as historical precedent for the imposition of martial law during the Civil War was not lost upon Lincoln and his political rivals. See Neely, *The Fate of Liberty,* 199–202 (concluding that "Democratic party traditions in no way specially prepared the Democracy of the Civil War era to defend civil liberties from martial assault.")

35. Winthrop, *Military Law and Precedents,* 832–833. One historian described General Winfield Scott's order establishing military commissions as "unique in American military law." Bauer, *The Mexican War,* 327.

36. Offenses included "Assassination, murder, poisoning, rape, or the attempt to commit either, malicious stabbing or maiming, malicious assault and battery, robbery, theft, the wanton destruction of churches, cemeteries, or other religious edifices and fixtures, the interruption of religious ceremonies, and the destruction, except by order of a superior officer, of public or private property." In addition, "the purchase by Mexicans or civilians in Mexico, from soldiers, of horses, arms, ammunition, equipments or clothing" were identified as crimes subject to the jurisdiction of the military commissions under the General Order. G.O. 20, February 19, 1847, amended by G.O. 190 and 287, quoted in Winthrop, *Military Law and Precedents,* 832.

37. Ibid.

38. As the commissions convened with regularity by order of General Scott, as well as Generals Wool and Zachary Taylor, they frequently heard cases involving other offenses not explicitly provided for in the General Order. Thus, the commissions dealt with cases of "'Manslaughter,' 'Burglary,' 'Picking Pockets,' 'Carrying a concealed weapon,' 'Threatening the lives of soldiers,' 'Riotous conduct,' 'Attempting to pass counterfeit money,' 'Obtaining money under false pretences,' 'Fraud,' 'Attempt to defraud the United States,' [and] 'Introducing spirituous liquor into U.S. barracks.'" Bauer notes that shortly after the re-issue of the order in April 1847, "The hanging of a camp follower on April 10 for the rape and robbery of a Mexican woman had a salutary effect on those in the army who might have been tempted to follow suit." Bauer, *The Mexican War,* 253.

39. Howard Levie states that the council of war was established "for the purpose of dealing with members of gangs of brigands who were infesting the roads

of Mexico, preying on all who passed, without regard to nationality." Levie, *Terrorism in War,* 411.

40. Price, *The Origins of the War with Mexico;* Frederick Merk, "Dissent in the Mexican War" in Morison et al., *Dissent in Three American Wars,* 35–63; and Schroeder, *Mr. Polk's War.*

41. Peterson, *The Great Triumvirate,* 422–23. As Forrest McDonald observes, Calhoun's fears about the dangerous precedent established here were fully realized only fifteen years later, with its application against his own state at Fort Sumter. McDonald, *States' Rights and the Union,* 151.

42. For example, it was the Mexican War that prompted the writing of Henry David Thoreau's *On Civil Disobedience* (1849).

43. Charles Francis Adams called the preamble "one of the grossest national lies that was ever deliberately told." Boston Whig (d), June 2, 1846, quoted in Morison, et al., *Dissent in Three American Wars,* 40.

44. Thus, members of Congress opposed to Polk's policies in Mexico, such as Senator John C. Calhoun of South Carolina and John M. Niles of Connecticut, stressed the dangers attendant upon an embrace of the All-Mexico movement in racial terms. McDonald, *States' Rights and the Union,* 153. Columbus Delano, the abolitionist Whig representative from Ohio, voiced a sentiment shared by many in speaking of the Mexicans as "a sad compound of Spanish, English, Indian and negro bloods . . . resulting, it is said in the production of a slothful, indolent, ignorant race of beings." Quoted in ibid. Such sentiments were common among the American armies as well. Johnson, *Winfield Scott,* 193–94.

45. Bauer, *The Mexican War,* 223; Bergeron, *The Presidency of James K. Polk,* 101; Johnson, *Winfield Scott,* 165–70.

46. Neely, *The Fate of Liberty,* 40.

47. Bishop, *Justice Under Fire,* 80–83.

48. Halleck, *International Law,* 782.

49. Bauer, *The Mexican War,* 223, 253; Bauer notes that the order amounted to an invocation of "unwritten 'Martial Law,' i.e., natural law as applied within the military sphere." Ibid., 327. See also Neely, *Fate of Liberty,* 40.

50. Ibid. See Scott, *Memoirs of Lieut.-General Scott,* 2: 393; and Halleck, *International Law,* 783.

51. Scott, *Memoirs,* 394.

52. Ibid., 395.

53. Ibid.

54. Ibid., 395–96. Scott's assessment seems largely to have withstood the test of time. Historians generally praise his conduct of the war and his ability to keep a tight lid on the inevitable depredations committed by the invading army under his charge. See Johnson, *Winfield Scott,* 207; and Peskin, *Winfield Scott and the Profession of Arms,* 194–95.

55. The strategy as it was carried out in Veracruz, for example, "had a noticeable impact as the townspeople began to accept the American occupation with little resistance." Johnson, *Winfield Scott,* 179, 187–89. Volunteers in the American army complained of the disproportionably harsh punishments they received in comparison to Mexican offenders. Ibid., 192–93; 165–81.

56. Ibid., 181.

57. Bauer, *The Mexican War,* 327.

58. Peskin, *Winfield Scott and the Profession of Arms,* 194–205

59. Rossiter, *Constitutional Dictatorship,* 223.

60. Ibid., 224.

61. Resolved in Lincoln's favor by the Supreme Court in the *Prize Cases.* "Proclamation Calling Militia and Convening Congress," April 15, 1861; and "Proclamation of Blockade," April 19, 1861, in Lincoln: *Speeches and Writings,* 232–234. The legal question of the blockade order was resolved in Lincoln's favor by the Supreme Court in *The Prize cases,* 67 U.S. 635 (1863). Edwin Stanton, Executive Order No. 1, "Relating to Political Prisoners, February 14, 1862, available at http://www.presidency.ucsb.edu/ws/index.php?pid=69792.

62. Randall, *Constitutional Problems,* 121–23. "This reluctance appears in the fact that only a qualified suspension was ordered in 1861, that the military authorities were enjoined to use the power sparingly, that the action was taken during a recess of Congress, and that an early opportunity was taken to lay the matter before the special session of Congress convened for the emergency in the summer of '61." Ibid., 121; see Neely, *The Fate of Liberty,* ch. 1. Neely's superb work on civil liberties in the Civil War is the authoritative study of this subject, and in this section I rely upon his findings. Any errors of course remain my own.

63. Randall, *Constitutional Problems,* 128–29.

64. US. Stat. at large, XII, 755.

65. Neely, *The Fate of Liberty,* 36.

66. Neely quotes the constitutional historian Andrew C. McLaughlin's ominous pronouncement in 1936, "That a president armed with the 'war power,' may some day wreck the whole constitutional system is theoretically possible, and the dictator, if he ever appears, may discover precedents in the conduct of Lincoln." Ibid., 230.

67. Rossiter, *Constitutional Dictatorship,* 235. The desperate conditions that called forth the proclamation emerge in its opening lines: "Whereas, it has become necessary to call into service not only volunteers but also portions of the militia of the States by draft in order to suppress the insurrection existing in the United States, and disloyal persons are not adequately restrained by the ordinary processes of law from hindering this measure and from giving aid and comfort in various ways to the insurrection . . . [the order was given.]" Abraham Lincoln, Proclamation Suspending the Writ of Habeas Corpus (September 24, 1862), in Lincoln, *Speeches and Writings,* 371.

68. Ibid.

69. Neely notes that the September 24 order actually served as a mere "gloss on a *fait accompli*," the stamp of approval for an earlier series of orders issued by Lincoln's Secretary of War, Edwin Stanton, which suspended the writ throughout the United States on August 8. It was during the month following these orders that worst excesses of the entire war took place. It was "the lowest point for civil liberties in the North during the Civil War, the lowest point for civil liberties in U.S. history to that time, and one of the lowest for civil liberties in all of American history." The orders, aimed mainly at resistance to "the first national conscription" in the history of the country, led to widespread abuses in the form of "wrong-headed," arbitrary arrests at an unprecedented rate, one that would not be matched again for the rest of the war. Neely, *The Fate of Liberty*, 53, 51–74. Thus, this nadir for civil liberties coincided with the low point in the Union's fortunes during the war.

70. In his count of the number of arrests post–February 1862—i.e., the time when Stanton took over internal security matters—Neely exceeds the 13,535 figure that had generally been accepted among historians, pushing it closer to 14,000, but he also notes that this tally is "of less significance in the history of civil liberties" than it was ever previously imagined. This is because "a majority of the arrests would have occurred whether the writ was suspended or not. They were caused by the mere incidents or friction of war, which produced refugees, informers, guides, Confederate defectors, carriers of contraband goods, and other such persons as came between or in the wake of large armies." Thus, "the total number of civilians in military prisons in the North, whatever that was, would not equal the number of 'arbitrary arrests.'" Simply not enough information is available to tell us much about the significance of these numbers. Ibid., 233–34.

71. Randall, *Constitutional Problems*, 155.

72. Abraham Lincoln, Message to Congress in Special Session, July 4, 1861, in Lincoln, *Speeches and Writings*, 246, 252–53.

73. While Lincoln's words may be "embarrassing" when "read with our current sensitivity to civil liberties," it is surely wrong as a matter of historical, biographical, and textual accuracy to assert that Lincoln was merely engaged here in making cynical (if noble) excuses for permitting "the exigencies of war to restructure the government." Fletcher, *Our Secret Constitution*, 37–38. If Lincoln's recognition of a need, in extreme circumstances, to suspend the privilege of *habeas corpus* is a source of embarrassment, then, apparently, the same should be said of the Constitutional text which explicitly provides for the same. Neither does the context of this and other Lincoln speeches and actions substantiate the contention that Lincoln enjoyed a "casual attitude toward formal constitutional institutions, such as the writ of habeas corpus." Ibid., 5. As Lincoln himself averred in this same speech, the text made it his responsibility to see to the

preservation, protection, and defense of the Constitution and to "take care that the laws be faithfully executed." Article II, Sec. 3. With "the whole of the laws which were required to be faithfully executed" suffering resistance, "and failing of execution, in nearly one-third of the States," the President faced more of a bind than that presented by a putative "secret" desire to "reinvent the United States." See text below, and accompanying notes.

74. Jaffa, *A New Birth of Freedom,* 363.

75. Ibid., 364.

76. Lincoln, Reply to the Ohio Democratic Convention (June 29, 1863), in Lincoln, *Speeches and Writings,* 466, 468.

77. Neely, *The Fate of Liberty,* 41.

78. Randall, *Constitutional Problems,* 159.

79. Fletcher, *Our Secret Constitution,* 84. "For much of the war, it was not clear who was in charge of the state." Ibid.

80. Randall and Donald, *The Civil War and Reconstruction,* 235.

81. Randall, *Constitutional Problems,* 175.

82. Randall and Donald, *The Civil War and Reconstruction,* 236.

83. Neely, *The Fate of Liberty,* 171.

84. Ibid., 171–72.

85. Gunther Rothenberg, "The Age of Napoleon," in Howard, Andreopoulos, and Shulman, eds., *The Laws of War,* 86–97.

86. United States War Department, *General Orders of the War Department,* no. 151, 1863, 2: 169–70 (Derby & Miller, 1864), [hereinafter, *General Orders*].

87. Neely, *The Fate of Liberty,* 168–69, 35, 162.

88. Ibid., 162–63. Typical was the case of one Matthew Miller, convicted for attempted smuggling of military goods "for the use and benefit of the rebels." The death sentence in the case was annulled. The record was determined to be "fatally defective and thus, "inoperative" for it failed to show "that the members of the Commission were sworn, or that two-thirds concurred in the sentence." *General Orders,* 2: 190.

89. Randall, *Constitutional Problems,* 175.

90. *General Orders,* 2: 158–59.

91. Nichols, *Lincoln and the Indians,* 87.

92. Ibid., 99.

93. Carol Chomsky, "The United States–Dakota War Trials: A Study in Military Injustice," 43 Stan. L. Rev. 13 (1990), gives a detailed account of the case, though the author gives short shrift to the fact that Lincoln was absorbed in fighting the Civil War at the same time.

94. To her credit, Chomsky does not give in to moral over-simplification in recounting the tragic events. She observes in a footnote, for instance, that Colonel Sibley agonized with the weight of his judicial responsibility, writing to his wife: "I have to review all the proceedings, and decide the fate of each indi-

vidual. This power of life, and death, is an awful thing to exercise, and when I think of more than three hundred human beings are [sic] subject to that power, lodged in my hands, it makes me shudder. Still, duty must be performed, and judgment visited upon the guilty." Ibid., 93, note 494.

95. Ibid., 13, 29–34. Chomsky's account also evinces the exceptional courage of officers such as Colonel Stephen Miller, who was charged with keeping the condemned prisoners and who managed to stave off the mob violence that constantly threatened.

96. Statement of Major-General Burnside, in response to Habeas Corpus Proceedings, May 11, 1863 [hereinafter, Burnside, Answer], in *The Trial of Hon. Clement L. Vallandigham, by a Military Commission: and the Proceedings under his Application for a Writ of Habeas Corpus in the Circuit Court of the United States for the Southern District of Ohio* at 41 (Cincinnati: Rickey and Carroll, 1863).

97. G.O. No. 38, ibid., 7.

98. Proceedings of a Military Commission, April 21, 1863. Ibid., 32.

99. Ibid., 9–33; and Randall, *Constitutional Problems,* 176–77.

100. Rossiter, *Constitutional Dictatorship,* 237, note 43.

101. *Ex Parte Vallandigham,* 1 Wall. 243, (Feb. 1864).

102. Ibid.

103. Shelby Foote, *The Civil War: A Narrative,* 1: 247.

104. Burnside, Answer, 41–42.

105. Ibid.

106. Donald, *Lincoln,* 443–44.

107. Abraham Lincoln, To Erastus Corning and Others, June 12, 1863, in Lincoln, *Speeches and Writings,* [hereinafter, *Corning Letter*] 454–463.

108. Ibid., 455.

109. Ibid., 456–57.

110. Ibid., 458.

111. Ibid.

112. Ibid., 460.

113. The problem is perennial, going to the delicate balance between liberty and security. See *Schneiderman v. United States,* 63 S. Ct. 1333, 320 U.S. 118 (1943). The Supreme Court majority in *Schneiderman,* a case involving the canceling of a naturalization decree on the basis of the petitioner's involvement in the Communist Party, came to rest on the other side of the balance, over vigorous dissent from Chief Justice Stone, who argued that "a man can be known by the ideas he spreads as well as by the company he keeps."

114. Corning Letter, 458–59. Thus, Lincoln had asserted in his Special Address to Congress after the outbreak of war, "the people will save their government, if the government itself, will do its part, only indifferently well." "Message to Congress in Special Session," July 4, 1861, in Lincoln, *Speeches and Writings,* 246, 254.

115. Lincoln, Reply to the Ohio Democratic Convention, June 29, 1863, in ibid., 466, 468–69.

116. "Copperheads" were Northerners who sympathized with the cause of the Confederacy.

117. See Rehnquist, *All the Laws but One*, 75–88, for a contextual explanation for why such a conspiracy at such a late point in the war was not as unreasonable and hopeless as might first appear.

118. *Ex Parte Milligan*, 71 U.S. (4 Wall.) 2.

119. Ibid.

120. While the dissent "would judge the validity of governmental action by the ordinary canons of appropriateness and necessity to the exercise of an express power," Justice Davis "would import into the Constitution a mechanical test derived from English constitutional history of a period when rigid lines had seemed the only means of controlling the prerogative." Fairman, *The Law of Martial Rule,* 162.

121. Neely, *The Fate of Liberty*, 176. Rossiter and Longaker, *The Supreme Court and the Commander in Chief,* 39. See the list of authorities catalogued by Charles Fairman in support of his contention that "at no time has the dictum in Mr. Justice Davis' opinion been accepted as having settled the law for the future." Fairman, *The Law of Martial Rule,* 163.

122. Neely, *The Fate of Liberty,* 175–84.

123. Corwin, *The President,* 165–66, quoted in ibid., 184.

124. Neely, *The Fate of Liberty,* 176–77.

125. *State v. Stillman*, 7 Cold., 352, quoted in Winthrop, *Military Law and Precedents,* 834, note 75.

126. The opening section of the Act stated, "Whereas no legal State governments or adequate protection for life or property now exists in the rebel states of Virginia, North Carolina, South Carolina, Georgia, Mississippi, Alabama, Louisiana, Florida, Texas, and Arkansas; and whereas it is necessary that peace and good order should be enforced in said States until loyal and republican State governments can be legally established . . ."; quoted in ibid., 848.

127. Randall, *The Civil War and Reconstruction,* 558–600

128. Winthrop, *Military Law and Precedents*, 853.

129. Sefton, *The United States Army and Reconstruction,* 31, 35.

130. Ibid. It was this category of adjudication that later would figure prominently in the use of military commissions in the aftermath of the Second World War.

131. Neely, *The Fate of Liberty,* 177–78.

132. Randall, *The Civil War and Reconstruction,* 643–44, note 4.

133. Though not without its shortcomings, at this time the best available scholarly treatment of Andersonville and the Wirz trial remains Marvel, *Andersonville: The Last Depot.*

134. See Rehnquist, *All the Laws but One*, 138–69.

135. Sefton, *The United States Army and Reconstruction*, 5–6. Sefton's work provides an excellent, thorough account of the Army's involvement in the post-war Reconstruction South, which this portion of the chapter follows. He concludes that "the fact that such discretion existed complicates the evaluation of the Army's performance but facilitates the study of comparative statesmanship." Ibid., 7, 253, 30.

136. "The object of the Government," said General Henry W. Slocum, "is not to screen this class from just punishment; not to encourage in them the idea that they can be guilty of crime and escape its penalties; but simply to ensure to them the rights of free men, holding them, at the same time, subject to the same laws by which other classes are governed." Quoted in ibid., 44–45, 46.

137. G.O. 3, AGO, Jan. 12, 1866, RG94, NA, quoted in ibid., 70.

138. Ibid., 37–38.

139. Ibid., 23. Sherman deplored the "reprehensible arrangement of districts" effected by General Pope in Georgia in the run-up to the 1867 convention. Pope's partisan gerrymandering "gave the Negroes and their white allies a vastly greater potential for controlling the convention than their registered voting strength warranted." Ibid., 165–66.

140. Ibid., 146. Some of the generals were quite sparing in their use of military commissions. Thus, General George Gordon Meade, charged in December 1867 with command of the Third Military District, comprising the departments of Alabama, Georgia, and Florida, tried only thirty-two people by military commission in the entire division over the eight months of his tenure in command. Ibid., 172.

CHAPTER 2

1. For discussion of the vast reassessment and reform of overall military policy prompted by the British Army's unsatisfactory performance in the Boer War, see John Gooch, "Britain and the Boer War," in Andreopoulos and Selesky, eds., *The Aftermath of Defeat*, 40–58.

2. Charles Townshend, "Martial Law: Legal and Administrative Problems of Civil Emergency in Britain and the Empire, 1800–1940," 25 *The Historical Journal* 167, 173 (1982) [hereinafter, Townshend]. I am indebted to Professor Townshend's article for the following summary of the Eyre controversy.

3. Orwell's observation in the next century restated the same agonizing problem of the clash of principles at the point of impact of cultures: "But there is one thought which every white man . . . thinks when he sees a black army marching past. 'How much longer can we go on kidding these people? How long before they turn their guns in the other direction?'" George Orwell, "Marakech," in Orwell, *The Collected Essays*, 1: 127.

4. The perennial nature of the problem is, again, perhaps best captured in Orwell's famous essay on the bitter ironies of empire, "Shooting an Elephant": "[it was] as I stood there with the rifle in my hands, that I first grasped the hollowness, the futility of the white man's dominion in the East. Here was I, the white man with his gun, standing in front of the unarmed native crowd—seemingly the leading actor of the piece; but in reality I was only an absurd puppet pushed to and fro by the will of those yellow faces behind. I perceived in this moment that when the white man turns tyrant it is his own freedom that he destroys. He becomes a sort of hollow, posing dummy . . . For it is the condition of his rule that he shall spend his life in trying to impress the 'natives,' and so in every crisis he has got to do what the 'natives' expect of him. He wears a mask, and his face grows to fit it." Ibid., 1: 46.

5. Charles Callwell, *Small Wars—Their Principles and Practice* (1896), quoted in Asprey, *War in the Shadows,* 1: 203. As Asprey notes, Callwell revised his work to incorporate the lessons of the Anglo-Boer conflict of 1899–1902, in which he served with distinction.

6. Townshend, 174.

7. Richard A. Cosgrove, "The Boer War and the Modernization of British Martial Law," 44 *Military Affairs* 124, (1980) [hereinafter, Cosgrove].

8. Fairman, *The Law of Martial Rule,* 141–42.

9. Ceylon debate, 1 April 1851. 115 H.L. Debates, 3rd series, col. 880, quoted in Townshend, 172. The point was reiterated in the instructions on martial law promulgated by Lord Kitchener in 1900. Parliamentary Papers Relating to the Administration of Martial Law in South Africa (1902) [hereinafter, *Parliamentary Papers*].

10. 11 Hansard's Parl. Deb. N.S., 1046, cited in Clode, *Military Forces of the Crown,* 486.

11. Amery, ed., *The Times History,* 6: 544.

12. Ibid.

13. Martial Law Order, 30 January 1900, in *Parliamentary Papers,* 23. The order is signed, in typical fashion, "KITCHENER OF KHARTOUM, Chief of Staff, Cape Town."

14. To this end, the order stipulated that any regulations promulgated by the commander exercising martial rule "should be so framed as to interfere as little as possible with the civil rights of peaceable inhabitants, and their freedom to pursue their ordinary avocations." Ibid. See also, Chief of Staff's Circular Memorandum No. 7, 3 February 1900, in ibid., 26 (stating that "non-military offenses such as theft, assault, rape, etc." should normally be dealt with by the local magistracy).

15. In typical fashion, the order lists six separate categories of offenses suitable for trial by military courts: treason or sedition; enlisting in the enemy's forces; aiding or abetting the enemy; trading or supplying goods to the enemy;

sabotage of bridges, railways, etc.; and breaches of martial law regulations issued by the regional military commanders. All other offenses were "to be left to the Civil Court to deal with in ordinary course." Ibid.

16. Chief of Staff's Circular Memorandum No. 7, 3 February 1900, in *Parliamentary Papers*, 26.

17. Ibid.

18. Ibid.

19. *Notice*, 22 April 1901, in *Parliamentary Papers*, 75.

20. See Martial Law Order, 30 January 1900, paragraph 8, in ibid., 23.

21. The term has entered into the vocabulary of military strategic analysis as a result of the innovative "Center of Gravity," or COG, theory developed by Colonel John Worden in the planning and execution of the American air operation in the Persian Gulf War in 1991. Though the term may be anachronistic in the literal historical sense, it is nevertheless apposite to this aspect of British strategy in the Boer War.

22. Pakenham, *The Boer War*, 526–27.

23. Kipling, "Ubique," in *The Five Nations* (1903). Kipling, whose remarkable prescience anticipated much of the grief and horrors of the twentieth century, viewed the exhaustion of British imperial nerve in the Boer War as spelling the doom of the British empire, marking the point of incipient decline of the *pax Britannia* that, despite its faults, had been a source of stability and order in international affairs. See, Gilmour, *The Long Recessional*, passim.

24. British law officers regarded the decision to annex as premature on the basis of international law principles. Spies, *Methods of Barbarism?*, 58–59.

25. Amery, *The Times History*, 548.

26. Spies, *Methods of Barbarism?*, 69–71.

27. "During the early months of the war few officers could be spared from active operations in the field to carry on the administration of martial law, and those that could be detailed had no previous experience of their duties, and did not understand fully the nature of the powers they were called upon to exercise. The principal objections urged against the extension of the area under martial law were the want of system in its administration and the delay in investigating the cases of persons arrested under it. There was a tendency throughout the Colony, from the Ministry on downwards, to make complaints against the military administration, and owing to the novelty of the situation, it was inevitable that some awkward incidents should arise." Amery, *The Times History*, 549.

28. Dicey, *Introduction to the Study of the Law of the Constitution*, 187.

29. Spies, *Methods of Barbarism?*, 303.

30. Ibid.

31. For a representative Afrikaner account, see Dietlof van Warmelo, *On Commando* 172–73.

32. Albert Grundlingh, "The War in Twentieth-Century Afrikaner Consciousness," in Omissi and Thompson, eds., *The Impact of the South African War*, 23–24.

33. Spies, *Methods of Barbarism?*, 142. As Spies observes, the measure violated Hague principles as well as contemporary standards of customary international law. Ibid. The camps received criticism not only on humanitarian grounds. Kipling sardonically remarked that the camps allowed "the guerrillas . . . to behave like 'Apaches . . . having the time of their lives' while the British were 'looking after their wives and kids so they [had] nothing to worry about.'" Gilmour, *The Long Recessional*, 154.

34. For a detailed account of the inspections of the camps, see, Great Britain, Concentration Camps Commission, *Report on the Concentration Camps in South Africa, by the Committee of Ladies Appointed by the Secretary of State for War; Containing Reports on the Camps in Natal, the Orange River Colony, and the Transvaal* (1902). Among its primary aims, the commission sought "how to account for the extraordinary high death-rate" in the camps, and noted the "pestilential atmosphere" of the tents. Ibid., 14, 16.

35. State Attorney J. C. Smuts to President Kruger, 3 June 1901, in Smuts, *Selections from Smuts Papers*, Hancock and Van Der Poel, eds., 1: 154–55.

36. Warwick, *Black People and the South African War*, 145–62.

37. For a recent popular, somewhat tendentious pro-Boer account documenting injustices suffered by Boer regulars and non-combatants in the British military tribunals, see, Jooste and Webster, *Innocent Blood*. The work demonstrates that the injuries suffered still rankle among the Afrikaner people.

38. The evidence collected by the Royal Commission of Inquiry contains a detailed appendix, itemizing the courts of inquiry that were conducted to investigate numerous British troop surrrenders, especially in the early campaigns of the war. See Appendix 55, "Papers Relating to South African Surrenders," in Great Britain, Royal Commission on the War in South Africa, *Appendices to the Minutes of Evidence taken before the Royal Commission on the War in South Africa*, Cd. 1792, at 372, ff. (1903).

39. Ibid., 403.

40. Ibid., 404–6.

41. See, ibid.; and Great Britain, Royal Commission on the War in South Africa, *Minutes of Evidence taken before the Royal Commission on the War in South Africa*, vol. 1, 2 Cd. 1790 (1903); and Report of His Majesty's Commissioners Appointed to Inquire into the Military Preparations and other Matters Connected with the War in South Africa, Cd. 1789 (1903).

42. Pakenham, *The Boer War*, 163.

43. Judd and Surridge, *The Boer War*, 99.

44. Ibid.

45. Ibid.

46. For discussion of the unease and discomfort experienced by the British administration, from Chamberlain on down, over the imposition of martial law in the Cape, see Townshend, 176–79. British leniency was widely noted and sharply criticized by imperial unionists like Kipling, who was "flabbergasted" by the nation's "'silly, sentimental methods,'" both in its manner of conducting the war and of addressing the transgressions of Cape rebels. Gilmour, *The Long Recessional,* 154.

47. The oath is reproduced in *Parliamentary Papers,* 10.

48. Amery's account, noting that some of the Boer marauders reached to within thirty-five miles of Cape Town itself, emphasized the urgency and appropriateness of the decree: "with a large portion of the population openly or latently disloyal, it was imperative to take more severe action to prevent the invader receiving reinforcements in men, arms, or horses. Gradually, the regulations enforced were rendered more severe, till, towards the end of the war, in those districts in which active operations were in actual or threatened progress, consideration for the inhabitants had to give way in large measure, to military requirements. Dutch farmers now found that they could no longer openly express their sympathy with the invaders, and that assistance given to the Boer bands was fraught with danger to themselves. More even than passive neutrality was required of them." Amery, *The Times History,* 559.

49. Pakenham, *The Boer War,* 515.

50. J. Smuts to L. Botha, 23 January 1901, in Smuts, *Smuts Papers,* 1: 357.

51. Quoted in Amery, *The Times History,* 553–54.

52. See text below.

53. Commandant Kritzinger himself was not captured until the night of December 16. South Africa Despatches, Despatch by General Lord Kitchener, 8 January 1902, relative to Military Operations in South Africa, Cd. 824, p. 11 (1902).

54. Jooste and Webster, *Innocent Blood,* 228–29, contains charts detailing citizenship and ages of the executed, places, method of execution, and charges. The number given by Jooste and Webster for the Transvaal and Free State is the highest of any available source. They include twenty-four executions without trial in this number. In many of these cases, there is little reliable evidence to go on.

55. A transcript and summarized witness testimony in the trial appears in *Parliamentary Papers,* 251.

56. For a detailed summary of the trial and witness testimony, see *Parliamentary Papers,* 251ff.

57. Jooste and Webster repeat the argument throughout their account of the Scheepers case. Jooste and Webster, *Innocent Blood,* 149–64. Yet as Pakenham asserts, this had largely been a fiction from the very outset, from the perspective of both sides, as "Africans . . . played a central role as non-combatants serving

both armies," though "no one will ever know the total number of black 'Boers,' or black British, many of whom were forced labourers." He gives the number of 40,000 as a "conservative estimate." Despite the invisibility of these black laborers throughout the history of white South Africa, "behind every white artisan there had always been a black man, and so now, behind every white man with a rifle was a black man with a spade, hewing out the white man's trenches, driving his ox wagons and mule wagons, guarding his cattle; diggers and drivers and drovers, as ubiquitous and docile as the cattle themselves—and (to most white men) as invisible." Pakenham, *The Boer War,* 580.

58. For a summary, see Jooste and Webster, *Innocent Blood,* 129.

59. Thus, in view of the damaging prolongation of hostilities, Ian Rawlinson had advised summary executions of the "cold blooded [Boer] ruffians" as the best means of securing "the future peace of the country." Quoted in Pakenham, *Boer War,* 595. Leniency continued to prevail on the Boer side with the release of the prisoner Lieutenant-General Lord Methuen—veteran of Modder River and Magersfontein and the only British general whom the Boers succeeded in capturing—though by this point in time, March 1902, the war's denouement was rapidly coming into clearer focus.

60. Pakenham, *The Boer War,* 582.

61. De Wet, *Three Years' War (October 1899–June 1902)* (1902) 322. De Wet continued his description: "The blockhouses themselves were sometimes round, sometimes angled erections. The roofs were always of iron. The walls were pierced with loop-holes four feet from the ground, and from four to six feet from each other . . . Between the blockhouses were fences, made with five strands of barbed-wire. Parallel with these was a trench, three feet deep and four to five feet across the top, but narrower at the bottom. Where the material could be procured, there was also a stone wall to serve as an additional obstacle. Sometimes there were two lines of fences, the upper one—erected on top of the earth thrown up from the trench—consisting of three or four strands only. There was thus a regular network of wires in the vicinity of the blockhouses—the English seemed to think that a Boer might be netted like a fish. If a wild horse had been trapped there, I should have liked to have been there to see, but I should not have liked to have been the wild horse." Ibid., 323

In De Wet's estimation, the blockhouse scheme had been a great waste of resources. His description of his own break through the blockhouse lines demonstrated how "this wonderful scheme of the English prolonged the war for at least three months." Ibid. De Wet found the British adoption of the strategy of "night attacks" to have been a far more effective method. Thus, he argued, it was the British imitation of their opponents' irregular guerrilla tactics that became "the most difficult of the enemy's tactics with which we had to deal." Ibid., 324.

62. Fairman, *The Law of Martial Rule,* 141–42.

63. Report of the Royal Commission Appointed to Inquire into Sentences Passed under Martial Law, iv, November 1902.

64. Ibid.

65. Ibid., Schedules II and III.

66. Ibid., Schedule III, 62.

67. Amery, *The Times History*, 556.

68. Judd and Surridge, *The Boer War*, 234.

69. Quoted in Ibid.

70. See, e.g., Jooste and Webster, *Innocent Blood*, 22.

71. *Ex parte Marais*, 1902 App. Cas. 109 (P.C. 1901).

72. Ibid., 110.

73. See, e.g., *Elphinstone v. Bedreechund*, 1 Knapp, P.C. 316; In re Sup. Ct. Rep. 173 (1900); *The Queen v. Gildenhuys* id. 266; *Queen v. Bekker* id. 340; *Morcom v. Postmaster General* 21 N. S. Natal Law Rep. 32 (1900). The approach of the courts in such cases is summarized in Fairman, *The Law of Martial Rule*, 64–65.

74. Ibid., 114.

75. Ibid., 115.

76. Ibid. The Judicial Committee had occasion to affirm the assertion in a later case, arising out of the native insurrection in Natal of 1906

77. Edward S. Corwin, "Martial Law, Yesterday and Today," 47 *Political Science Quarterly* 96, 102 (1932).

78. Amery, *The Times History*, 559.

79. Ibid, 561–52.

80. In his eighth and final edition of an authoritative and influential treatise on constitutional law, Dicey relied extensively on this colloquy for his treatment of the subject of martial rule. It is surely more than mere coincidence that this edition was produced during the middle of Britain's next major military engagement, this time the world conflagration of the Great War. Dicey, *Introduction to the Study of the Law of the Constitution* (8th ed., 1915) (1982), 396.

81. H. Erle Richards, "Martial Rule," 70 Law Quarterly Review, 141.

82. Cyril Dodd, The Case of Marais, 70 Law Quarterly Review 143, 144 (1902).

83. Ibid., 144.

84. Ibid., 145.

85. Ibid.

86. Ibid.

87. Ibid., 147.

88. Ibid.

89. Ibid., 149.

90. Frederick Pollock, "What is Martial Law?" 70 Law Quarterly Review 152, 154 (1902).

91. For an interesting and scholarly historical study examining the role of military influences on the development of cultural, legal, and political institutions, see Downing, *The Military Revolution and Political Change.*

92. Frederick Pollock, "What is Martial Law?" 70 Law Quarterly Review 155 (1902).

93. In this way, Kitchener's martial law instructions conceded too much.

94. Ibid., 156.

95. Ibid., 156.

96. *Tilonko v. Attorney-General of Natal* A.C. 93, 94 (1907).

97. Ibid.

98. Ibid.

99. Ibid., 94–95.

100. Cosgrove, 125.

101. Ibid.

102. Mahan, *The Story of the War in South Africa (1899–1900)* (1901), 1.

103. Amery, *The Times History,* 571–72. Moving forward in history, other striking comparisons arise, for instance, with the French administration of martial rule during the Algerian conflict. See, e.g., Alistair Horne, *A Savage War of Peace: Algeria 1954–1962* (1972); and Ambler, *The French Army in Politics,* 149–204.

104. Despatch by General Lord Kitchener, 23 June 1902, relative to Military Operations in South Africa, in *South Africa Despatches,* Cd. 986, p. 3 (1902). Earlier in the month Kitchener had expressed his relief that all the participants would be spared the futility of "a further prolongation of a useless guerrilla struggle," and offered his "tribute of respect . . . to those of the Boer leaders, who, facing privation and danger at the head of their commandos up to the very last moment, have at length been manly enough to bow to the inevitable, and far-seeing enough to accept the generous terms accorded by His Majesty's Government." Despatch, General Lord Kitchener, 1 June 1902, relative to Military Operations in South Africa, in *South Africa Despatches* Cd. 984, p. 3 (1902). Major-General Locke Elliot, Commander in the Midland District of the Orange River colony, commented upon De Wet in this manner: "De Wet appears a man of great character and firmness, and after living with him for 10 days, I have no hesitation in saying that he intends using his great influence, loyally, to further the interests of the British government, and to maintain a lasting peace." General Remarks, Pretoria, 18 June 1902, MG E Locke Elliot, in *South Africa Despatches,* Cd. 986, Appendix, 36 (1902).

Chapter 3

1. Rossiter, *Constitutional Dictatorship,* 79.

2. Ibid.

3. "English public law does not *want* to anticipate the crisis situation, and the sacrifices of principle that it will demand; it organizes matters once it appears. On the contrary, French public law admits in advance that in periods of crisis, non-military individuals may in certain cases be tried in military tribunals." (italics in original) Joseph- Barthélemy, "Le Droit Public en Temps de Guerre," 4: "Diminution des garanties des citoyens devant la répression pénale," 33 Revue du droit public 73, 76 (1916). (This article appeared serially in five separate installments from 1915–1916.) The observation indirectly points to another fundamental structural contrast: the fact that the foundational distinction in civil law systems between public and private law finds no ready analogue in the Anglo-American common law tradition. See generally, Merryman, *The Civil Law Tradition.* This further points to a distinction arising out of the fact noted by the French comparatist, René David, that French criminal law falls under the "public" category, and as such for a Frenchman, "is not and cannot be law in the strict sense," since law "can only develop in the area of relations between individuals, where the state is an impartial arbiter. In criminal as in administrative law, the government is required to play a more active role. Society's interest is obviously and directly involved. A Frenchman will allow the government a degree of discretion, and even arbitrariness, that is hard to reconcile with the certainty characteristic of legal principles. The assumption predominates that society's interest requires that one trust the police." David, *French Law,* 119–20. These startling observations cast a wide shadow over the developments related in the following account.

4. Law of August 9, 1849.

5. Law of April 9, 1878.

6. Subsequent to the legislative creation of the regime of *l'état de siege,* additional emergency measures, originating in the Parliament, by executive decree, and even by judicial initiative have been adopted at various times to address a wide variety of crisis conditions. See text, *infra.*

7. Art. 36, Constitution of 1958.

8. A. Bosc, "Les Actes de Gouvernement et la Théorie des Pouvoirs de Guerre," 43 Revue du droit public 186, 244 (1926).

9. Law of 1849, para. 9.

10. The 1849 statute provides, in broad terms, the basis for the jurisdiction of the conseils de guerre: "Les tribunaux militaires peuvent être saisis de la connaissance des crimes et délits contre la sûreté de la République, contre la Constitution, contre l'ordre et la paix publique, quelle que soit la qualité des auteurs principaux et des complices." ("Military tribunals may adjudicate crimes and misdemeanors against the security of the Republic, against the Constitution, and against public order and peace, whatever the status of the principal actors and accessories.") Law of August 9, 1849, Article 8. Two competing interpretations existed as to the precise meaning of "crimes and misdemeanors against

public security." According to one understanding, the phrase contemplated a reference back (*renvoi*) to the corresponding title in the criminal code. According to the other interpretation, the article contained only a general principle, allowing military authorities the discretion to determine whether or not, in a given case, a crime or offense constituted a threat to order and public safety. The weight of the evidence appears to support the latter view: "The legislative intent was clear; it was nevertheless difficult to find the juridical formula to insert in a statutory text. Thus the legislature limits itself to giving to the military authority a very large discretionary power (*pouvoir d'appréciation*), counting on its ability to exercise such authority with discernment, counting most of all upon the supervisory control, even under the regime of a state of siege, that the governmental authority is called to exert over the military." Barthélemy, 4: 97–102, 102.

11. "From the point of view of the opportunity of a declaration, of the extent, and duration of the state of siege, the government of the Republic at the time of the war of 1914 has shown itself much more energetic than the imperial government in analogous circumstances." Barthélemy, 1, 32 Revue du droit public 134, 153 (1915).

12. Ibid.

13. Welch, *Justice and the Genesis of War,* 119.

14. Kissinger, *Diplomacy,* 203. In actual practice, France's mobilization order preceded the German order by an hour, though the effect was the same whatever the precise order of events. Keegan, *The First World War,* 68.

15. Becker, *La France en guerre,* 66.

16. The plan of Field Marshal Alfred von Schlieffen, Chief of the German General Staff from 1891–1906, called for a lightning strike against France from the north, moving five armies across the Belgian frontier in a great semi-circular pincer movement that would destroy the French armies in a decisive battle and bring Paris to submission within forty-two days. This would free up the German armies to race eastward via railroad in order to defeat the slowly mobilizing Russian armies on the eastern front.

17. For detailed discussion of the German invasion of Belgium from the point of view of international law, see, Garner, *International Law and the World War,* 2: 186–230. See also, Horne and Kramer, *German Atrocities.*

18. The "dirty war" of the *francs-tireurs* of 1870–71 is discussed in Wawro, *The Franco-Prussian War,* 237–38, 309.

19. Horne and Kramer, *German Atrocities,* 77, concluding, "Organized civilian resistance on a scale commensurate with German reactions in August 1914 is an historical impossibility."

20. Such was the (now discredited) allegation of, e.g., Müller-Meiningen, *Der Weltkrieg und "der Zusammenbruch des Volkerrecht."*

21. Horne and Kramer, *German Atrocities,* 9–78. Thus, "the substantive phenomenon was German *belief* in a People's War, which constituted a massive case of collective self-suggestion, probably unparalleled in a modern army. A million men were swept by a delusion which mistook the fantasy of the franc-tireur war for reality" (italics in original). Ibid., 77.

22. Ibid., 74. To be sure, the fear occasioned by the actions of the German army led to exaggeration and embellishment in the re-telling of events. But the actual offenses were bad enough. From the first day, the massacres included the summary execution of Belgian priests as well as ordinary civilians. Tuchman, *The Guns of August,* 173. The ancient medieval university town of Louvain suffered severe damage. Among the more serious allegations, Germans were charged with "systematically firing upon hospitals, ambulances, stretcher bearers, and dressing stations . . . [illegal uses of the Red Cross flag]; transporting munitions in ambulances, with maltreating the wounded, etc." in Belgium. Garner, *International Law and the World War,* 1: 498.

23. Keegan, *The First World War,* 111. Indeed, the French command structure was such that Joffre, in his position as "supreme commander with war powers, could not be overruled by ministers or even the President." Ibid., 109–10.

24. Ibid., 21. With the adoption of a new law in 1982, revising the Codes of Criminal Procedure and of Military Justice, the permanent courts of the Armed Forces were finally dismantled. Act No. 82–621, July 21, 1982.

25. "In fact, the state of siege, proclaimed the 2nd of August, 1914, has brought about a *collaboration* between, rather than an outright *substitution* of military for civilian authorities; formally, the public acts by which this collaboration is articulated have frequently carried the joint signatures of authorities from the two categories: prefects and regional commandants of the departments, prefect of police and Governor of Paris" (italics in original). Barthélemy, 1: 137. Thus the French scheme upended Justice Davis's bright-line rule from the Milligan case: "Martial rule can never exist where courts are open, and in the proper and unobstructed exercise of their jurisdiction." The present danger, while not *per se* imposing an obstruction on the activities of the civil courts, rendered the American justice's tidy arrangement irrelevant at best.

26. It was a formula repeated in the opinions of the Cour de Cassation pertaining to the conseils de guerre, (see, e.g., Arrêt, Cour de Cassation, July 22, 1915, B. 155, 286; and July 22, 1915, B. 159, 292).

27. Arrêt, Cour de Cassation, November 18, 1915, B. 217, 399.

28. This "public-private" distinction is fundamental to the legal regimes of civil law countries and has no immediate analogue in the common law tradition, though there has been some recent blending of the traditions. David and Brierley, *Major Legal Systems,* 74–82.

29. Rossiter, *Constitutional Dictatorship,* 95; Barthélemy, 3: "La Gouvernement et la loi," 32 Revue du droit public 548–49 (1915). In the reconstruction South, too, alcohol-related cases formed a significant share of the offenses tried by military commission. There, civilians were often tried for "selling liquor to soldiers" and violating licensing requirements for the sale of alcohol in hotels and inns. Sefton, *The United States Army and Reconstruction,* 146.

30. Becker, *La France en guerre,* 67. One of the more sensational cases to test the limits of the discretion of the conseils de guerre, the *Affaire Bolo et Porchère,* involved an international espionage ring. Among other offenses, co-defendant Marie-Paul Bolo, a French national, was convicted for having exchanged intelligence communications with the enemy—from Switzerland in 1915—via the former viceroy of Egypt and the Pacha Youssouf Saddik, as well as of having received payments from the German government while in the United States in 1916 in furtherance of a plan to use the media to influence French opinion in favor of the Central powers. On appeal, both the Conseil de Revision and the Cour de Cassation affirmed Bolo's conviction and death sentence, acknowledging the competence of the military tribunals to try crimes committed *à l'étranger,* by a civilian. Arrêt, Cour de Cassation, April 2, 1918, B. 79, p. 131. See also, 45 Journal du droit international 638–43; 659–66 (1918).

31. One French theorist, commenting generally on the institutionalization of exceptional executive powers, posits the theoretical benefit provided by its explicit legality, while acknowledging that in practice, ineluctably, "emergency powers, once institutionalized, offer fewer guarantees for the safeguarding of democracy than if the laws remain silent on the subject, allowing to circumstance the attentions giving rise to such powers." Leroy, *L'Organisation constitutionnelle,* 41.

32. Bulletin de la jurisprudence française, reporting on Conseil de Guerre, 2nd region (Paris), July 2, 1915; and Conseil de Revision permanent de Paris, July 21, 1915, in 42 Journal du droit international 617–19 (1915).

33. Mérignhac and Lémonon, *Le Droit des gens,* 1: 177.

34. Journal officiel de la République Française, Séance du Senat du 23 mars 1916, pr 185–197 (March 24, 1916) quoted in ibid., 874, 880.

35. Malvy took to the defense in a letter to the Parisian journal *La Liberté,* dated December 26, 1915. The virulence of his protest gives some indication of the direction from which the winds of critique were coming:

> I would surely abstain from responding to your articles regarding foreigners in France and the repression of espionage if I did not consider there to be a true national danger in allowing a demoralizing idea to gain further credit in public opinion, the idea that the administration over which I have charge does not employ against internal enemies [*les ennemis de l'intérieur*] all the vigilance and energy that is necessary in the tragic circumstances we currently face.

> As the minister responsible for public peace and order, I have the duty to rise up against all that which is susceptible of harming the admirable state of morale of the Nation and, in response to press campaigns that may sow disquiet and mistrust, to issue a call to public opinion, a call for calm and level-headedness [*sang-froid*].

Among other measures to his credit, Malvy records the establishment of 52 concentration camps for the sequestration of Austro-German nationals, and the expulsion of over 5,000 potentially disloyal foreigners. The editorial response is equally illuminating. The minister's figures give cause for greater alarm, not calm and security: in sixteen months, only 42 convictions in the conseils de guerre for the offense of espionage, both in the zone of the armies and in the interior—and none in the city of Paris. This despite the police's accumulation of some 27,000 *dossiers* (i.e., criminal investigatory files) opened against possible espionage suspects in Paris alone! Since it is beyond all reasonable conjecture to presume that each and every one of these cases amounted to nothing more than a "false alarm," the minister is guilty either of gross incompetence or of unjustifiable solicitude for the suspects. Lettre de M. Malvy, ministre de l'intérieur à M. Georges Berthoulat, directeur de la Liberté, and response, *La Liberté*, December 26, 1915, quoted in 43 Journal du droit international 155–60 (1916). Needless to say, there is no hint in the entire exchange given to the consideration that a greater crack-down on civil liberties would be tantamount to a cession of victory to the other side.

36. Journal officiel de la République Française, Senate Proceedings, March 23, 1916, at 185–97 (March 24, 1916) reproduced in ibid., 874, 880. The transcript of the Senate debate continues in ibid., 1188–1203; and concludes in 44 Journal du droit international 570–86 (1917).

37. Ibid., 583.

38. "Espionage and illegal residence in the entrenched camp of Paris," *Le Figaro*, January 18, 1916, reproduced in ibid., 544–45.

39. "The Affaire Hochel," *Le Temps*, July 18, 1915, reporting results of Conseil de Guerre, 15th region, (Marseilles, undated), reproduced in "Faits et Informations," 42 Journal du droit international 479–80 (1915).

40. Conseil de Guerre, Dunkerque, June 18, 1914, reported in ibid., 774.

41. The French law setting penalties for the offense of espionage as applied during the First World War, the Law of April 18, 1886, is reproduced in 44 Journal du droit international 779–83 (1917).

42. "Faits et Informations," reporting results of Conseil de Guerre, 3rd region (Paris, undated) in 45 Journal du droit international 456 (1918). For additional reports of cases in the conseils de guerre addressing espionage, see, e.g., l'affaire Theissen, results of Conseil de Guerre, 1st region, (Boulogne-sur-Mer), September 24, 1915, reported in "Faits et Informations," 42 ibid., at 998–99 (1915).

Theissen, a Belgian national, was chief of German espionage operations in Belgium. Captured in Brussels in early August 1914 and then sent to Britain, where he was shifted from prison to prison, he was eventually turned over to French authorities for adjudication. Interestingly, the Conseil de Guerre refrained from imposing the death sentence; instead, it condemned him to be permanently deported to a fortified security facility. See also the reports of the following representative sample of cases: the results of Conseil de Guerre, Dunkerque, June 18, 1915, reported in ibid., 774 (1915); l'affaire Heck, the execution of a spy reported at ibid., 1227 (Heck, an Alsatian reporting troop movements to the German authorities from within France, was condemned to death by three different conseils de guerre); l'affaire Bacchle, report of 3rd Conseil de Guerre (Paris, undated), summarized at ibid., 1227; and l'affaire Dei Pasi, report of 3rd Conseil de Guerre (Paris, January 5, 1916), summarized in *Le Figaro,* January 6, 1916, reproduced in ibid., 44: 586–87.

43. *Gazette des tribunaux,* August 22–24, 1915, reporting results of Conseil de Guerre, 3rd region, August 20, 1915, in ibid., at 776–77.

44. Ibid., reporting results of Conseil de Guerre, 2nd region (undated).

45. Ibid., reporting results of Conseil de Guerre, 3rd region (undated).

46. *Gazette des tribunaux,* July 31, 1915, reporting results of Conseil de Guerre, Lyon-Rhône, 14th region (undated), in ibid., 776.

47. Farcy, *Les Camps de concentration français,* 134.

48. Ibid., 90–91. For an emotionally charged personal account of the trial of one such suspect, convicted before a Paris military tribunal, see Menendez Valdés, *French Justice: Seven Months Under Sentence of Death.* Menéndez Valdés, an engineer from Spain, was apprehended by French authorities in May 1918, after making contacts with Germans in France. He suffered brutal treatment at the hands of police interrogators and finally appeared before a tribunal of seven officers on August 27. At the conclusion of his day-long trial, he received the death sentence for "intelligence with the enemy." Menéndez Valdés appealed to have his case reheard by a different military tribunal, on grounds of 1) insufficient evidence; 2) insufficient means of defense; 3) injury and maltreatment at the hands of his captors; and 4) the state of intoxication of three out of the seven military judges on his panel. Ibid., 125. After Menéndez Valdés had languished in prison for seven months, awaiting execution of the sentence, President Poincaré commuted it to penal servitude for life in French Guiana. He succeeded in escaping the prison camp there and returned to Spain in February 1922.

49. Farcy, *Les Camps de concentration français,* 90–91.

50. "It suffices to dissect the past history of the person in question in order to thicken the dossier [*epaisser le dossier*] and thereby prompt a removal that in fact rests on nothing more than the appearance before a conseil de guerre or on charges likely to lead to such an appearance." Ibid.

51. By the time of the Parisian government's removal to Bordeaux on September 2, 1914, thousands of Belgian refugees had converged on the city from the north, even while its own inhabitants were fleeing south by the tens of thousands. Over a third of Paris's peacetime population of three million left the city in these opening weeks of the war. Gilbert, *The First World War,* 65.

52. The problem assumed truly serious proportions in the First World War. See Speed, *Prisoners, Diplomats, and the Great War,* 141ff.

53. Garner, *International Law and the World War,* 1: 75.

54. Consideration of those structures which were fitted with the recession of "the sea of faith" for a new purpose in a new century, prompts echoes of the sardonic jibe of Solzhenitsyn's Solovetsky prisoners, "A holy place is never empty." Solzhenitsyn, *The Gulag Archipelago,* 2: 31.

55. For a description of conditions in the camps and comparisons with similar camps and internment arrangements in other countries during the First World War, see Speed, *Prisoners, Diplomats, and the Great War.* See also, Cahen-Salvador, *Les Prisonniers de guerre.*

56. Saint-Bonnet, *L'État d'exception,* 18. See also, Leroy, *L'Organisation constitutionnelle.*

57. See the summary provided in Saint-Bonnet, ibid., 9–23. The war produced a plethora of studies and doctoral theses devoted to the institutions of the state of siege, and the conseils de guerre. In addition to the works referred to throughout this chapter, see, e.g., Hermann Bekaert, *Le Code du conseil de guerre* (Brussels, 1945), providing a summary of the developments of the law concerning the conseils de guerre in Belgium; Col. Augier et Le Poittevin, *Droit pénal militaire* (Paris, 1918); M. le Commandant C. Louitz, *L'Organisation des conseils de guerre* (Paris, 1927); Henri Marie Joseph Xavier de Tanoüarn, *Étude de la compétence des tribunaux militaires en temps de paix* (Algiers, 1937); Capt. Edme Pinseau, *La Compétence des tribunaux militaires d'après la loi du 9 Mars 1928* (Besancon, 1929); Albert Stamm, *Étude de la compétence des tribunaux militaires en temps de paix* (Nancy, 1932). Without exception, such works engage in a theoretical and technical examination of the statutory framework, rather than in detailed exposition of the facts of particular cases in which such laws have been applied. The contrast with treatments of similar subjects from states with common law traditions is striking. The examiners come to their material with different questions; and the material itself has been shaped within a different juridical context. The differences reflect fundamental variances between the common law and civil law traditions.

58. The onset of crisis provoked a reversion to pre-constitutional, despotic forms. "But the progress of modern constitutionalism has led to the establishment in advance of a kind of 'public law in time of crisis,' and the corresponding attempt to achieve conciliation between the rights of citizens and the needs of exceptional discipline in times of disturbance. A preventive law drafted in periods

of calm allows for the opportunity of further elaboration and tailoring; it also presents the advantage of providing advance warning to citizens of the sacrifices that will be expected of them at the point of crisis." Barthélemy, 1: 136.

59. Saint-Bonnet, *L'État d'exception,* 362.

60. Arrêts, Conseil d'Etat, August 6, 1915, *Delmotte* and *Senmartin.* See, Gaston Jèze, "Notes de jurisprudence, jurisprudence judiciaire," 33 Revue du droit public 407 (1916).

61. Barthélemy, 1: 138.

62. "The Conseil de Guerre of the armies has no fixed position; it moves with the unit to which it is attached; its jurisdictional competence is personal, first and foremost, exercising authority over the military members of the unit; but it extends also, for a set category of offenders and infractions, over the territory actually occupied by the unit." Barthélemy, 4: 79.

63. A 1915 decision of the Cour de Cassation clarified that any infraction committed in time of war, on French soil, and in the *zone des armées*—as determined by decision of the Minister of War—constituted, for these purposes, an offense committed in the presence of the enemy. Arrêt, Cour de Cassation, November 18, 1915, B. 215, 393.

64. Title II, Book IV, Code de Justice Militaire, 1857.

65. Arrêts, Cour de Cassation, April 27, 1917, B. 109, 177; and August 26, 1920, B. 378, 610.

66. Barthélemy, 4: 82. The harshness of this aspect of the law of procedure was somewhat mitigated by circular instructions issued by the government urging commanders to involve defense counsel, to the extent possible, at an earlier stage of the process. Ibid., 83.

67. Ibid., 83–84.

68. "The legislator fears that the military judge may allow himself to be softened in his response to individual cases, and that, by an indulgent admission of mitigating circumstances, he should compromise the superior interests of military discipline." Ibid., 90.

69. Romain, *L'Etat de siège politique,* 424–29.

70. Ibid, 411–13.

71. Art. 81, Code de Justice Militaire.

72. Arrêt, Cour de Cassation, January 10, 1918, B. 3, 3. The brief report of the case in the Official Bulletin of the decisions of the Cour de Cassation provides no indication of the facts and circumstances of Haïm's crime.

73. Romain, *L'Etat de siège politique,* 443.

74. This was the nature of the decrees of January 7, 1915, prohibiting the sale of absinthe and the opening of new establishments for the sale or consumption of alcohol. "Thus, the Government forces the hand of the Chambers, by means of a process of dubious constitutionality, but which is new and interesting: rather

than go through the process of drafting a law, it makes—on a matter falling within the legislative domain—a *decree,* which has a certain validity in and of itself, which is immediately executory, and which will remain so until such time as the Chambers take the positive step of a *contrary solution*" (italics in original). Barthélemy, 5: 563–64. For a discussion of the French government's censorship activities, see Barthélemy, 2: 310–59.

75. Joffre addressed the government in Bordeaux in no uncertain terms, citing insubordination, desertion, and malingering as principal offenses requiring the jurisdiction of the special courts: "Up until now, I had thought that the rapid procedure of the conseils de guerre of the armies furnished sufficient means of action. But I have come to the realization that the difficulty of observing regular forms in the actual situation, and the 24-hour delay imposed by the law, greatly impede their capacity for setting [deterrent] examples—examples that are actually indispensable. Consequently, I request that you decree, as a matter of urgency, the establishment of courts-martial, composed of three members, which will adjudicate without delay all flagrant offenses, notably pillaging, malingering, desertion, and insubordination, the judgments of which will be subject to immediate execution." Quoted in Hélie, *Competence des conseils de guerre,* 107. See also Barthélemy, 4: 110–11.

76. "It is a hard but certain necessity that the fear of terrible punishment should maintain before the enemy those who would be tempted to abandon their post and thereby sow panic, and compromise the outcome of battles; that he who gives way to the fear of losing his life in glory, should be assured of losing it in shame;—it is necessary, by the same prospect of terrifying punishment, to stop those who would favor the enemy by their maneuvers: traitors and spies;—it is necessary, finally, that the army should find in its rearguard, among a nation shaped by rigorous discipline, the material and moral support to which it has a right . . . These ideas are self-evident. To the exceptional need for order and discipline, it is necessary to have appropriate means; this requires a particularly rigorous punitive repression." Barthélemy, Ibid, 73–74.

77. Ibid., 112.

78. Decree dated September 6, 1914, quoted in Hélie, *La Competence des conseils de guerre,* 106–7. The French Foreign Minister, René Viviani, reported on September 22, 1915, a little over a year after the introduction of the summary tribunals, that 840 prosecutions had been conducted, with 345 acquittals, 420 sentences to hard labor or imprisonment, and approximately 80 death sentences. Subsequent figures submitted to the Senate, compiled between the date of the decree, September 6, 1914 and October 31, 1915, reported 798 defendants, 517 guilty findings, 109 death sentences, 221 to imprisonment, and 281 aquittals. Barthélemy, 4: 112–13. A 35–40% acquittal rate surely provides some balance of perspective from which to assess the much-maligned special courts.

79. Ibid, 114–15. "In creating this legal procedure, simple and swift for application in time of war, the National Assembly thought to give all necessary satisfaction to the exigencies of military discipline, and, consequently, to render all illegal punitive procedures futile."

80. "These courts-martial, composed of three judges, with extremely simplified procedures, allowed for the adjudication of flagrant offenses in a few hours, and allowed too for the immediate execution of sentence. In such cases, there was no longer any check. This system handed to the military authorities the power of life and death over their men. In practice, these military courts demonstrated restraint, but they presented unquestionable dangers. In fact the system in place allowed for the maintenance of strict army discipline. But it could not avoid the condemnation and execution of innocents—there were such cases—and defied every true judicial rule. Becker, *France en Guerre,* 67–68. See also the comments of M. Etienne Flandin, President, Séance de la Société Générale des Prisons, May 17, 1916, discussing the "Fonctionnement et competence des tribunaux militaires" reproduced in 40 Revue pénitentiare et de droit penal: Bulletin de la Société Générale des Prisons 221–22 (1916).

81. Becker, *The Great War and the French People,* 217–35. Even then, there did not appear to be cause for concern of an imminent collapse of law and order in any of the departments. Ibid., 235.

82. "There is a lack of equilibrium in the functioning of parliamentary control: it proceeds by fits and starts; at times the Parliament grants a general absolution, at other times it asserts a right of stickling and excessive surveillance over details. One would almost be tempted to conclude that the Parliament fails to exercise its supervisory responsibility but under the goad of political passion or party interest." Barthélemy, 4: 117.

83. See, e.g., Germany, Austwärtiges Amt, *The Belgian People's War, a Violation of International Law.*

84. Willis, *Prologue to Nuremberg,* 12–13.

85. Yet the devastating carnage of the war *in toto* rendered such Manichean pronouncements largely meaningless. Roberts, "*Land Warfare: From the Hague to Nuremberg,*" in Howard et al., eds., *The Laws of War,* 126.

86. For discussion of one such effort at "l'encerclement judiciare" of the Central powers, see the comments of M. Lucien Normand, Séance de la Société Générale des Prisons, November 22, 1916, discussing the "Répression des Crimes de Guerre," reproduced in 40 Revue pénitentiare et de droit penal: Bulletin de la Société Générale des Prisons 398–403 (1916).

87. Willis, *Prologue to Nuremberg,* 13. In France, "stories of outrage—the destruction of the Cathedral at Rheims, tales of pillage and rape, accounts of murder of prisoners—dominated the news." Ibid. German juridical theory attempted to justify such action, prohibited under the normal law of nations, by recourse to the doctrine of exceptionality known as *Kriegsraison,* or *ratio belli.*

A. Mérignhac, "De la Sanction des infractions au droit des gens commises, au cours de la guerre européenne par les empires du centre," 24 Revue générale de droit international public 5, 18 (1917) (providing a representative selection of German legal authorities explicating the *Kriegsraison* doctrine) [hereinafter, Mérignhac, "De la Sanction des infractions"]. The same rationale would form the basis of defenses mounted by the accused at Nuremberg.

88. Garner, *International Law and the World War,* 1: 472.

89. See, e.g., Louis Renault, "De l'Application du droit pénal aux faits de guerre," 42 Journal du droit international 313 (1915); and addressing the Séance de la Société Génerale des Prisons, 1915, re: "Application du droit pénal aux faits de guerre," reproduced in 39 Revue pénitentiare et de droit penal: Bulletin de la Société Générale des Prisons 406 (1915); Mérignhac, "De la Sanction des infractions"; M. Rene Garraud, Professor of Criminal Law at the University of Lyon, addressing the Séance de la Société Génerale des Prisons, January 19, 1916, re: "Application du Droit Pénal aux Faits de Guerre" reproduced in 40 Revue pénitentiare et de droit penal: Bulletin de la Société Générale des Prisons 20 (1916).

90. "What security would the application of punitive law over crimes committed in time of war afford, if such application could not be made by the army to which the criminals belong?" Indeed, the German military manual on the law of war itself anticipated the possibility of *foreign*—even enemy—criminal sanctions against German violators of such laws, in the event they became prisoners in the course of war. Renault, "De l'Application du droit pénal aux faits de guerre," 328, 320–21.

91. The foregoing summary follows the discussion of M. Rene Garraud, Professor of Criminal Law at the University of Lyon, addressing the Séance de la Société Génerale des Prisons, January 19, 1916, re: "Application du droit pénal aux faits de guerre," reproduced in 40 Revue pénitentiare et de droit penal: Bulletin de la Société Générale des Prisons 20–32 (1916).

92. At the Versailles Peace Conference, these formed a portion of the thirty-two separate categories of war crimes compiled by the Allies. The entire list is given in Mérignhac and Lémonon, *Le Droit des gens* 2: 592–93.

93. Garner, *International Law and the World War,* 1: 472. Subsequent studies have tended to bear out the claim that German pillaging was "pitiless, arbitrary, and anarchical," and occurred on a massive scale, especially in the early weeks of the war. German prisoners and dead were regularly found to be loaded down with plunder. Phillipson, *International Law and the Great War,* 229–38, See, e.g., Horne and Kramer, *German Atrocities,* passim.

94. Conseil de Guerre, 17th corps, (Toulouse), July 16, 1915, cited in Mérignhac, "De la Sanction des infractions," 35–36.

95. "Condamnation d'un soldat allemand pillar, incendiare et assassin, par la Justice Militaire Française," Conseil de Guerre, 10th region (Rennes), February 26, 1915, reported in 42 Journal du droit international 54–56.

96. Garner, *International Law and the World War,* 1: 75–76.

97. Extract from the note-book of Private Hassemer, 8th Army Corps, September 3, 1914, quoted in *Germany's Violations of the Laws of War 1914–15*, Compiled Under the Auspices of the French Ministry of Foreign Affairs, at 155 (J. O. P. Bland, ed., trans. William Heinemann Publishers, 1915).

98. Extract from the notebook of Private Karl Scheufele, 3rd Bavarian Regiment of Landwehr Infantry (undated), quoted in ibid., 183.

99. "5 Oct. Evening march on the road to Arras. Evening 14 *Turcos* from the 3/train (2 groups) summarily shot." (Translation mine.) Extract from the diary of Private Joh. Nusser, 3rd Bavarian Regiment, Reserve, October 5, 1914, quoted in ibid., 69. In the original English translations accompanying the German texts, the term *standrechtlich* is incorrectly translated (an understatement) as "according to martial law," or "court-martial." See also, ibid., 138, 215, 29, 31–33, 34–35, 36–39, 41–42, 51, 52, 55–57, 59–60.

100. *Rapports et procès-verbaux d'enquête de la commission instituée en vue de constater les actes commis par l'ennemi en violation du droit des gens*, Documents rélative à la Guerre X–XI–XII, 184–95 (Paris, 1919). See also, *Les Violations des lois de la guerre par l'Allemagne*, publication faite par les soins du Ministère des Affaires Étrangères (Paris, 1915).

101. René Garraud, "Application du Droit Pénal aux Faits de Guerre," Séance de la Société Générale des Prisons, January 19, 1916, 14 Revue pénitentiaire et de droit pénale 28 (1916).

102. Mérignhac, "De la Sanction des infractions," 36. See also, Mérignhac and Lémonon, *Le Droit des gens* 2: 564–65.

103. Willis, *Prologue to Nuremberg,* 14.

104. Garner, *International Law and the World War,* 1: 493–94. For discussion of the treatment of captured aviators on the Western front, and the relatively negligible incidence of actual reprisals against allied prisoners, see Ibid., 494–96.

105. Jackson, *The Prisoners,* 77. But see also Cahen-Salvador, *Les Prisonniers de guerre* (presenting an account of generally pervasive reprisal and counter-reprisal actions). None of these works addresses in detail the question of reprisals taken in response to trials or potential trials in military tribunals. Usually, reprisals took the form of retaliation for perceived maltreatment of prisoners—e.g., forced labor or unsanitary conditions.

106. Helmuth Mende, "Deutsche Militarrechtspflege im besetzten feindlichen Gebiet unter besonderer Berucksichtigung Belgiens," in *Der Gerichtsaal,* 86: 207–28, (1919), quoted in Fraenkel, *Military Occupation and the Rule of Law,* 24.

107. For a sympathetic German treatment of the German administrative regime in Belgium, see Ludwig von Köhler, *The Administration of the Occupied Territories, Belgium*, vol. 1, esp. 64–70.

108. Garner, *International Law and the World War*, 2: 85–92.

109. Ibid., 96. These figures included 100 death sentences; over 11,000 of the convicted were ordered into confinement. Mass deportations to Germany began in the autumn of 1916.

110. The case is discussed in more detail in ibid., 97–105. See also, A. A. Hoehling, *Edith Cavell* (London, Cassell & Co., 1958), and Ambroise Got, trans., ed., *The Case of Miss Cavell.*

111. Garner observes an interesting set of comparisons with the cases of female spies executed by Belgian and French governments on the charge of spying, and that of the female co-conspirator, Mary Surratt, executed by order of the military commission which investigated President Lincoln's assassination: Cavell had not been charged with spying or with conspiring to assassinate a head of state—offenses generally punishable by death—but with aiding individuals in escaping occupied territory. "She had done nothing to reveal German military movements, nor had she furnished the enemy with any information of military value . . . In the case of Mrs. Surratt, it may also be remarked that the trial was public; she was allowed the fullest right of defence; the right of appeal was allowed, and the military commission which found her guilty accompanied its verdict with a recommendation for clemency. There was no attempt to conceal the fact of the trial from the public, nor was she hurried to her death within a few hours after the trial in order to forestall an appeal and a possible pardon." In all of these respects, Surratt had received greater fairness at the hands of her trial by military commission than Cavell saw from the German military court. Garner, *International Law and the World War,* 2: 102–3.

112. Kagan, *On the Origins of War, and the Preservation of Peace,* 297. The discussion of post-war developments in this section follows the narrative of Willis, *Prologue to Nuremberg*, which remains the authoritative study of the Leipzig trials.

113. The focus on German atrocities spawned a vast number of studies dedicated to the subject of criminal liability for violations of the laws of war. For a representative compilation, see, Garner, *International Law and the World War,* 1: 472, note 2.

114. See, e.g., Quincy Wright, "The Legal Liability of the Kaiser," 37 *American Political Science Review* 120 (1919). The catalogue of thirty-two categories of war crimes cited by the Allies at the peace conference, as well as a list and description of the principal persons sought for indictment by France, is given in Mérignhac and Lémonon, *Le Droit des gens,* 2: 592–98. The list included Crown-Prince Rupprecht of Bavaria, General von Bülow, Commandant of the 2nd Army, Friedrich-Wilhelm of Hohenzollern, Imperial Crown Prince, Marshall von Hindenburg, and General Ludendorff.

115. Nevertheless, evidence provided by military "proclamations, daily issues of orders, depositions of victims and witnesses, received during the course of the

governmental *commissions d'enquête*, thanks to papers, letters and other documents found or seized from the baggage or person of the wounded and prisoners" all provided elements of proof for the trial of cases in the conseils de guerre. Mérignhac and Lémonon, *Le Droit des gens*, 2: 566.

116. Eyck, *A History of the Weimar Republic*, 1: 187–88.

117. Of all the early prosecutions in the 1914 conseils de guerre, it was the trial of four of Stenger's troops of the 53rd German infantry brigade, convicted of the massacre of innocent civilians in the same incident, that attracted great attention in France and led to calls for action against Stenger at the conclusion of the war. Willis, *Prologue to Nuremberg*, 13–14. The notorious order given by General Stenger and its consequences, along with other similar orders, are discussed in Mérignhac and Lémonon, *Le Droit des gens* 1: 257–59.

118. Horne and Kramer, *German Atrocities*, 351.

119. Jean Martet, "M. Clemenceau and the Versailles Peace Treaty," 9 *Journal of the Royal Institute of International Affairs* 783, 796 (1930).

120. Eyck, *Weimar Republic*, 1: 110.

121. Willis, *Prologue to Nuremberg*, 147.

122. George F. Kennan in *Diplomatic History of the United States*, 6: 717.

123. For the complete text of the Rhineland Agreement of June 28, 1919, see Fraenkel, *Military Occupation and the Rule of Law*, Appendix I, 233–36.

124. Benvenisti, *The International Law of Occupation*, 52. Benvenisti provides an overview of the Reichsgericht's jurisprudence with regard to the occupation; see Ibid., 52–58.

125. The relevant sections of Foch's instruction, along with supplemental rules promulgated by the Interallied Conference of November 22, 1918, are provided in Jaer, *L'Armée belge d'occupation*, 72.

126. Fraenkel, *Military Occupation and the Rule of Law*, 48–49.

127. Law of April 3, 1955.

128. French Code of Criminal Procedure, Art. 700.

129. See "France's Riots: An Underclass Rebellion," in *The Economist*, November 12, 2005, 25; available at http://www.economist.com/displaystory.cfm?story_id=E1_VTPVSJV.

130. French Constitution, Art. 16, 1958.

131. Barthélemy, 1: 153.

132. See, Aguiló Bonnín, *Estado de sitio; jornadas septembrinas de 1985 en Bolivia;* Amparo Serrano, *Uso y abuso del estado de sitio*; Correia, *Estado de sítio e de emergência em democracia;* Cruz Villalon, *El estado de sitio y la constitución;* Gallon Giraldo, *Quince años de estado de sitio en Colombia;* Navarro de la Ossa, *La constitución y el estado de sitio;* Núñez Carvallo, *El estado de sitio y el habeas corpus;* Reyes Matta, Andrés Richards, Cárdenas, eds., *Chile bajo el estado de sitio;* Sanchez Viamonte, *Ley marcial y estado de sitio;* Posada Viana and Matallana Eslava, *Estado de sitio y legalidad marcial en Colombia.*

This is only a partial, representative sample from the extensive Latin American literature on states of emergency and the state of siege. Consideration of the relatively sparse literature on similar topics within the common law tradition makes for a striking contrast.

Chapter 4

1. "As I Please," 18, *Tribune,* March 31, 1944, in Orwell, *Essays*, 575, 577.

2. Albert G. D. Levy, "The Law and Procedure of War Crime Trials," 37 Am. J. Int. Law 1052, 1062–23 (1943). For additional literature on the Leipzig trials, see, Mullins, *The Leipzig Trials;* George G. Battle, "The Trials Before the Leipsic Supreme Court of Germans Accused of War Crimes," 8 Va. L. Rev. 1 (1921); Glueck, *War Criminals—Their Prosecution and Punishment.*

3. See, e.g., Bradley F. Smith, *Reaching Judgment at Nuremberg* and *Road to Nuremberg;* Willis, *Prologue to Nuremberg.*

4. Blum, *From the Morgenthau Diaries*, 3: 397–98, 341–83.

5. As to war crimes, the main difference in the competing plans had to do with the treatment of the major war criminals. Morgenthau sought summary execution for a select number of "archcriminals." "The attack on such advocacy of drumhead justice was led by Secretary of War Henry Stimson. Prompt justice based on fair legal procedures, Stimson argued, was 'consistent with the advance of civilization' and would 'have all the greater effect upon posterity.' Stimson made clear that he had in mind trials before military commissions." Stimson's advocacy of military commissions was a measured *ameliorative* response to the harsh, lawless approach of summary executions. Dower, *Embracing Defeat,* 445–56.

6. See, e.g., William M. Wiecek, "Sabotage, Treason, and Military Tribunals in World War II," in Ernst and Jew, eds., *Total War and the Law*, 43–74 [hereinafter, Wiecek]. In a characteristic post–9/11 editorial, Ann-Marie Slaughter, then Professor of International Law at Harvard Law School, argued that "Military commissions have been used rarely in the past, principally to try spies caught behind enemy lines." Presumably, Professor Slaughter was extrapolating from the *Ex Parte Quirin* decision of the Supreme Court, a case involving the trial of enemy spies. Ann-Marie Slaughter, "Al Qaeda Should Be Tried before the World," *New York Times,* November 17, 2001, A21.

7. The Chairman of the United Nations War Crimes Commission, charged with publishing the law reports of the military commissions, Lord Wright of Durley, thus stated his assessment of the significance of these records: "I cannot sufficiently emphasise what I regard as the great importance of these reports from the point of view of the future development of International Law as applied to war crimes." Already, by October 1946, when Lord Wright wrote, hundreds of such trials had been convened. United Nations War Crimes Commission, *Law*

Reports of Trials of War Criminals, Selected and Prepared by the United Nations War Crimes Commission (1947), x.

8. Gerry J. Simpson, "War Crimes: A Critical Introduction," in McCormack and Simpson, eds., *The Law of War Crimes,* 6.

9. Hawaii Organic Act, ch. 339, § 67, 31 Stat.141 (1900).

10. Fairman, *The Law of Martial Rule,* 249.

11. See Anthony, *Hawaii under Army Rule,* and "Martial Law, Military Government and the Writ of Habeas Corpus in Hawaii," 31 Calif. L. Rev. 477 (1943); Fairman, "The Supreme Court on Military Jurisdiction: Martial Rule in Hawaii and the Yamashita Case," 59 Harvard Law Review 833 (1946); see also Harry N. and Jane L. Scheiber, Bayonets in Paradise: A Half-Century Retrospect on Martial Law in Hawaii, 1941–1946," 19 U. of Hawaii L. Rev. 477 (1997); and more generally, Corwin, *Total War and the Constitution.*

12. See, Fisher, *Military Tribunals and Presidential Power,* 130–39. In his own account, Fisher provides more detail on some of the appellate cases from this period. But what is lacking in his account is context. Individuals are simply brought into court—and then the narrative proceeds. There is little or no attempt to present reasons for any of the actions taken by military authorities. The obvious questions—why was it deemed necessary to take away the liberties of a Mr. Zimmerman or a Mr. Glockner or a Mr. Seifer? what were the circumstances in which such actions occurred?—are hardly given consideration. Were they arrested and held on grounds of murder, treason, shoplifting, having German surnames? The silence leaves the reader with the impression that taking away liberties is simply what military authorities do to people if given the chance. Moreover, apparently, courts exist, not to ensure that justice is done in specific cases, but to "defend citizen rights against military rule." Ibid., 130. Given the premises, the conclusions are rarely in doubt.

13. The proclamation by which this transfer was accomplished is reproduced in Fairman, *The Law of Martial Rule,* 252. Jurisdiction over "judicial proceedings, both criminal and civil" was returned to the civil authorities at this time. Exceptions were made for criminal prosecutions against military members and cases involving the violation of military orders. The commander also reserved the right to retain jurisdiction over particular cases. Ibid.

14. Executive Order 9185, "Appointing a Military Commission," *Federal Register* 7: 5103 (1942).

15. *Ex parte Quirin* et al., 317 U.S. 1 (1942).

16. Ibid, 28–29.

17. Ibid, 31.

18. Ibid, 30–33, cf. the authorities cited therein, notes 9 and 10. See also the long list of cases tried against alien spies during the War of Independence, the War of 1812, and the Civil War, cited at ibid., 42–44, note 14.

19. Ibid., 35–37.

20. Ibid., 37–38. One of the petitioners, Hermann Haupt, had argued that, as an American citizen, he could not be tried by the commission.

21. Ibid., 39–40.

22. Ibid., 45–46.

23. Ibid., 21–22.

24. Wiecek concludes that this amounted to a "less than candid, . . . unpersuasive intellectual exercise"—a straining at gnats and swallowing camels in order "to legitimate trial before a military panel that would not be inconvenienced" by basic constitutional protections; "it did not even rise to the level of a lawyer's distinction without difference." Allowing for context, such conclusions appear tendentious at best. Wiecek, 53–54.

25. Ibid., 55.

26. *Ex parte Quirin,* 37.

27. Fairman, *The Law of Martial Rule,* 166.

28. Wiecek, 55.

29. Churchill noted that in the first seven months of 1942, which witnessed a "terrible massacre of shipping along the American coast, . . . the Allied losses in the Atlantic from U-boats alone amounted to over three million tons." The countervailing payout in enemy losses was negligible. Winston S. Churchill, *The Second World War,* vol. 4, *The Hinge of Fate*: (1951), 123 [hereinafter, Churchill, *Hinge of Fate*].

30. Ibid, 125.

31. Admiral Dönitz, convicted at Nuremberg of having waged a "war of aggression" and sentenced to ten years' imprisonment at Spandau, received a spirited and extraordinary defense from a broad international array of military, political, and literary luminaries, including, *inter alia,* T. S. Eliot and Justice William O. Douglas; see Thompson and Strutz, eds., *Doenitz at Nuremberg.*

32. Quoted in Padfield, *War Beneath the Sea,* 306.

33. Churchill, *Hinge of Fate,* 117.

34. Ibid.

35. Ibid., 130. Dönitz calculated the November total to exceed 900,000 tons. See Padfield, *War Beneath the Sea,* 305.

36. Indeed, "there was . . . some criticism of the Court for taking the case at all and for dealing so thoroughly with the constitutional issues raised. Even some of our liberals explained that while we ought, of course, to be scrupulous to administer impartial justice according to our traditional American rule of law, we ought not in the midst of a total war to waste time, money, and manpower by this ludicrous judicial ritual in the case of a group of enemy criminals who should have been shot at sunrise without more ado." Robert E. Cushman, "The Case of the Nazi Saboteurs," 36 Am. Pol. Sci. Rev. 1089 (1942).

37. Fairman, *The Law of Martial Rule,* 250.

38. A. Wigfall Green, "The Military Commission," 42 Am. J. Int. Law 832 (1948).

39. G. A. Finch, "Retribution for War Crimes," 37 Am. J. Int. Law 84 (1943).

40. The Commission "was an international body formed and created by its member governments." United Nations War Crimes Commission, *History of the United Nations War Crimes Commission,* 127, 113–34. The Soviet Union did not participate.

41. Ibid., 113.

42. For a catalogue of the range of views represented among the Allied nations, see Albert G. D. Levy, "The Law and Procedure of War Crime Trials," 37 Am. J. Int. Law 1052, 1055–57 note 11 (1943). On the movement to establish an international criminal court, see ibid., 1070–81.

43. "Statement Signed by President Roosevelt, Prime Minister Churchill and Premier Stalin Regarding Atrocities," in Memorandum to President Roosevelt from the Secretaries of State and War and the Attorney General, January 22, 1945, Document I, in *Report of Robert H. Jackson, United States Representative to the International Conference on Military Trials*, London 1945, pp. 11, 12 (1949). The Moscow Conference, held between October 18 and November 1, 1943, was attended by U.S. Secretary of State Cordell Hull, and his British and Soviet counterparts, Anthony Eden and Vyacheslav Molotov, respectively. It was also determined at this time to pursue a policy of unconditional surrender.

44. Taylor, *The Anatomy of the Nuremberg Trials,* 270 [hereinafter, Taylor, *Nuremberg Memoir*].

45. C. Arnold Anderson, "The Utility of the Proposed Trial and Punishment of Enemy Leaders," 37 Am. J. Int. Law 1081 (1943).

46. Kennan, *Memoirs,* 175–76.

47. Lord Wright, "Introduction," United Nations War Crime Commission, *History of the United Nations War Crimes Commission,* 5 (1948). The United States designated the Office of the Judge Advocate General of the Army as its National Office. Great Britain followed suit in 1946, transferring its National Office from the Treasury Solicitor's Office. Ibid., 121–22.

48. Trial of the Major War Criminals Before the International Military Tribunal, Nuremberg (November 14, 1945–October 1, 1946), Documents, 2309-PS. 30: 158, 161–62 (1948).

49. Ibid., 161.

50. Ibid, 4.

51. Appleman, *Military Tribunals and International Crimes,* 267.

52. Ibid.

53. The Allies had tried 2,724 Japanese for alleged war crimes, and had convicted and sentenced 2,284. Acting Political Adviser in Japan (Sebald) to the

Secretary of State, (Tokyo, June, 3 1948), in Foreign Relations of the United States 6: 807–8 (1948).

54. Levie, *Terrorism in War,* 135–39. Levie provides a sampling of the cases tried by military commissions at 98–135, *passim.* No satisfactory breakdown of the numbers has yet been produced. Levie states that "it is difficult to understand the deficiencies in the availability of acceptable statistics on war crimes trials" from the countries of Western Europe and the United States, though the lack of verifiable numbers is more understandable with regard to the Soviet Union and the then Communist countries of Eastern Europe. It does appear that at least some of the confusion in numbers can be attributed to the fact that multiple defendants were often tried in a single numbered case. Ibid., 139.

55. Höss was convicted of membership in a criminal organization, the Nazi party, and of genocide, and was executed. In its decision, the Tribunal found that the defendant had "participated in the murder of . . . at least 2,500,000 people, mainly Jews." Trial of Obersturmbannführer Rudolf Franz Ferdinand Höss, Supreme National Tribunal of Poland (March 11–29, 1947), in *UNWCC Law Reports* 7: 11, 17 (1948) [hereinafter, *Law Reports*]. For discussion of the Supreme National Tribunal, its jurisdiction and powers, see Annex, in ibid., 91ff. Polish national criminal courts and military criminal courts also dealt with war crimes cases.

56. Rulings on procedural matters were usually made without explanation.

57. These differences in the style of the reports are attributable to particular differences among the procedures and policies of the various national military tribunals.

58. *Law Reports,* 1: 22–34.

59. Ibid., 29–30.

60. Ibid., 30.

61. Cited in Appendix, ibid., 33–34.

62. As Hannah Arendt would later observe in the case of Adolf Eichmann, we cannot but conclude that Dostler "acted fully within the framework of the kind of judgment required of him: he acted in accordance with the rule, examined the order issued to him for its 'manifest' legality, namely regularity; he did not have to fall back upon his 'conscience,' since he was not one of those who were unfamiliar with the laws of his country. The exact opposite was the case." According to Arendt, the plausibility of a 'natural law' argument for the substitution of "a sense of justice grounded in the depths of every man" in place of "familiarity with the law" depended upon "the assumption that the law expresses only what every man's conscience would tell him anyhow." Arendt, *Eichmann in Jerusalem,* 293.

63. Taylor, *Nuremberg Memoir,* 254.

64. Ibid.

65. *Law Reports,* 1: 30.

66. Taylor, *Nuremberg Memoir,* 255.

67. *Law Reports,* 1: 200.

68. Hon. Robert H. Jackson, "Forward," in ibid., xiv.

69. *Law Reports,* 1: 61.

70. Ibid., 210; the letter is reproduced at ibid., 172.

71. Arendt, *Eichmann in Jerusalem,* 288–89.

72. *Law Reports,* 1: 20–22.

73. The commission found all of the defendants guilty and sentenced Klein, Ruoff and Willig to be hanged. The rest of the defendants received sentences of confinement at hard labor, for varying lengths of time, from life (Wahlmann) to twenty-five years (Huber).

74. Cited in "Trial of Gustav Becker, Wilhelm Weber and 18 Others," Permanent Military Tribunal at Lyon (concluded July 17, 1947), reported in *Law Reports,* 7: 67, 68.

75. Ibid.

76. Ibid.

77. Judgment of the Permanent Military Tribunal at Metz, concluded October 8, 1947, cited in ibid., 71.

78. Trial of Franz Holstein and Twenty-Three Others, Judgment of Permanent Military Tribunal at Dijon (completed February 3, 1947), reported in *Law Reports,* 8: 22.

79. The complete record of the trial, running some 749 pages, has been published and forms the basis for much of the discussion that follows. Raymond Phillips, ed., *Trial of Josef Kramer and Forty-Four Others (The Belsen Trial),* (London, 1949) [hereinafter, *Belsen Trial*].

80. *Law Reports,* 2: 128.

81. Ibid., Annex II, 1: 116.

82. Ibid., Annex I, 105–10. Ibid., 126.

83. Quoted in ibid.

84. Indeed, other nations appear to have relied on the authority of the American Supreme Court opinions. See Levie, *Terrorism in War,* 258 and *passim.*

85. Ibid., 126. For more detailed discussion of the Canadian War Crimes Regulations, see *Law Reports,* Annex, 4: 125. Application of the Regulations by a Canadian Military Court can be examined in the Abbaye Ardenne Case, the Trial of S.S. Brigadefuhrer Kurt Meyer, Canadian Military Court, Aurich, Germany (December 10–28, 1945), in Ibid., 97ff. Meyer was tried for having given a "take no prisoners" order and for his responsibility in the killing of prisoners of war. The Convening Authority commuted the military court's death sentence to confinement for life.

For discussion of the Australia War Crimes Act, see *Law Reports,* 5: 94. For application of the Act by an Australian Military Court, see ibid., 32, "The Trial of Captain Eitaro Shinohara and Two Others," Australian Military Court, Rabaul

(March 30–April 1, 1946). The defendants in the Shinohara case were tried and convicted of having failed to provide a fair and proper trial in regard to native inhabitants they had tried for acts of resistance against Japanese authorities.

86. Ibid., 85, 108 ("a Military Court may take into consideration any oral statement or any document appearing on the face of it to be authentic provided the statement or document appears to the Court to be of assistance in proving or disproving the charge, notwithstanding that such statement or document would not be admissible in evidence in proceedings before a Field General Court-Martial"). Exceptions were made for secondary evidence of statements made by witnesses who were dead or unavailable; official documents of Allied or enemy governments; reports of the International Committee of the Red Cross or by members of the medical profession; reports or depositions from military courts of inquiry; diaries or letters; and copies of documents.

87. *Belsen Trial,* 141–44; Appendix III, ibid., 654ff., contains affidavits and statements that were read out in court. Those portions of the statements which received an objection from defense are omitted from the record.

88. Ibid., 45.

89. Ibid.

90. Ibid., 85.

91. Ibid., 79–80.

92. Taylor, *Nuremberg Memoir,* 271.

93. Arendt, *Eichmann in Jerusalem,* 5.

94. *Belsen Trial,* 522–23.

95. Arendt, *Eichmann in Jerusalem,* 12. In the Eichmann trial, no answer was given. Yet "one could easily have found an answer had he permitted his imagination to dwell for a few minutes on the fate of those Dutch Jews who in 1941, in the old Jewish quarter of Amsterdam, dared to attack a German security police detachment. Four hundred and thirty Jews were arrested in reprisal and they were literally tortured to death [in the camps] . . . For months on end they died a thousand deaths, and every single one of them would have envied his brethren in Auschwitz and even in Riga and Minsk. There exist many things considerably worse than death, and the S.S. saw to it that none of them was ever very far from their victims' minds and imagination." Ibid.

96. *Law Reports,* Annex I, I: 109.

97. Taylor, *Nuremberg Memoir,* 271.

98. Piccigallo, *The Japanese on Trial,* 160–62, 173. This, and subsequent paragraphs in this section dealing with the Pacific Theater, summarize some of the findings of Piccigallo's ground-breaking account. This work continues to be the standard of reference on this subject. For its thoroughness and comprehensive scope, no comparable work specifically devoted to war crimes tribunals exists to cover the war in its geographic entirety, or for that matter, any of the other conflicts discussed in this survey.

The Chinese major general serving as military court member "prefaced the opening of the first war crimes trial held in the Peiping-Tientsin area by declaring his determination to try all cases 'according to military law.' Despite 'bestial wartime Japanese behavior,' he further asserted, his court intended to dispense justice, not revenge." This first trial prosecuted five Japanese charged with murdering Chinese civilians—the most frequently charged offense in the Chinese trials. All five were found guilty; four out of five received the death penalty, and the fifth received five years' hard labor with confinement. Ibid. quoting *China Press,* April 9, 18, 1946, pp. 162–63.

99. Total number of trials and accused, Ibid., 48. In Manila, "eight thousand residents were killed and over seven thousand were mistreated, maimed and wounded without cause of trial. Hundreds of females were beaten and raped, their breasts and genitals abused and mutilated. The military Commission concluded that the Filipino people, including thousands of women and children, were tortured, starved, beaten, bayoneted, clubbed, hanged, burned alive and subjected to mass executions rarely rivaled in history, more than 30,000 deaths being revealed by the record. Prisoners of war and civilian internees suffered systematic starvation, torture, withholding of medical and hospital facilities and execution in disregard of the rules of international law. . . . [There] were systematic . . . [executions] with indescribable bestiality of little girls and boys only months or even days old." In Batangas Province, Luzon Island, alone, "sixteen thousand unarmed non-combatant civilians were killed between November 1944 and April 1945. Individuals were shot, bayoneted and buried alive. Three hundred Filipinos were forced to leap into a deep well into which heavy weights were dropped. Those who survived were shot. Three to four hundred civilians were bayoneted, shot and immolated in another incident. Prisoners of war were mistreated and were compelled to catch and consume cats, pigeons and rats. Over fifteen hundred Americans were crowded into the cramped cargo hold of a Japanese steamship. They were starved and driven to dementia, wildly attacking one another and sucking their victims' blood." General Headquarters United States Army Forces, Pacific Office of The Theater Judge Advocate, Review of the Record of Trial by a Military Commission of Tomoyki Yamashita, General, Imperial Japanese Army, reprinted in Whitney, *The Case of General Yamashita,* 60, 72–73, 69.

100. "General Yamashita's headquarters were at Fort McKinley until December 23, 1944, where four hundred disabled American prisoners of war were held from October 31, 1944 until January 15, 1945. The prisoners were crowded into one building, furnished (with) no beds or covers and kept within the enclosure of a fence extending thirty feet beyond each side of the building. Their two meals a day consisted of one canteen cup of boiled rice, mixed with greens; once a week the four hundred men were given twenty-five to thirty pounds of rotten meat, filled with maggots. Occasionally they would go a day or two without

water and at times were reduced to eating grass and sticks they dug in the yard. These conditions existed within walking distance of General Yamashita's headquarters; yet, while recognizing a duty to prevent such occurrences, and despite his testimony that had he foreseen or known of these conditions he would have 'concentrated all [his] efforts toward preventing it,' he never conducted nor directed the conduct of an inspection of the facilities." Major William H. Parks, "Command Responsibility for War Crimes," 62 Mil. L. Rev. 1, 27, 29 (1973), [hereinafter, Parks]. *Law Reports,* 1: 30, 34–35.

101. Parks, 37.

102. See Wiecek, 60–64 (characterizing the majority opinion as mere "minimalist . . . evasion"; and the dissenting opinions as "eloquent," "moving," "vehement, yet idealistic"); Lael, *The Yamashita Precedent;* Whitney, *The Case of General Yamashita;* and Reel, *The Case of General Yamashita* (Reel served on Yamashita's defense team at the trial). As Levie observes, "just as the dissents in the Supreme Court have received far more publicity than the majority opinion, so the Reel book has received far more publicity than more moderate and unbiased discussions of the Yamashita case." Levie, *Terrorism in War,* 159, note 68.

103. In fact, the records of both tribunals clearly do attribute such knowledge to the general. Levie, *Terrorism in War,* 161–63; and "Command Responsibility," 8 USAFA J. of Leg. Studies 1, 15, note 13.

104. Piccigallo, *The Japanese on Trial,* 73. More cases in the UNWCC *Law Reports* relate to this offense than to any other.

105. Ibid.

106. Australia War Crimes Act, §§ 9(1), 10, quoted in Piccigallo, *The Japanese on Trial,* 125–26. While the relaxation of the rules of evidence was the source of most of the criticism of the Australian military courts, even such critics admitted that the courts were administered with fairness and impartiality. Ibid., 139.

107. Ibid., 128–29.

108. Ibid.

109. Ibid., 130.

110. Ibid., 95.

111. Ibid., 120.

112. Ibid., 139.

113. Ibid., 173.

114. Ibid., 183.

115. Ibid., 197.

116. Ibid., 208.

117. The variety of offenses tried before the various Allied military commissions is reflected in a small sampling of cases reported in the initial five volumes of UNWCC *Law Reports*, including the killing of survivors of a sunken ship (the Peleus Trial, vol. I, case no. 1); the shooting/killing of unarmed prisoners of war (the Dostler case, vol. I, case no. 2; the Jaluit Atoll case, vol. I, case no. 6; the

Dreierwalde case, vol. I, case no. 7; the Essen Lynching case, vol. I, case no. 8; the trials of Gunther Thiele and Georg Steinert, vol. III, case no. 14; the trial of Peter Back, vol. III, case no. 15; the trials of Albert Bury and Wilhelm Hafner, vol. III, case no. 16; the trials of Anton Schosser, Josef Goldbrunner, and Alfons Jacob Wilm, vol. III, cases nos. 17 and 18; the trial of Major Karl Rauer and six others, vol. IV, case no 23; trial of Kurt Student, vol. IV, case no. 24; the trial of Karl Buck and ten others, vol. V, case no. 29; the trial of Karl Adam Golkel and thirteen others, vol. V, case no. 30); the incitement to kill prisoners of war, and inactivity while under a duty to protect them, and the false and illegal trial of prisoners of war and civilians (the trial of Lieutenant-General Shigeru Sawada and three others, vol. V, case no. 25; the trial of Captain Eitaro Shinohara and two others, vol. V, case no. 27; the trial of Lieutenant General Harukei Isayama and seven others, vol. V, case no. 32; the trial of General Tanaka Hisakasu and five others, vol. V, case no. 33); the killing of prisoners of war without trial, as well as treason, espionage (the Almelo trial, vol. I, case no. 3); the liability of civilians for killing Allied nationals by means of injections (the Hadamar trial, vol. I, case no. 4); the scuttling of U-Boats in violation of the Instrument of Surrender (the Scuttled U-Boats case, vol. I, case no. 5); the complicity of German industrialists in the murder of interned Allied civilians by means of poison gas (the Zyklon B case, vol. I, case no. 9); the killing and ill-treatment of concentration camp occupants (the Belsen trial, vol. II, case no. 10); the responsibility of a military commander for offenses committed by his troops (trial of General Tomoyuki Yamashita, vol. IV, case no. 21); the incitement by a commander to his men to deny quarter to opposing troops (the Abbaye Aredenne case, vol. III, case no. 22); and murder (the trial of Sergeant-Major Shigeru Ohashi and six others, vol V., case no. 26; the trial of Captain Eikichi Kato, vol. V, case no. 28).

118. For a wider array of cases, still representing a small fraction of the total number, see, Levie, *Terrorism in War,* passim.

119. Piccigallo, *The Japanese on Trial,* 214.

120. Ibid., 213.

121. Ibid. The same point is developed in Dower, *Embracing Defeat,* 443–84. See also, Maguire, *Law and War,* 169.

122. Taylor, *Nuremberg Memoir,* 269.

123. Kennan, "Memorandum," in United States, Foreign Relations: The Far East and Australia 6: 718 (1948).

124. Marshall Green, Division of Northeast Asian Affairs, "Memorandum of Conversation" (May 28, 1948), in ibid., 6: 788, 794. The May 1948 meeting between Kennan and various American and British foreign policy officials had concluded: "It was firmly agreed that the purge and the war crimes trials were ill-conceived, [and] psychologically unsound." Ibid.

125. Acting Political Adviser in Japan (Sebald) to the Secretary of State, Tokyo, (December 24, 1948), in ibid., 936–937.

126. Buscher, *The U.S. War Crimes Trial Program,* 22.

127. Department of State Policy Statement, Washington, August, 26, 1948 in Foreign Relations of the United States, 1948: Germany and Austria 2: 1297, 1303.

128. Buscher, *The U.S. War Crimes Trial Program,* 65, 70ff., 159.

129. See, e.g., Brackman, *The Other Nuremberg;* Tusa and Tusa, *The Nuremberg Trial;* Minear, *Victors Justice.*

130. But see, Benjamin B. Ferencz, "Nuremberg Trial Procedure and the Rights of the Accused," 39 J. Crim. L. & Criminology 144 (1948) (defending the process and program of the International Tribunal).

131. Buscher explicitly states this to have been a failure on the part of the Allies.

132. Telegram, Sebald to Secretary of State, Tokyo, November 24, 1948 (containing text of General McArthur's review of the war crimes sentences) in Foreign Relations of the United States, Far East and Australasia 6: 908.

133. Smith, *The Road to Nuremberg,* 260.

134. Report to the President by Mr. Justice Jackson, October 7, 1946, International Conference on Military Trials, *Report of Robert H. Jackson,* 440.

135. Smith, *Road to Nuremberg,* 260.

136. Department of State Policy Statement, Washington, August, 26, 1948 in Foreign Relations of the United States, Germany and Austria, 2: 1297, 1303.

137. Howard Levie countenances the argument that trial by military commission may no longer be a legitimate means of trying prisoners of war, as a result of the combination of Articles 85 and 102 of the 1949 version of the Geneva Prisoner of War Convention. Levie also notes that these provisions apply only to captured enemies who qualify for prisoner of war status. Levie, *Terrorism in War,* 258–59. See also Robinson O. Everett and Scott L. Silliman, "*Forums for Punishing Offenses Against the Law of Nations,*" 29 Wake Forest Law Review 509, 517–20 (1994), (suggesting the military commission remains an appropriate forum for trying prisoners of war).

138. Appleman, *Military Tribunals and International Crimes,* 268.

Chapter 5

1. Arendt, *On Violence,* 52.

2. The point was made by George Kennan in his assessment of the International Military Tribunals for Japan.

3. *Hamdan v. Rumsfeld,* 126 S. Ct. 2479, 2759 (2006) (Stevens, J.).

4. For a detailed account including historical background for the attacks, see National Commission on Terrorist Attacks upon the United States, *9/11 Commission Report* [hereinafter, *9/11 Commission Report*].

5. See, e.g., Neal K. Katyal and Laurence H. Tribe, "Waging War, Deciding Guilt: Trying the Military Tribunals," 111 Yale L. J. 1259 (2002).

6. Michael J. Kelley, "Understanding September 11th—An International Legal Perspective on the War in Afghanistan," 35 Creighton L. Rev. 283 (2002). It is revealing that Kelly uses examples like the Hindenburg disaster, the landing of Apollo 11 on the moon, or the assassination of President Kennedy as points of comparison. Such analogies minimize the fact that these were deliberate, mass lethal attacks on the nation's critical governmental, military, and financial centers by ostensibly responsible moral agents. This despite the fact that the victim count on September 11, 2001, exceeded the number of casualties at Pearl Harbor.

7. Habeck, *Knowing the Enemy,* 7.

8. See, Bin Laden's Letter to America, *Observer Worldview*, November 24, 2002, reproduced in *9/11 Commission Report,* 63. Also available at http://observer.guardian.co.uk/worldview/story/0,11581,845725,00.html. See also, e.g., Shaykh Usamah Bin-Muhammad Bin-Ladin, Ayman al-Zawahiri, Abu-Yasir Rifa'I Ahmad Taha, Shaykh Mir Hamzah, and Fazlur Rahman, World Islamic Front Statement of February 23, 1998, in Laqueur, ed., *Voices of Terror,* 410, 412; ("The ruling to kill the Americans and their allies—civilians and military—is an individual duty for every Muslim who can do it in any country in which it is possible to do it, in order to liberate the al-Aqsa Mosque and the holy mosque [Mecca] from their grip, and in order for their armies to move out of all the lands of Islam, defeated and unable to threaten any Muslim").

9. Usama Bin Muhammad Bin Laden, "Declaration of War Against the Americans Occupying the Land of the Two Holy Places (Expel the Infidels from the Arab Peninsula)," *The Idler* 3, no. 165 (September 13, 2001).

10. See *9/11 Commission Report,* 59; see also, Cohen, *Obligations of Leadership*. For a more comprehensive description of the pattern of radical Islamic terror attacks on American interests, see, Norman Podhoretz, "World War IV: How it Started, What it Means, and Why We Have to Win," *Commentary* 17–54 (September, 2004).

11. Authorization for Use of Military Force Joint Resolution (Public L. No. 107–40, 115 Stat. 224). See also, the USA Patriot Act of 2001, Pub. L. No. 107–56, 115 Stat. 272, regarding domestic national security.

12. 124 S. Ct. 2633 (2004).

13. U.N. Doc. S/RES/1373 (2001), available at http://usinfo.state.gov/is/Archive_Index/UN_Security_Council_AntiTerrorism_Resolution.html.

14. Detention, Treatment and Trial of Certain Non-Citizens in the War Against Terrorism, 66 Fed. Reg. 56,833 (November 16, 2001), available at http://www.white-house.gov/news/releases/2001/11/20011113–27.html.

15. Military Order, §4(b).

16. Ibid., §4(c).

17. The Secretary of Defense's sixteen-page summary of rules and procedures is detailed in U.S. Department of Defense, Military Commission Order No. 1 (March 21, 2002), available at http://www.defenselink.mil/news/commissions.html ;

Procedures for Trials by Military Commissions of Certain Non-U.S. Citizens in the War Against Terrorism, 32 C.F.R. pts. 10–17 [hereinafter, Trial Procedures].

18. This in turn may be due to a more general aggressive interventionism on the part of judges throughout the West. For a perceptive scholarly treatment of the development and expansion of the doctrine of judicial review, see, e.g., Carrese, *The Cloaking of Power.*

19. 542 US 466 (2004).

20. The court cited as precedent a case involving a federal district court's assertion of *habeas* jurisdiction over a defendant indicted in a state felony proceeding in Kentucky, a six-to-three decision authored by Justice William Brennan. *Braden v. 30th Judicial Circuit Court of Kentucky*, 410 US 484 (1973).

21. 542 US 466, 497–98 (Scalia, J., dissent).

22. Ruth Wedgwood, "The Supreme Court and the Guantanamo Controversy," in Berkowitz, ed., *Terrorism, the Laws of War, and the Constitution,* 159, 162.

23. 124 S. Ct. 2633 (2004).

24. Ibid, 2648.

25. Ibid, 2641–42.

26. Oliver O'Donovan, "The Loss of a Sense of Place," in O'Donovan and O'Donovan, *Bonds of Imperfection* 296, 320.

27. See Victor Davis Hanson, "The Fruits of Appeasement," *City Journal*, Spring 2004, 32–45.

28. Donald Kagan, "Terrorism and the Intellectuals," 37 *Intercollegiate Review* 3 (2002). See, e.g., the statements of the emir of the Jihad Group, Egypt, and al-Qaeda deputy, Ayman al Zawahri: "Tracking down the Americans and the Jews is not impossible. Killing them with a single bullet, a stab, or a device made up of a popular mix of explosives or hitting them with an iron rod is not impossible. Burning down their property with Molotov cocktails is not difficult. With the available means, small groups could prove to be a frightening horror for the Americans and the Jews." Ayman al Zawahiri, Knights Under the Prophet's Banner, London Al-Sharq al-Awsat in Arabic, December 12, 2001, Foreign Broadcast Info. Service, trans., Document no. FBISNES-2001–1212 , excerpted in Laqueur, ed., *Voices of Terror,* 426, 432. See also, Habeck, *Knowing the Enemy,* and *The 9/11 Commission Report.*

29. Professor Harold Koh makes a similar observation, but with the criminal justice response ultimately in view. Koh, "Preserving American Values: The Challenge at Home and Abroad," in Talbott and Chanda, eds., *The Age of Terror*, 158 [hereinafter, Koh, Preserving American Values"].

30. Vattel, *The Law of Nations*, 257–58.

31. Ibid.

32. Grotius, *The Rights of War and Peace,* 3: 1246–47. The section follows with illustrative examples from classical antiquity to more recent times.

33. Geneva Convention Relative to the Treatment of Prisoners of War, August 12, 1949, art. 4(2), 6 U.S.T. 3316, 75 U.N.T.S. 135.

34. Ibid., Art. 5. United States Army regulations adopt the same basic provision: "[I]n accordance with Article 5, [GPW], if any doubt arises as to whether a person, having committed a belligerent act and been taken into custody by the US Armed Forces, belongs to any of the categories enumerated in Article 4, such persons shall enjoy the protection of the present Convention until such time as their status has been determined by a competent tribunal." U.S. Dept. of Army, Reg. 190–8, Enemy Prisoners of War, Retained Personnel, Civilian Internees and Other Detainees para. 1–6 (October 1, 1997).

35. Gesturing, perhaps, in the direction of the canard that "one person's terrorist is another's freedom fighter," the drafters of Protocol I in 1977 blurred the effect of the traditional distinction, by "[r]ecognizing . . . that there are situations in armed conflicts where, owing to the nature of the hostilities an armed combatant cannot . . . distinguish himself . . . [from the civilian population]." Protocol I Additional to the Geneva Conventions of 1949, 1125 U.N.T.S. 3, Art. 44(3), (June 8, 1977). The United States has refused to ratify Protocol I, largely for this reason.

36. Secretary of the Navy, Memorandum: Implementation of Combatant Status Review Tribunal Procedures for Enemy Combatants detained at Guantanamo Bay Naval Base, Cuba, Enclosure 1, Combatant Status Review Tribunal Process (July 29, 2004), available at http://www. defenselink.mil/news/Ju12004/d20040730comb.pdf.

37. Detainee Treatment Act of 2005, Pub. L. 109–148, 119 Stat. 2739 (internal divisions omitted).

38. 344 F. Supp. 2d 152 (2004).

39. Ibid., 166.

40. Ibid., 167.

41. This distinction, apparently so critical to the District Court's ruling, raises practical questions: How much additional investigation, how many further questions would it be necessary to ask, how much more testimony would be needful—having once determined a defendant's combatant status—in order to assess its *legality* under the GPW? Only four criteria must be considered. And these criteria, established with the military decision-maker in the field in mind, are not intended to provide the subject matter for protracted complex litigation. The GPW requires only a "competent tribunal." Would not the same basic set of facts be applied in both determinations? Nevertheless, the Court sent the case back, requiring a separate inquiry, if not an entire new system of inquiry, for addressing the legality question.

42. 415 F. 3d 33, 38 (2005).

43. *Hamdan,* 126 S. Ct. at 2759.

44. Ibid., at 2718–19 (Scalia, J., dissenting).

45. *Federalist* No. 23, p. 147 (Hamilton). Similar points about the relative strengths of the different branches have been repeated by luminaries of the Supreme Court throughout its history. See, e.g., Justice Holmes's remarks in *Moyer v. Peabody*, 212 U.S. 78, 85 (1909): "When it comes to a decision by the head of the State upon a matter involving its life, the ordinary rights of individuals must yield to what he deems the necessities of the moment. Public danger warrants the substitution of executive process for judicial process. [Citations omitted.] This was admitted with regard to killing men in the actual clash of arms, and we think it obvious, although it was disputed, that the same is true of temporary detention to prevent apprehended harm." See also Justice Robert Jackson in *Chicago & Southern Air Lines, Inc. v. Waterman Steamship Corp.*, 333 U.S. 103, 111 (1948): "It would be intolerable that courts, without the relevant information, should review and perhaps nullify actions of the Executive taken on information properly held secret. Nor can courts sit *in camera* in order to be taken into executive confidences. But even if courts could require full disclosure, the very nature of executive decisions as to foreign policy is political, not judicial. Such decisions are wholly confided by our Constitution to the political departments of the government, Executive and Legislative. They are delicate, complex, and involve large elements of prophecy. They are and should be undertaken only by those directly responsible to the people whose welfare they advance or imperil. They are decisions of a kind for which the Judiciary has neither aptitude, facilities nor responsibility and which has long been held to belong in the domain of political power not subject to judicial intrusion or inquiry." And see also Justice Sutherland in *U.S. v. Curtiss-Wright*, 299 U.S. 304, 319–20 (1936): "It is important to bear in mind that we are here dealing not alone with an authority vested in the President by an exertion of legislative power, but with such an authority plus the very delicate, plenary and exclusive power of the President as the sole organ of the federal government in the field of international relations—a power which does not require as a basis for its exercise an act of Congress, but which, of course, like every other governmental power, must be exercised in subordination to the applicable provisions of the Constitution. It is quite apparent that if, in the maintenance of our international relations, embarrassment—perhaps serious embarrassment—is to be avoided and success for our aims achieved, congressional legislation which is to be made effective through negotiation and inquiry within the international field must often accord to the President a degree of discretion and freedom from statutory restriction which would not be admissible were domestic affairs alone involved. Moreover, he, not Congress, has the better opportunity of knowing the conditions which prevail in foreign countries, and especially is this true in time of war. He has his confidential sources of information. He has his agents in the form of diplomatic, consular and other officials. Secrecy in respect of information gathered by them may be highly necessary, and the premature disclosure of it productive of harmful results." The

examples could be multiplied. In the last-quoted passage, Justice Sutherland referred to similar pronouncements by the Senate Committee on Foreign Relations of 1816, John Marshall and President Washington to establish the point.

46. Geneva Convention Relative to the Treatment of Prisoners of War art. 3, *adopted* Aug. 12, 1949, 6 U.S.T. 3316, 75 U.N.T.S. 135.

47. Ari Fleischer, White House Spokesman: Special White House Announcement Re: Application of Geneva Conventions in Afghanistan, February 7, 2002, available at http://www.whitehouse.gov/news/releases/2002/02/20020207-13.html (last visited November 9, 2006).

48. Reisman and Antoniou, *The Laws of War,* xxiii.

49. UCMJ Art. 104, 106 (2002).

50. Surely any similarities here with the "problems of definition" identified by Sir Karl Popper and noted in the introduction to this work are purely coincidental.

51. Deputy Secretary of Defense Gordon England, Department of Defense Memorandum, "Application of Common Article 3 of the Geneva Conventions to the treatment of detainees in the Department of Defense," available at http://www.nimj.org/documents/Application%20of%20Common.pdf.

52. Public Law 366, 109th Cong., 2d sess., 120 Stat. 2600 (Oct. 17, 2006).

53. § 948c and §948d(a).

54. § 948d(b).

55. § 948 (a)(1) and (2).

56. § 948h.

57. § 948i(a) and (b).

58. § 948j(b).

59. § 948m; and 949m. This section also provides that if circumstances or physical conditions make it "unreasonable" to procure 12 available members, the convening authority is authorized to specify a lesser number, no fewer than 9. § 949m(c)(2).

60. § 948r(a)(b) and (d).

61. § 948s.

62. § 949a.

63. § 949a(2)(E).

64. § 949j.

65. § 949d.

66. § 9491. A standard regular court-martial instruction identifies this requirement as "the highest burden of proof known to the law."

67. § 949m.

68. § 948e.

69. § 949a(3)(d).

70. § 949b.

71. § 950b.

72. § 950f.

73. § 950g.

74. § 950i.

75. The statute defines terrorism as killing or inflicting great bodily harm, or intentional acts of wanton disregard for human life, done "in a manner calculated to influence or affect the conduct of government or civilian population by intimidation or coercion, or to retaliate against government conduct." § 950v(b)(24).

76. § 950v(b)(1)—(28).

77. Ibid., Sec. 5(a).

78. Ibid., Sec. 6(a)(2).

79. "As provided by the Constitution and by this section, the President has the authority for the United States to interpret the meaning and application of the Geneva Conventions and to promulgate higher standards and administrative regulations for violations of treaty obligations which are not grave breaches of the Geneva Conventions." Ibid., Sec. 6(a)(3).

80. Thus, Justice Jackson writing for a Court majority discussed the question of enforcement of prisoners' rights under the Geneva Conventions: "These prisoners claim to be and are entitled to its protection. It is however, the obvious scheme of the Agreement that responsibility for observance and enforcement of these rights is upon political and military authorities. Rights of alien enemies are vindicated under it only through protests and intervention of protecting powers as the rights of our citizens against foreign governments are vindicated only by Presidential intervention." Johnson v. Eisentrager, 339 U.S. 763, 789 n. 14. (1950).

81. MCA, Sec. 7(e)(1).

82. Ibid., Sec. 7(e)(2).

83. *Hamdan*, 126 S. Ct. at 2839 (Thomas, J., dissenting).

84. Evan J. Wallach, "Afghanistan, Quirin and Uchiyama: Does the Sauce Suit the Gander?" Army Law 18, 46 (2003). A similar opinion characterizes Michal R. Belknap, "A Putrid Pedigree: The Bush Administration's Military Tribunals in Historical Perspective," 38 Cal. W. L. Rev. 433 (2002).

85. Traditionally, the law of war and the principles of just war theory upon which it is based form two sets of guiding principles. The first category, the *jus ad bellum,* deals with issues attending the decision to go to war. The second set of principles, the *jus in bello,* addresses the conduct of warfare itself. Formulated in various ways, the *jus in bello* basically requires that commanders consider the military necessity of a proposed action, balance this military significance against the likelihood and extent of collateral damage—"proportionality"—and discriminate between lawful and unlawful targets.

86. Lon L. Fuller, "Human Interaction and the Law," 14 Am. J. Jurisprudence 1 (1969). On the "Prisoner's Dilemma" and the related "vocabulary of Game Theory," see the chapter entitled "The Puzzle of Cooperation" in Ellickson,

Order Without Law, 156–66; see also Schelling, *The Strategy of Conflict.* A similar point, emphasizing both the reality of custom, and its limits, is made more recently in Goldsmith and Posner, *The Limits of International Law,* chapter 1.

Though military officers come from widely differing societies and cultures, there is a commonality of purpose within this group that makes it possible to view officers as well as the soldiers they command as members of a distinct "community"—Clausewitz used the term "guild"—on the order of the geographically separated, but professionally connected members of "the international whaling community" of Ellickson's example from the nineteenth century. See Ellickson, *Order Without Law,* 192–95. Indeed, a case can be made that military professionals have more in common with one another than with the domestic civilian cultures which they respectively represent. The same cannot be said of terrorists, it must be acknowledged.

Early examples of the "cooperative principle" can be found in the fifteenth-century Chronicles of the late Middle Ages. See, Keen, *The Laws of War in the Late Middle Ages.* In this regard, see also the observations of Lon Fuller on the subject of customary law in "Human Interaction and the Law," 14 American J. Jurisprudence 1, 23 (1969): "Paradoxically, the tacit restraints of customary law between enemies are more likely to develop during active warfare than during a hostile stalemate of relations; fighting one another is itself in this sense a 'social' relation since it involves communication."

87. Most significant in this regard is the effect of the al-Qaeda terror attacks upon Spanish commuter trains in the days leading up to national elections in Spain. The attacks contributed to the defeat of the incumbent prime minister's conservative government, and to the withdrawal of Spanish troops from the allied coalition in Iraq. "Spain Aftershock: Bombs Affect Election and the War in Iraq," *Detroit Free Press*, March 16, 2004, A1; available at http://web2.westlaw.com/result/-Ihttp://web2.westlaw.com/result/-Ihttp://web2.westlaw.com/result/—Il

88. See, Hanson, *The Western Way of War* (arguing that a kind of "convention" or "reciprocal agreement" characterized the Western "way of war," which sought a one-time decisive event that would paradoxically limit and contain the destructiveness of armed combat by virtue of its very brutality and finality. This has been superseded by the need to fight against non-Western opponents "who dare not face us in battle," raising the specter of an unending conflict of vague, potentially limitless proportions. Ibid., 223, xxix.) See also Laqueur, *No End to War.*

89. Keen, *The Laws of War in the Late Middle Ages,* chapter 4, "The Authority of Military Courts," 45–59.

90. Goldsmith and Posner, *The Limits of International Law,* 39, 43.

91. Bauer, *The Mexican War,* 327.

92. *Madsen v. Kinsella*, 343 U.S. 341, 346–47 (1952). The case involved the *habeas* petition of a dependent wife accused of murdering her active-duty military

husband. The Court found this civilian could be tried in a military commission convened in American-occupied West Germany.

93. See, e.g., Michael Walzer, "Can There be a Decent Left?" 49 *Dissent* 19, 20 (April 1, 2002) [hereinafter, Walzer, "Decent Left?"]. Walzer argues that the Boer War offers insight into the question as to whether there is "any way of escaping the politics of guilt and resentment on the home ground of a superpower." For although the war aroused "fierce opposition . . . in England, . . . such opposition "wasn't marked, despite the cruelty of the war, by the kind of self-hate that we have seen in the American left [in the wake of the September 11, 2001, attacks]. Nor were the 'little Englanders' hostile to English politics and culture; they managed to take a stand against the empire without alienating themselves from its home country."

94. See, e.g., the "Guidelines for beating and killing hostages" in the Al-Qa'eda Manual, excerpted in Laqueur, ed., *Voices of Terror,* 403, 406; see also, Habeck, *Knowing the Enemy,* 126–29.

95. See, e.g., Meron, *War Crimes Law Comes of Age.*

96. Judge Robertson favorably referenced the arguments in his *Hamdan* opinion, *Hamdan v. Rumsfeld,* 344 F. Supp. 2d 152, 163, citing Neil McDonald and Scott Sullivan, "Rational Interpretation in Irrational Times: The Third Geneva Convention and the 'War on Terror'," 44 Harv. Int'l L. J. 301, 310 (2003); and Lawyers Committee for Human Rights, "Assessing the New Normal: Liberty and Security for the Post-September 11 United States," 77–80 (2003).

97. Chief Warrant Officer Durant, U.S. Army Special Operations, along with his crew, was shot down in his UH-60 Black Hawk helicopter in the battle over Mogadishu in October 1993. The lone survivor of the crash, Durant was held prisoner in solitary confinement for ten days before American forces secured his release. Durant's memoir gives the account of his captivity see, Durant, *In the Company of Heroes.*

The elision of the two cases forms part of the argument of the District Court judge in *Hamdan v. Rumsfeld,* 344 F. Supp. 152, 163 (2004).

98. See Kenneth Anderson, "The Role of the Lawyer in War: The Role of the United States Military Lawyer in Projecting a Vision of the Laws of War," 4 Chi. J. Int'l L. 445, 463 (2003).

99. See, e.g., Koh, "Preserving American Values."

100. Richard A. Posner, "Security Versus Civil Liberties," *Atlantic Monthly,* December 2001.

101. David, *French Law,* 119–20.

102. 18 USC 1385. The "Posse Comitatus Act" does provide for exceptions to this general policy where they are expressly authorized by the Constitution or by Act of Congress. Interestingly, the Act arose out of the experience of the South in the aftermath of the Civil War. See Matthew Carlton Hammond, "The Posse Comitatus Act: A Principle in Need of Renewal," 75 Wash. U. L. Q. 953 (1997).

103. As we have seen, the jurisdiction of the conseils de guerre *permanents* has since been eliminated in France.

104. See, e.g., Harold Hongju Koh, "The Case Against Military Commissions," 96 American J. of Int'l Law 337, 341 (2002). See also Jim Davis, "Note, A Cautionary Tale: Examining the Use of Military Tribunals by the United States in the Aftermath of the September 11 Attacks in Light of Peru's History of Human Rights Abuses Resulting from Similar Measures," 31 Ga. J. Int'l & Comp. L. 423 (2003).

105. Montesquieu, *The Spirit of the Laws,* Parts III, IV and V.

106. Horne, *A Savage War of Peace,* 353.

107. *Madsen v. Kinsella*, 343 U.S. 341, 348.

108. Numerous observers and commentators have drawn the analogy. Moreover, the connection with fascism is not unique to post–9/11 commentary. For a respected scholarly pre–9/11 work, identifying militant Islamic radicalism and terror with "clerical fascism," see, Laqueur, *Fascism: Past, Present, Future,* 147–69. As Mary Habeck argues, the problem of proper nomenclature extends to the characterization of the conflict itself. "The term 'war on terror' has never been satisfactory because it suggests that this is a war against a tactic, that there is no agency (or enemy), and that it will be difficult if not impossible to know when the war is won. Changing the name to something like 'the war on jihadis' or 'the war on jihadism,' will differentiate the extremists from other Muslims, give the war an enemy with a definite ideology and objectives, and suggest that there is an end point to work toward." Habeck, *Knowing the Enemy,* 175.

109. Lewis, *The Crisis of Islam,* 137. (Lewis observes that "[f]or Usama bin Ladin, his declaration of war against the United States marks the resumption of the struggle for religious dominance of the world that began in the seventh century." Ibid., 162.)

110. See Andrew Sullivan, "The Agony of the Left: What the War has Wrought," *Wall Street Journal*, October 10, 2001, A21.

111. Thus, "religious motives" cannot "really count" in the modern world, since "theology, on this view, is just the temporary, colloquial idiom in which the legitimate rage of oppressed men and women is expressed." Walzer, "Decent Left," 21. In another place, Walzer argues: "We need a combined cultural-religious-political explanation that has to focus, I think, on the creation of an Enemy, a whole people who are ideologically or theologically degraded so that they are available for murder." Walzer, *Arguing About War* 132. See also, Habeck, *Knowing the Enemy.*

112. George Weigel, "Iraq: Then & Now," 162 *First Things* 34, 37 (April, 2006). See also, e.g., Susan Sachs and Judith Miller, "Under Eye of U.N., Billions for Hussein in Oil-for-Food Plan," *New York Times*, August 13, 2004, A1, available at http://query.nytimes.com/gst/abstract.html?res=FA0913F93F5B0C708DDDA10894DC404482; Claudia Rosett, "The Oil-for-Food Scam: What Did

Kofi Annan Know, and When Did He Know It?," *Commentary* 15–22 (May, 2004); Owen Bowcott, "Report Reveals Shame of UN Peacekeepers: Sexual Abuse by Soldiers 'Must be Punished,'" *London Guardian*, March 25, 2005, A1.

113. Goldsmith and Posner, *The Limits of International Law,* 225.

114. Ignatieff, *The Warrior's Honor,* 160. The same point is elaborated in the recent work of Jeremy Rabkin, *Case for Sovereignty,* and *Law Without Nations?*

115. For treatment of the concept of "revolutions in military affairs," see, e.g., Krepinievich, "Cavalry to Computer," 30–42.

116. Kennan, Memorandum, in *Foreign Relations: The Far East and Australia* 6-718 (1948).

117. Elshtain, *Just War Against Terror,* 165.

118. Charles Krauthammer, "Man for a Glass Booth," *Washington Post*, December 9, 2005, A31.

119. *Terminiello v. Chicago*, 337 U.S. 1, 35 (1948) (J. Jackson, dissenting).

120. Liddell Hart, *Strategy,* 328.

121. The current modes of warfare imposed by the exponents of terror exacerbate this perennial problem: "Controlling the tempo of a crisis is often critical to its resolution . . . [Yet] the luxury of considered action may be one of the biggest casualties of September 11." Paul Bracken, "Rethinking the Unthinkable," in Talbott and Chanda, eds., *The Age of Terror,* 171, 186.

122. "Let justice be done, though the heavens fall." Sometimes stated in the form *fiat justitia et pereat mundus*—"let justice be done, though the world should perish."

123. See Sowell, *A Conflict of Visions.*

124. Interesting in this context is the conclusion of one of the prominent critical histories of the Tokyo War Crimes trials, which asserts that "to limit the options to trial by national courts, summary execution and international trial à la Tokyo is in itself evidence of political immaturity . . . [In a sense], the Tokyo trial was harmful rather than helpful. It prolonged our immersion in the unreal world of our dreams. In this sense, perhaps, summary executions might have been preferable." Minear, *Victors' Justice,* 179–80.

125. It seems that the concept of war is here to stay, at least for the foreseeable future, even though the attempt is made to define it out of existence, for instance, by substituting terms such as "aggression" or "conflict." Jovan Babic, "War Crimes: Moral, Legal or Simply Political?," in Jokić, *War Crimes and Collective Wrongdoing,* 57, 64 (arguing that "basic documents of the current world organization . . . talk only of aggression and don't even mention war as such. This has the consequence that war is reduced to a kind of police raid in which it is predetermined which side of the conflict is in the right.")

126. Bass, *Stay the Hand of Vengeance,* 283.

127. Power, "*A Problem from Hell,*" criticizes America's recent failures to stop genocide through humanitarian intervention.

128. Ironically, as Justices Thomas and Alito noted in dissent, the *Hamdan* decision preempts this retrospective function, in its *prospective* declaration of the illegitimacy of military commission methods, before any actual commission had been given a chance to put any such methods into practice.

129. *Korematsu v. United States*, 323 U.S. 214 (1944).

130. Letter to Erastus Corning and others, June 12, 1863, in Lincoln, *Speeches and Writings, 1859–1865*, p. 457.

131. U.S. District Judge John G. Koetl praised Stewart for her advocacy on behalf of "the poor, despised and dispossessed" in the course of his sentencing remarks. Michael Powell, "Lawyer Sentenced for Aiding Terrorist Client; 28 months is Far Less Than Prosecutors Sought," *Washington Post*, October 16, 2006, A3.

Notes to Conclusion

1. Henri Guernut, Preface, in Réau, *Les Crimes des conseils de guerre*, ix.

2. The title of Robert Sherrill's Vietnam-era contribution speaks for itself. Sherrill, *Military Justice is to Justice as Military Music is to Music.* (The line has been attributed, variously, to Georges Clemenceau commenting on the Dreyfus affair and to Groucho Marx.)

3. Thus, in his "deliberate choice to rely extensively on historical examples," McCormack notes the existence, over time, of a "broad acceptance of the principles of restrictions on the conduct of war, [and] personal responsibility for excesses of those limitations and legal processes for the imposition of penal sanctions against those convicted of such excesses." Timothy McCormack, "From Sun Tzu to the Sixth Committee," in McCormack and Simpson, eds., *The Law of War Crimes*, 36–37. McCormack further notes the important role played by national military tribunals throughout this tradition. Ibid., 31–63.

4. See, e.g., Borch, *Judge Advocates in Combat;* and Brigadier General Charles A. Dunlap, Jr., "The Role of the Lawyer in War," 4 Chi. J. Int'l Law 479 (2003). Military training and education in the laws of armed conflict now extend even to obligations concerning the protection of the environment during military actions. See, e.g., Merrit P. Drucker, "The Military Commander's Responsibility for the Environment," 11 *Environmental Ethics* 135 (1989); and Peter J. Richards and Michael N. Schmitt, "Mars meets Mother Nature: Protecting the Environment During Armed Conflict," 28 Stetson L. Rev. 1047 (1999). In identifying the characteristics of "military genius," what he identified as "a very highly developed mental attitude for a particular occupation," Clausewitz emphasized the need for "a sensitive and discriminating judgment . . . a skilled intelligence to scent out the truth." Clausewitz, *On War*, 100, 101.

5. Cohen, *Supreme Command*, 113 (commenting on allegations of Churchill's "personal harshness").

6. Military Order, November 13, 2001. The point is forcefully brought home in a recent work of the British statesman Robert Cooper: In the contemporary "nightmare of the modern, . . . chaos does not represent a threat of the kind we are used to—an armed attack by the military of an aggressive neighbouring state." Thus, "We may not be interested in chaos but chaos is interested in us. In fact, chaos, or at least the crime that lives within it, needs the civilized world and preys upon it . . . At its worst, in the form of terrorism, chaos can become a serious threat to the whole international order. Terrorism represents the privatization of war, the pre-modern with teeth." Moreover, "[i]n the jungle, one must use the laws of the jungle. In this period of peace in Europe, there is a temptation to neglect defences, both physical and psychological." Cooper, *The Breaking of Nations,* 64–65, 77, 62.

7. In a speech given on October 6, 2005, President Bush announced that the United States and its allies had disrupted ten different serious terror plots since September 11, 2001. David E. Sanger, "10 Plots Foiled Since Sept. 11, Bush Declares," *New York Times,* October 7, 2005, A1. On the same day, on the same page of the same newspaper, a conspiracy involving over a dozen people was reported to be targeting the New York City subway system. William K. Rashbaum, "New York Named in Terror Threat Against Subways," *New York Times,* October 7, 2005, A1.

8. Richard A. Posner, "Security Versus Civil Liberties," *Atlantic Monthly,* December 2001. The same argument forms the backbone of the work of Donald Kagan, *On the Origins of War, and the Preservation of Peace.*

9. Lowell S. Gustafson, "Thucydides and Pluralism," in Gustafson, ed., *Thucydides' Theory of International Relations,* 174, 185.

10. These competing views reflect the larger complex of trans-Atlantic tensions examined in a much-discussed work, Robert Kagan, *Of Paradise and Power.*

11. Guelke, *The Age of Terrorism and International Political System,* 192.

12. Ibid., citing R. J. Vincent, *Concluding Observations,* in Freedman et al., *Terrorism and International Order*, 106. As memories of September 11, 2001, fade, these kinds of arguments once again gain traction. Yet according to recent revelations from the Soviet archives, now being published for the first time as part of the Yale "Annals of Communism" series, these terror-skeptics do not even seem to have gotten it right on the matter of Communism in 1950s America. See, e.g., Klehr, Haynes, and Firsov, *The Secret World of American Communism.*

13. Here I would join in the caution of Michael Howard, who observes an ongoing ironic tension within the "liberal conscience" between its ideals of justice, truth, and peace and the need to buttress such noble principles by the prudential application of force. Howard's evaluation of the history of this "liberal tradition" is heavily qualified by the candid acknowledgment of its manifest

shortcomings. To be sure, the cumulative effect of the qualifications could be said to be tantamount to damning the tradition with faint praise: "This does not mean that the liberal tradition in thinking about war and peace has been totally self-deluding and false. It has certainly been a tradition often marred by naiveté, by intellectual arrogance, by ignorance, by confused thinking and sometimes, alas, by sheer hypocrisy." Nevertheless, it remains possible to acknowledge the "progress" of the last two centuries in establishing universal standards "to which all states virtually without exception pay at least lip-service." Howard, *War and the Liberal Conscience,* 134. The narrative of the intervening decades regrettably affords little scope for improving the picture.

Bibliography

OFFICIAL DOCUMENTS

France. Commission instituée en vue de constater les actes commis par l'ennemi en violation du droit des gens. *Rapports et procès-verbaux d'enquête de la commission instituée en vue de constater les actes commis par l'ennemi en violation du droit des gens, documents rélative à la guerre.* Vols. 10–12. Paris: Imprimerie nationale, 1919.

France. Ministère des affaires étrangères. *Germany's Violations of the Laws of War 1914–15, Compiled Under the Auspices of the French Ministry of Foreign Affairs.* Edited and translated by J. O. P. Bland. London: William Heinemann Publishers, 1915. Originally published as *Les Violations des lois de la guerre par l'Allemagne, publication faite par les soins du Ministère des Affaires étrangères.* (Paris, Imprimerie nationale, 1915).

Germany. Auswärtiges Amt. *The Belgian People's War, a Violation of International Law.* Translations from the Official German White Book, Published by the Imperial Foreign Office. New York: Press of John C. Rankin, Co., 1915.

Great Britain. Concentration Camps Commission. *Report on the Concentration Camps in South Africa, by the Committee of Ladies Appointed by the Secretary of State for War, Containing Reports on the Camps in Natal, the Orange River Colony, and the Transvaal.* Cd. 893. London: H.M. Stationer's Office, Eyre & Spottiswoode, 1902.

Great Britain. Royal Commission on the War in South Africa. *Appendices to Minutes of Evidence taken before the Royal Commission on the War in South Africa.* Cd. 1792. London: H.M. Stationer's Office, Wyman and Sons, 1903.

Great Britain. Royal Commission on the War in South Africa. *Minutes of Evidence taken before the Royal Commission on the War in South Africa.* 2 vols. Cd. 1790–1791. London: H.M. Stationer's Office, Wyman and Sons, 1903.

Great Britain. Army. *Parliamentary Papers Relating to the Administration of Martial Law in South Africa.* 2 vols. Cd. 981, 1423. London: H.M. Stationer's Office, 1902–03.

Great Britain. Royal Commission Appointed to Inquire into Sentences Passed Under Martial Law. *Report.* Cd. 1364. London: H.M. Stationer's Office, 1902.

Great Britain. War Office. *South Africa Despatches by Lord Kitchener relative to Military Operations in South Africa.* Cd. 984, 986. London: H.M. Stationer's Office, 1901–1902.

International Committee of the Red Cross. *The Geneva Conventions of August 12, 1949.* Geneva, Switzerland: ICRC Publications, 1949.

International Conference on Military Trials. *Report of Robert H. Jackson, United States Representative to the International Conference on Military Trials, London 1945.* Washington, DC: US Government Printing Office, 1949.

The Tokyo Judgment: The International Military Tribunal for the Far East (I.M.T.F.E.), 29 April 1946–12 November 1948. Edited by B. V. A. Röling and C. F. Ruter. 2 vols. Amsterdam: APA-University Press, 1977.

The Trial of Hon. Clement L. Vallandigham, by a Military Commission: and the Proceedings under his Application for a Writ of Habeas Corpus in the Circuit Court of the United States for the Southern District of Ohio. Cincinnati: Rickey and Carroll, 1863.

United Nations War Crimes Commission. *History of the United Nations War Crimes Commission and the Development of the Laws of War.* London: H.M. Stationer's Office, 1948.

United Nations War Crimes Commission. *Law Reports of Trials of War Criminals. Selected and Prepared by the United Nations War Crimes Commission.* 15 vols. London: Published for the United Nations War Crimes Commission by Her Majesty's Stationer's Office, 1947–1949.

United States. Foreign Relations of the United States. Declassified U.S. State Department documents, organized according to place and year.

United States. Journals of the Continental Congress, 1774–1779. Edited by Worthington Chauncey Ford. 2 vols. Washington, DC: U.S. Government Printing Office, 1905.

United States. National Commission on Terrorist Attacks upon the United States. *9/11 Commission Report.* Washington, DC: U.S. Government Printing Office, 2004.

United States War Department. *General Orders of the War Department, embracing the years 1861, 1862 and 1863. Adapted specially for the use of the Army and Navy of the United States.* 2 vols. New York: Derby & Miller, 1864.

JOURNALS CONTAINING ARTICLES ON DEVELOPMENTS IN THE LAW AND REPORTS OF CASES

42 Journal du droit international 617 (1915).
43 Journal du droit international 155 (1916).
44 Journal du droit international 570 (1917).
70 Law Quarterly Review 143 (1902).

Revue du droit public.
Revue pénitentiaire et de droit pénale.

BOOKS AND ARTICLES

Acer, Eleanor. *Assessing the New Normal: Liberty and Security for the Post–September 11 United States*. New York: Lawyers Committee for Human Rights, 2003.

Aguiló Bonnín, Federico. *Estado de sitio: apuntes para la historia de las jornadas septembrinas de 1985 en Bolivia*. Cochabamba, Bolivia: Asamblea Permanente de Derechos Humanos, 1985.

Ambler, John Steward. *The French Army in Politics: 1945–1962*. Columbus, OH: Ohio State University Press, 1966.

Amery, Leo, ed. *The Times History of the War in South Africa, 1899–1902*. 7 vols. London: S. Low, Marston & Co., 1909.

Amparo Serrano, Luz. *Uso y abuso del estado de sitio*. Bogotá, Colombia: Editorial Temis Librería, 1980.

Andreopoulos, George J., and Harold E. Selesky, eds. *The Aftermath of Defeat: Societies, Armed Forces and the Challenge of Recovery*. New Haven, CT: Yale University Press, 1994.

Anthony, Joseph Garner. *Hawaii under Army Rule*. Stanford, CA: Stanford University Press, 1955.

Appleman, John Alan. *Military Tribunals and International Crimes*. Westport, CT: Greenwood Press, 1954.

Arendt, Hannah. *Eichmann in Jerusalem: A Report on the Banality of Evil*. New York: Viking Press, 1963.

———. *On Violence*. New York: Harcourt, Brace & World, 1970.

Asprey, Robert B. *War in the Shadows: The Guerrilla in History*. 2 vols. Garden City, NY: Doubleday, 1975.

Barthélemy, Joseph. "Le Droit public en temps de guerre." Pt. 1. 32 Revue du Droit Public 134 (1915).

———. Pt. 2. "La Liberté d'opinion et la censure," 32 Revue du Droit Public 310 (1915).

———. Pt. 3. "La Gouvernement et la loi," 32 Revue du Droit Public 548 (1915)

———. Pt. 5. "Les Pouvoirs Publics et le Commandement Militaire," 33 Revue du Droit Public 552 (1916).

———. Pt. 4. "Diminution des garanties des citoyens devant la répression pénale," 33 Revue du Droit Public 73 (1916).

Bass, Gary J. *Stay the Hand of Vengeance: The Politics of War Crimes Tribunals*. Princeton, NJ: Princeton University Press, 2000.

Baudrillard, Jean. *The Spirit of Terrorism*. Translated by Chris Turner. New York: W. W. Norton & Co., 2002.

Bauer, K. Jack. *The Mexican War: 1846–1848*. New York: Macmillan, 1974.

Becker, Jean-Jacques. *La France en guerre, 1914–1918: La Grande mutation.* Bruxelles: Editions Complexe, 1988.

———. *The Great War and the French People.* Translated by Arnold Pomerans. Dover, NH: Berg Publishers, 1985.

Benvenisti, Eyal. *The International Law of Occupation.* Princeton, NJ: Princeton University Press, 1993.

Bergeron, Paul H. *The Presidency of James K. Polk.* Lawrence, KS: University Press of Kansas, 1987.

Berkowitz, Peter, ed. *Terrorism, the Laws of War, and the Constitution: Debating the Enemy Combatant Cases.* Stanford, CA: Hoover Institution Press, 2005.

Bethke-Elshtain, Jean. *Just War against Terror: The Burden of American Power in a Violent World.* New York: Basic Books, 2003.

Bishop, Joseph W., Jr. *Justice Under Fire: A Study of Military Law.* New York: Charterhouse Books, 1974.

Blum, John Morton. *From the Morgenthau Diaries.* Vol. 3 *Years of War, 1941–1945*. Boston: Houghton Mifflin Co., 1967.

Borch, Frederic L. *Judge Advocates in Combat: Army Lawyers in Military Operations from Vietnam to Haiti.* Honolulu, HI: University Press of the Pacific, 2004.

Bosc, A. "Les Actes de gouvernement et la théorie des pouvoirs de guerre," 43 Revue du Droit Public 186 (1926).

Brackman, Arnold. *The Other Nuremberg: The Untold Story of the Tokyo War Crimes Trials.* New York: William Morrow & Co., 1987.

Buscher, Frank M. *The U.S. War Crimes Trial Program in Germany, 1946–1955*. New York: Greenwood Press, 1989.

Cahen-Salvador, Georges. *Les Prisonniers de guerre (1914–1919)*. Paris, Payot, 1929.

Callwell, Col. Charles E. *Small Wars—Their Principles and Practice.* London: H.M. Stationer's Office, Harrison and Sons, 1896.

Carrese, Paul O. *The Cloaking of Power: Montesquieu, Blackstone and the Rise of Judicial Activism.* Chicago: University of Chicago Press, 2003.

Carnahan, Burrus M. "Reason, Retaliation and Rhetoric: Jefferson and the Quest for Humanity in War," 139 Military Law Review 83 (1993).

Chomsky, Carol. "The United States–Dakota War Trials: A Study in Military Injustice," 43 Stanford Law Review 13 (1990).

Churchill, Winston S. *The Second World War.* 6 vols. Boston: Houghton Mifflin, 1948–1951.

Clausewitz, Carl Von. *On War.* Edited and translated by Michael Howard and Peter Paret. Princeton, NJ: Princeton University Press, 1984.

Clode, Charles M. *The Military Forces of the Crown: Their Administration and Government.* London: J. Murray, 1869.

Cohen, Eliot A. *Obligations of Leadership: The Khobar Towers Bombing and its Aftermath*. Washington D.C.: Paul H. Nitze School of Advanced International Studies, Johns Hopkins University, SAIS Publications 1997.

———. *Supreme Command: Soldiers, Statesmen, and Leadership in Wartime*. New York: The Free Press, 2002.

Coil, George. "War Crimes of the American Revolution," 82 Military Law Review 171 (1978).

Cooper, Robert. *The Breaking of Nations: Order and Chaos in the Twenty-First Century*. New York: Atlantic Monthly Press, 2003.

Correia, António Damasceno. *Estado de sítio e de emergência em democracia*. Lisbon: Vega, 1989.

Corwin, Edward S. "Martial Law, Yesterday and Today," 47 Political Science Quarterly 96 (1932).

———. *The President: Office and Powers—History and Analysis of Practice and Opinion*. New York: New York University Press, 1940.

———. *Total War and the Constitution*. Freeport, NY: Books for Libraries Press, 1947.

Cosgrove, Richard A. "The Boer War and the Modernization of British Martial Law." 44 Military Affairs 124 (1980).

Cruz Villalon, Pedro. *El estado de sitio y la constitución: la constitucionalización de la protección extraordinaria del estado (1789–1878)*. Madrid: Centro de Estudios Constitucionales, 1980.

David, René. *French Law: Its Structure, Sources and Methodology*. Translated by Michael Kindred. Baton Rouge: LA: Louisiana State University Press, 1972.

———, and John C. Brierley. *Major Legal Systems in the World Today: An Introduction to the Comparative Study of Law*. 2nd ed. New York: The Free Press, 1978.

De Wet, Christian Rudolf. *Three Years' War (October 1899–June 1902)*. New York: Charles Scribner's, 1902.

Dicey, Albert Venn. *Introduction to the Study of the Law of the Constitution*. 8th ed. London: MacMillan and Co., 1915.

Donald, David Herbert. *Lincoln*. New York: Touchstone Books, 1995.

Dower, John. *Embracing Defeat: Japan in the Wake of World War II*. New York: W. W. Norton & Co., 1999.

Downing, Brian M. *The Military Revolution and Political Change: Origins of Democracy and Autocracy in Early Modern Europe*. Princeton, NJ: Princeton University Press, 1992.

Dunlap, Brig. Gen. Charles A. Jr. "The Role of the Lawyer in War," 4 Chicago Journal of International Law 479 (2003).

Dunn, John. *The Political Thought of John Locke: An Historical Account of the Argument of the Two Treatises of Government*. Cambridge: Cambridge University Press, 1969.

Durant, Michael J., with Steven Hartov. *In the Company of Heroes*. New York: Putnam, 1993.

Ellickson, Robert C. *Order Without Law: How Neighbors Settle Disputes*. Cambridge, MA: Harvard University Press, 1991.

Ernst, Daniel R., and Victor Jew, eds. *Total War and the Law: The American Home Front in World War II*. Westport, CT: Praeger, 2002.

Eyck, Erich. *A History of the Weimar Republic*. 2 vols. Translated by Harlan P. Hanson and Robert G. L. Waite. Cambridge, MA: Harvard University Press, 1962.

Fairman, Charles. *The Law of Martial Rule*. 2nd ed. Chicago: Callaghan and Company, 1943.

———. "The Supreme Court on Military Jurisdiction: Martial Rule in Hawaii and the Yamashita Case," 59 Harvard Law Review 833 (1946).

Farcy, Jean-Claude. *Les Camps de concentration français de la premiere guerre mondiale, 1914–1920*. Paris: Anthropos, 1995.

Fidell, Eugene R., and Dwight H. Sullivan, eds. *Evolving Military Justice*. Annapolis, MD: Naval Institute Press, 2002.

Fisher, Louis. *Military Tribunals and Presidential Power: American Revolution to the War on Terrorism*. Lawrence, KS: University of Kansas Press, 2005.

———. *Nazi Saboteurs on Trial: A Military Tribunal and American Law*. 2nd ed. Lawrence, KS: University of Kansas Press, 2003.

Fletcher, George P. *Our Secret Constitution: How Lincoln Redefined American Democracy*. New York: Oxford University Press, 2001.

Foote, Shelby. *The Civil War: A Narrative*. 3 vols. New York: Random House, 1958–1974.

Fraenkel, Ernst. *Military Occupation and the Rule of Law: Occupational Government in the Rhineland, 1918–1923*. New York: Oxford University Press, 1944.

Franklin, Daniel P. *Extraordinary Measures: The Exercise of Prerogative Powers in the United States*. Pittsburgh, PA : University of Pittsburgh Press, 1991.

Freedman, Lawrence, et al. *Terrorism and International Order*. London: Routledge & Kegan Paul, 1986.

Fuller, Lon L. "Human Interaction and the Law," 14 American Journal of Jurisprudence 1 (1969).

Gallon Giraldo, Gustavo. *Quince años de estado de sitio en Colombia: 1958–1978*. Bogota: Librería y Editorial América Latina, 1979.

Garner, James Wilford. *International Law and the World War*. 2 vols. London: Longmans, Green and Co., 1920.

Gilbert, Martin. *The First World War: A Complete History*. New York: H. Holt, 1994.

Gilmour, David. *The Long Recessional: The Imperial Life of Rudyard Kipling*. New York: Farrar, Straus and Giroux, 2002.

Glueck, Sheldon. *War Criminals: Their Prosecution and Punishment.* New York: A. A. Knopf, 1944.
Goldsmith, Jack L., and Eric A. Posner. *The Limits of International Law.* New York: Oxford University Press, 2005.
Got, Ambroise, ed., trans. *The Case of Miss Cavell, from the Unpublished Documents of the Trial: The Property of a Former Commissary of the German Government.* London : Hodder and Stoughton Ltd., 1920.
Grotius, Hugo. *The Rights of War and Peace.* 1625. 3 vols. Edited by Richard Tuck. Translated by Jean Barbeyrac. Indianapolis, IA: Liberty Fund, 2005.
Guelke, Adrian. *The Age of Terrorism and the International Political System.* New York: I. B. Tauris Publishers, distributed by St. Martin's Press, 1995.
Gustafson, Lowell S., ed. *Thucydides' Theory of International Relations: A Lasting Possession.* Baton Rouge, LA: Louisiana State University Press, 2000.
Habeck, Mary. *Knowing the Enemy: Jihadist Ideology and the War on Terror.* New Haven, CT: Yale University Press, 2006.
Halleck, Henry W. *International Law; or, Rules Regulating the Intercourse of States in Peace and War.* New York: D. Van Nostrand, 1861.
Hamilton, Alexander, John Jay, and James Madison. *The Federalist.* Edited by Jacob E. Cooke. Middletown, CT: Wesleyan University Press, 1961.
Hammond, Matthew Carlton. "The Posse Comitatus Act: A Principle in Need of Renewal," 75 Washington University Law Quarterly 953 (1997).
Hanson, Victor Davis. "The Fruits of Appeasement." City Journal 14, no. 2 (2004): 32–45.
———. *The Western Way of War: Infantry Battle in Classical Greece.* Berkeley, CA: University of California Press, 1989.
Hélie, Philippe. *La Competence des conseils de guerre, principalement en temps de guerre et pendant l'état de siege.* Besançon: Imprimerie de l'Est, 1924.
Hickey, Donald R. *The War of 1812: A Forgotten Conflict.* Urbana, IL: University of Illinois Press, 1989.
Horne, Alistair. *A Savage War of Peace: Algeria 1954–1962.* New York: Viking Press, 1978.
Horne, John, and Alan Kramer. *German Atrocities, 1914: A History of Denial.* New Haven, CT: Yale University Press, 2001.
Howard, Michael. *War and the Liberal Conscience.* London: Temple, Smith, 1978.
Howard, Michael, George J. Andreopoulos, and Mark R. Schulman, eds. *The Laws of War: Constraints on Warfare in the Western World.* New Haven, CT: Yale University Press, 1994.
Huntington, Samuel P. *The Soldier and the State: The Theory and Politics of Civil-Military Relations.* Cambridge, MA: Belknap Press of Harvard University Press, 1959.
Ignatieff, Michael. *A Lesser Evil: Political Ethics in an Age of Terror.* Princeton, NJ: Princeton University Press, 2004.

———. *The Warrior's Honor: Ethnic War and the Modern Conscience*. London: Chatto & Windus, 1997.
In re Yamashita, 327 U.S. 1 (1946).
Jackson, Robert. *The Prisoners, 1914–18*. New York: Routledge, 1989.
Jaer, B. de. *L'Armée belge d'occupation et son droit de juridiction*. Liége, Belgium: G. Thone, 1928.
Jaffa, Harry V. *A New Birth of Freedom: Abraham Lincoln and the Coming of the Civil War*. Lanham, MD: Rowan & Littlefield Publishers, 2000.
James, Marquis. *The Life of Andrew Jackson*. Indianapolis, IA: Bobbs-Merrill, 1938.
Johnson, Timothy D. *Winfield Scott: The Quest for Military Glory*. Lawrence, KS: University Press of Kansas, 1998.
Jokić, Aleksandar, ed. *War Crimes and Collective Wrongdoing: A Reader*. Malden, MA: Blackwell Publishers, 2001.
Jooste, Graham, and Roger Webster. *Innocent Blood*. Claremont, South Africa: Spearhead, 2002.
Judd, Denis, and Keith Surridge. *The Boer War*. London: John Murray, 2002.
Kagan, Donald. *On the Origins of War, and the Preservation of Peace*. New York: Doubleday, 1995.
Kagan, Robert. *Of Paradise and Power: America and Europe in the New World Order*. New York: Alfred A. Knopf, 2003.
Katyal, Neal K., and Laurence H. Tribe, "Waging War, Deciding Guilt: Trying the Military Tribunals," 111 Yale Law Journal 1259 (2002).
Keegan, John. *The First World War*. New York: Alfred A. Knopf, 1999.
Keen, Maurice. *The Laws of War in the Late Middle Ages*. London: Routledge & Kegan Paul, 1965.
Kelley, Michael J. "Understanding September 11th—An International Legal Perspective on the War in Afghanistan," 35 Creighton Law Review 283 (2002).
Kennan, George F. *Memoirs: 1925–1950*. Boston: Little, Brown, 1967.
Kipling, Rudyard. *Complete Verse*. New York: Anchor Press, 1989.
Kissinger, Henry. *Diplomacy*. New York: Simon & Schuster, 1994.
Klehr, Harvey, John Earl Haynes, and Fridrikh Igorevich Firsov. *The Secret World of American Communism*. New Haven, CT: Yale University Press, 1995.
Koh, Harold Hongju. "The Case Against Military Commissions," 96 American Journal of International Law 337 (2002).
Köhler, Ludwig von. *The Administration of the Occupied Territories*. 1927. Translated by W. R. Dittmar. Washington, DC: Carnegie Endowment for International Peace, 1942.
Krepinevich, Andrew F. "Cavalry to Computer: The Pattern of Military Revolutions," The National Interest 37 (Fall, 1994): 30–42.
Lael, Richard L. *The Yamashita Precedent: War Crimes and Command Responsibility*. Wilmington, DE: Scholarly Resources, 1982.

Laqueur, Walter. *Fascism: Past, Present, Future.* New York: Oxford University Press, 1996.

———. *No End to War: Terrorism in the Twenty-First Century.* New York: Continuum, 2003.

———. Ed., *Voices of Terror: Manifestos, Writings and Manuals of Al Qaeda, Hamas, and Other Terrorists from Around the World and Throughout the Ages.* New York: Reed Press, 2004.

Leroy, Paul. *L'Organisation constitutionnelle et les crises.* Paris: Librairie générale de droit et de jurisprudence, 1966.

Levie, Howard S. *Terrorism in War—The Law of War Crimes.* Dobbs Ferry, NY: Oceana Publications, 1993.

Lewis, Bernard. *The Crisis of Islam: Holy War and Unholy Terror.* New York: Modern Library, 2003.

Liddell Hart, Sir Basil Henry. *Strategy.* 2nd ed. New York: Praeger, 1967.

Lincoln, Abraham. *Speeches and Writings, 1859–1865.* Edited by Don E. Fehrenbacher. New York: Library of America, 1989.

Locke, John. *Two Treatises of Government.* Edited by Peter Laslett. Cambridge: Cambridge University Press, 1988.

Lukacs, John. *At the End of an Age.* New Haven, CT: Yale University Press, 2002.

Lurie, Jonathan. *Arming Military Justice: The Origins of the United States Court of Military Appeals, 1775–1950.* Princeton, NJ: Princeton University Press, 1992.

Mahan, Alfred T. *The Story of the War in South Africa (1899–1900).* 3rd ed. London: S. Low, Marston and Co., Ltd., 1901.

Maguire, Peter. *Law and War: An American Story.* New York: Columbia University Press, 2000.

Martin, James Kirby, and Mark Edward Lender. *A Respectable Army: The Military Origins of the Republic, 1763–1789.* Arlington Heights, IL: H. Davidson, 1982.

Marvel, William. *Andersonville: The Last Depot.* Chapel Hill, NC: University of North Carolina Press, 1994.

McCormack, Timothy L. H., and Gerry J. Simpson, eds. *The Law of War Crimes: National and International Approaches.* Boston : Kluwer Law International, 1997.

McDonald, Forrest. *States' Rights and the Union: Imperium in Imperio, 1776–1876.* Lawrence, KS: University Press of Kansas, 2000.

McDonald, Neil, and Scott Sullivan. "Rational Interpretation in Irrational Times: The Third Geneva Convention and the 'War on Terror,'" 44 Harvard International Law Journal 301 (2003).

Menéndez Valdés, Manuel. *French Justice: Seven Months Under Sentence of Death.* Translated by Dora Round. London: Faber & Faber, Ltd., 1930.

Mérignhac, Alexandre G., and E. Lémonon. *Le Droit des gens et la guerre de 1914–1918.* 2 vols. Paris: L. Tenin, 1921.

Meron, Theodor. *War Crimes Law Comes of Age: Essays.* New York: Oxford University Press, 1998.

Merryman, John Henry. *The Civil Law Tradition: An Introduction to the Legal Systems of Western Europe and Latin America.* 2nd ed. Stanford, CA: Stanford University Press, 1985.

Minear, Richard H. *Victors' Justice: The Tokyo War Crimes Trial.* Princeton, NJ: Princeton University Press, 1971.

Montesquieu, Charles de Secondat, Baron de. *The Spirit of the Laws.* 1748. Translated and edited by Anne M. Cohler, Basia Carolyn Miller, and Harold Samuel Stone. Cambridge: Cambridge University Press, 1989.

Morison, Samuel Eliot, Frederick Merk, and Frank Freidel. *Dissent in Three American Wars.* Cambridge, MA: Harvard University Press, 1970.

Müller-Meiningen, Ernst. *Der Weltkrieg und "der Zusammenbruch des Völkerrechts."* Berlin: G. Reimer, 1917.

Mullins, Claude. *The Leipzig Trials: An Account of the War Criminals' Trials and a Study of German Mentality.* London: H. F. & G. Witherby, 1921.

Murphy, Sean D. "Terrorism and the Concept of 'Armed Attack' in Article 51 of the U.N. Charter," 43 Harvard International Law Journal 41 (2002).

Nanda, Ved P., ed. *Law in the War on International Terrorism.* Ardsley, NY: Transnational Publishers, 2005.

Navarro de la Ossa, Roberto. *La constitución y el estado de sitio.* Bogotá: Pontificia Universidad Javeriana, 1974.

Neely, Mark E., Jr. *The Fate of Liberty: Abraham Lincoln and Civil Liberties.* New York: Oxford University Press, 1991.

Nichols, David A. *Lincoln and the Indians: Civil War Policy and Politics.* Columbia, MS: University of Missouri Press, 1978.

Núñez Carvallo, Gabriel. *El estado de sitio y el habeas corpus: antecedentes de la reforma constitucional.* Asunción, Paraguay: Ediciones Ñanduti Vive, Intercontinental Editora, 1989.

O'Donovan, Oliver, and Joan Lockwood O'Donovan. *Bonds of Imperfection: Christian Politics, Past and Present.* Grand Rapids, MI: Eerdmans, 2004.

Omissi, David, and Andrew S. Thompson, eds. *The Impact of the South African War.* New York: Palgrave, 2002.

Orwell, George. *The Collected Essays, Journalism and Letters of George Orwell.* Edited by Sonia Orwell and Ian Angus. 4 vols. London: Secker & Warburg, 1968.

———. *Homage to Catalonia.* Boston: Beacon Press, 1955.

Padfield, Peter. *War Beneath the Sea: Submarine Conflict during World War II.* London: John Murray, 1995.

Pakenham, Thomas. *The Boer War.* New York: Random House, 1979.
Peskin, Alan. *Winfield Scott and the Profession of Arms.* Kent, OH: Kent State University Press, 2003.
Peterson, Merrill D. *The Great Triumvirate: Webster, Clay and Calhoun.* New York: Oxford University Press, 1988.
Phillips, Raymond, ed. *Trial of Josef Kramer and Forty-Four Others (The Belsen Trial).* London: W. Hodge, 1949.
Phillipson, Coleman. *International Law and the Great War.* London: T. Fisher Unwin, Ltd., 1915.
Piccigallo, Philip R. *The Japanese on Trial: Allied War Crimes Operations in the East, 1945–1951.* Austin, TX: University of Texas Press, 1979.
Pollock, Sir Frederick, and Frederic William Maitland. *The History of English Law Before the Time of Edward I.* 2d. ed. Cambridge: Cambridge University Press, 1899.
Popper, Karl R. *The Open Society and Its Enemies.* 2 vols. London: Routledge & Keegan Paul, 1945.
Posada Viana, Alfredo, and Jose Ivan Matallana Eslava. *Estado de sitio y legalidad marcial en colombia.* Bogota, Colombia: Pontificia Universidad Javeriana, 1987.
Power, Samantha. *"A Problem from Hell": America and the Age of Genocide.* New York: Basic Books, 2002.
Price, Glenn W. *Origins of the War with Mexico: The Polk-Stockton Intrigue.* Austin, TX: University of Texas Press, 1967.
Rabkin, Jeremy. *The Case for Sovereignty: Why the World Should Welcome American Independence.* Washington, DC: AEI Press, 2004.
———. *Law Without Nations? Why Constitutional Government Requires Sovereign States.* Princeton, NJ: Princeton University Press, 2005.
Ramsay, David. *The History of the American Revolution.* 1789. 2 vols. Edited by Lester H. Cohen. Indianapolis, IA: Liberty Classics, 1990.
Randall, James G. *Constitutional Problems under Lincoln.* Rev. ed. Urbana, IL: University of Illinois Press, 1951.
———, and David Donald. *The Civil War and Reconstruction.* 2d ed., rev. with enl. bibliography. Boston: Little, Brown 1969.
Réau, R.-G. *Les Crimes des conseils de guerre.* Paris: Editions du Progrès civique, 1925.
Reel, A. Frank. *The Case of General Yamashita.* Chicago: University of Chicago Press, 1949.
Rehnquist, William H. *All the Laws but One.* New York: Knopf, 1998.
Reisman, W. Michael, and Chris T. Antoniou, eds. *The Laws of War: A Comprehensive Collection of Primary Documents on International Laws Governing Armed Conflict.* New York: Random House, 1994.

Reyes Matta, Fernando, Jorge Andrés Richards, and Juan Pablo Cárdenas, eds. *Periodismo independiente—mito o realidad? Debates sobre militancia, profesionalismo, democracia y verdad con los directores de las revistas prohibidas y censuradas en Chile bajo el estado de sitio*. Santiago, Chile: Instituto Latinoamericano de Estudios Transnacionales, 1986.

Rhodehamel, John, ed. *The American Revolution: Writings from the War of Independence*. New York: Library of America, 2001.

Romain, Paul. *L'Etat de siège politique*. Albi, France: Imprimerie des orphelins-apprentis, 1918.

Rossiter, Clinton. *Constitutional Dictatorship: Crisis Government in the Modern Democracies*. Princeton: Princeton University Press, 1948.

———, and Richard P. Longaker. *The Supreme Court and the Commander in Chief*. Expanded edition. Ithaca, NY: Cornell University Press, 1976.

Rubin, Alfred P. "The New World Disorder: Applying the Geneva Conventions: Military Commissions, Armed Conflict, and Al-Qaeda," 26 Fletcher Forum of World Affairs 79 (2002).

Saint-Bonnet, François. *L'État d'exception*. Paris: Presses universitaires de France, 2001.

Sanchez Viamonte, Carlos. *Ley Marcial y Estado de Sitio en el Derecho Argentino*. Buenos Aires, Venezuela: Editorial Perrot, 1957.

Schelling, Thomas C. *The Strategy of Conflict*. Cambridge, MA: Harvard University Press, 1980.

Schroeder, John H. *Mr. Polk's War: American Opposition and Dissent, 1846–1848*. Madison, WI: University of Wisconsin Press, 1973.

Scott, Winfield. *Memoirs of Lieut.-General Scott, LL.D. Written by Himself*. 2 vols. New York: Sheldon, 1864.

Sefton, James E. *The United States Army and Reconstruction, 1865–1877*. Westport, CT: Greenwood Press, 1980.

Sherrill, Robert. *Military Justice is to Justice as Military Music is to Music*. New York: Harper & Row, 1970.

Smith, Bradley F. *Reaching Judgment at Nuremberg*. New York: Basic Books, 1977.

———. *The Road to Nuremberg*. New York: Basic Books, 1981.

Smuts, Jan Christiaan. *Selections from the Smuts Papers*. Edited by W. K. Hancock and Jean Van Der Poel. 7 Vols. Cambridge: Cambridge University Press, 1966–73.

Solzhenitsyn, Aleksandr I. *The Gulag Archipelago, 1918–1956: An Experiment in Literary Investigation*. Vol. 2. Translated by Thomas P. Whitney. New York: Harper & Row Publishers, 1975.

Sowell, Thomas. *A Conflict of Visions: Ideological Origins of Political Struggles*. New York: Basic Books, 2002.

Speed, Richard B., III. *Prisoners, Diplomats, and the Great War: A Study in the Diplomacy of Captivity*. New York: Greenwood Press, 1990.

Spies, S. B. *Methods of Barbarism?-Roberts and Kitchener and Civilians in the Boer Republics, January 1900–May 1902.* Cape Town, South Africa: Human & Rousseau, 1977.

Talbott, Strobe, and Nayan Chanda, eds. *The Age of Terror: America and the World after September 11.* New York: Basic Books, 2001.

Tapia-Valdes, J. A. "A Typology of National Security Policies," 9 Yale Journal of World Public Order 10 (1982).

Taylor, Telford. *The Anatomy of the Nuremberg Trials: A Personal Memoir.* New York: Knopf, 1992.

Thompson, H. K., Jr., and Henry Strutz, eds. *Doenitz at Nuremberg, a Reappraisal: War Crimes and the Military Professional.* New York: Amber Pub. Corp., 1976.

Tocqueville, Alexis de. *Democracy in America, 1835–1840.* Translated and edited by Delba Winthrop and Harvey Mansfield. Chicago: University of Chicago Press, 2000.

Townshend, Charles. "Martial Law: Legal and Administrative Problems of Civil Emergency in Britain and the Empire, 1800–1940," 25 The Historical Journal 167 (1982).

Tuchman, Barbara. *The Guns of August.* New York: Macmillan, 1962.

Turner, Robert F. *Repealing the War Powers Resolution: Restoring the Rule of Law in U.S. Foreign Policy.* Washington, DC: Brassey's, 1991.

———. *The War Powers Resolution: Its Implementation in Theory and Practice.* Philadelphia, PA: Foreign Policy Research Institute, 1983.

Tusa, Ann, and John Tusa. *The Nuremberg Trial.* New York: Atheneum, 1983.

Tushnet, Mark, ed. *The Constitution in Wartime: Beyond Alarmism and Complacency.* Durham, NC: Duke University Press, 2005.

Vattel, Emmerich de. *The Law of Nations or The Principles of Natural Law, Applied to the Conduct and to the Affairs of Nations and of Sovereigns.* 1758. Translated by Charles G. Fenwick. Buffalo, NY: William S. Hein & Co., 1995.

Walzer, Michael. *Arguing About War.* New Haven, CT: Yale University Press, 2004.

———. *Just and Unjust Wars.* 3rd. ed. New York: Basic Books, 2000.

Warmelo, Dietlof van. *On Commando.* London: Methuen, 1902.

Warwick, Peter. *Black People and the South African War.* New York: Cambridge University Press, 1983.

Wawro, Geoffrey. *The Franco-Prussian War: The German Conquest of France in 1870–1871.* New York: Cambridge University Press, 2003.

Welch, David A. *Justice and the Genesis of War.* New York: Cambridge University Press, 1993.

Wharton, Francis, ed. *A Digest of the International Law of the United States: Taken from documents issued by presidents and secretaries of state, and from decisions of federal courts and opinions of attorneys-general.* 3 vols. 2d ed. Washington, DC: Government Printing Office, 1887.

Whitney, Courtney. *The Case of General Yamashita: A Memorandum.* Tokyo, 1959.

Willis, James F. *Prologue to Nuremberg: The Politics and Diplomacy of Punishing War Criminals of the First World War.* Westport, CT: Greenwood Press, 1982.

Winthrop, William. *Military Law and Precedents* Washington, DC: Government Printing Office, 1920.

Yoo, John. "The Continuation of Politics by Other Means: The Original Understanding of War Powers," 84 California Law Review 167 (1996).

———. *The Powers of War and Peace: The Constitution and Foreign Affairs after 9/11.* Chicago: University of Chicago Press, 2005.

Index

About the Author

Peter Judson Richards (LLM, JSD, Yale) served on active duty in Europe and America in the United States Air Force Judge Advocate General's Corps and taught for three years in the Departments of Law and Political Science at the USAF academy. He currently holds the rank of Lieutenant Colonel in the USAF Reserves. He was appointed a fellow in law and history at Emory University (2005–2006). He has taught and published in the areas of law and politics, church-state relations, and international law and is currently Director of the Center of Law and Theology at Southern Baptist Theological Seminary in Louisville, Kentucky.

www.ingramcontent.com/pod-product-compliance
Ingram Content Group UK Ltd.
Pitfield, Milton Keynes, MK11 3LW, UK
UKHW012343110625
459581UK00011B/120

9 780814 775912